# Post-Cinematic Bodies

# Post-Cinematic Bodies

Shane Denson

meson press

**Bibliographical Information of the
German National Library**
The German National Library lists this publication in the
Deutsche Nationalbibliografie (German National Biblio-
graphy); detailed bibliographic information is available
online at http://dnb.d-nb.de.

Published in 2023 by meson press, Lüneburg, Germany
with generous support from the Deutsche
Forschungsgemeinschaft
www.meson.press

Design concept: Torsten Köchlin, Silke Krieg
Cover design: Mathias Bär
Cover art: Karin Denson, Giant Green Anemone (2023); glitch,
photomontage; 16x20 inches (detail)

ISBN (print): 978-3-95796-043-6
ISBN (PDF): 978-3-95796-044-3
DOI: 10.14619/0436

The digital edition of this publication can be downloaded
freely at www.meson.press.

# Contents

# Configurations of Film: Series Foreword

Scalable across a variety of formats and standardized in view of global circulation, the moving image has always been both an image of movement and an image on the move. Over the last three decades, digital production technologies, communication networks and distribution platforms have taken the scalability and mobility of film to a new level. Beyond the classical *dispositif* of the cinema, new forms and knowledges of cinema and film have emerged, challenging the established approaches to the study of film. The conceptual framework of index, *dispositif* and canon, which defined cinema as photochemical image technology with a privileged bond to reality, a site of public projection, and a set of works from auteurs from specific national origins, can no longer account for the current multitude of moving images and the trajectories of their global movements. The term "post-cinema condition," which was first proposed by film theorists more than a decade ago to describe the new cultural and technological order of moving images, retained an almost melancholic attachment to that which the cinema no longer was. Moving beyond such attachments, the concept of "configurations of film" aims to account for moving images in terms of their operations, forms and formats, locations and infrastructures, expanding the field of cinematic knowledges beyond the arts and the aesthetic, while retaining a focus on film as privileged site for the production of cultural meaning, for social action and for political conflict.

The series "Configurations of Film" presents pointed interventions in this field of debate by emerging and established international scholars associated with the DFG-funded Graduate Research Training Program (Graduiertenkolleg) "Konfigurationen des Films" at Goethe University Frankfurt. The contributions to the series aim to explore and expand our understanding of configurations of film in both a contemporary and historical perspective, combining film and media theory with media history to address key problems in the development of new analytical frameworks for the moving image on the move.

*What happens to film once it leaves the cinema,*
*and how can film studies account for the*
*migration, and transformation of its object?*
*— Funding Application DFG-Graduiertenkolleg*
*2279 "Configurations of Film"*

# Foreword

Laura Laabs and Clara Podlesnigg

Quoted above is the inaugural research question posed by the Graduate Research Training Program (*Graduiertenkolleg*) Configurations of Film. *Post-Cinematic Bodies*, Shane Denson's contribution to the Configurations of Film book series, can be seen as rephrasing that question in an intriguing way: what happens to the *body* once film has left the cinema, and how can film studies account for the migration, transformation, and bodily situation of its viewing/addressed subjects? However, Denson offers answers to both questions at once, thinking about post-cinematic objects and the bodies that experience, live, or even work with them. In this book, he urges us time and again "to pay especial attention to the ways that the user/viewer's body is interpellated and imagined, constructed or deconstructed, engrossed or expelled—how, in other words, post-cinematic bodies are subjected to the push and pull of correlative and discorrelative tendencies and forces" (Denson 2023, 117 in this volume).

In a strange coincidence, Shane Denson's Mercator Fellowship at Configurations of Film—where the idea for this book first originated—could itself serve as a case study for this book. Coming to us in November 2020, in the dark, pre-vaccine days of the pandemic, the online fellowship consisted of a string of meetings of our very own post-cinematic bodies brought together in grids on our at-home screens. Different time zones resulted in differently adjusted bodies for each of our virtual get-togethers. When we in Europe were having wine and beer to decompress after a long day, Denson was sipping coffee in California to get his day started. Even back then, he had already begun working through some of the philosophical implications of the strange, at once connected and isolated situation in which we all found ourselves (cf. Denson 2020b). Operationalizing the term "multistability," itself a thread that runs both through Denson's past works as well as *Post-Cinematic Bodies* (the concluding part of a trilogy[1]), he describes the ubiquitous but curious perceptual situation of online get-togethers with keen focus on the mediality of split screens enabling split attention on self and other, or self as other:

> The multistability of the screen now became even more apparent as we found our vision bouncing around between the many faces arrayed in grids across our screens, shifting from box to box, frame to frame, peering into each other's apartments, and quite often winding up looking at our own faces as if in a glitchy digital mirror. (Ibid., 317)

In this earlier essay, Denson describes and comes to grips with the heightened perceptual alertness, sometimes verging on alarm, provoked in connection with the pandemic situation and its demands on our bodies: situated, as they were, in a screen environment that both enabled us to enact our academic exchange and physically shielded us from each other's potentially dangerous, virus-emitting, bodily co-presence. The essay also anticipates some of the questions of embodiment in our contemporary media environment which are posed and answered in this volume.

---

1 The previous two parts of the trilogy are *Postnaturalism: Frankenstein, Film, and the Anthropotechnical Interface* (2014) and *Discorrelated Images* (2020a).

# Down the Rabbit Hole with
## *Post-Cinematic Bodies*

In line with this focus on multistability, reading *Post-Cinematic Bodies* similarly brought us into closer contact with our bodies while also leading us away from them. This is the kind of book that immediately makes you want to put its theses and arguments to the test. Through its rich descriptions of objects and cases it elicits the almost irresistible desire to dive down rabbit holes: open tabs, look things up online, check whether your own experience of an object analyzed correlates or dis-correlates with Denson's assertions. Reading along in this manner can feel like a scavenger hunt on a playground of glitchy experiential opportunities. At one point, you may find yourself pressing Q, W, O and P on your keyboard in an erratic fashion, trying to make the avatar of an Olympic runner move, but failing at every attempt of growing muscle memory. Another time, you may pick up your mobile device to check its technical specifications and find out whether a creepy-sounding camera technology has unknowingly been with you every time you picked that thing up. These are the moments when some of the central theses of this book become available to experience and make themselves felt in the reader's flesh. Denson never explicitly directs you away from his book. Even so, precisely because the book may not have every answer (nor does it pretend to), the ways in which it leads you to see and feel for yourself can be quite fun. For us, the process of reading this book started a whole chain of searches for more and more cases exemplifying momentarily felt effects or indices of dis/correlation.[2] This is not only a testimony to *Post-Cinematic*

---

2    These are some exemplary findings of ours: "STAR WARS Tilt Brush – Spaceships Battle Paint Drawing in VR." Dong Yoon Park. January 2, 2017. Video, https://youtu.be/9Bx6nDjxC24. The creator of this video, a *Star Wars* fan, designer and creative technologist, uses Google's Tilt Brush, an application for 3D room scale painting in VR to create a battle scene featuring his favorite spaceship models from the franchise.

*Bodies'* timeliness, but also to the ways in which research and knowledge transfer go hand in hand.

One of those moments of parallel ruthless rabbit holing led us to a video tour of the "Google Data Center Security: 6 Layers Deep" (Google Cloud Tech 2020). Produced by Google and shared on YouTube in June 2020, the video functions both as an advertisement for Google's self-proclaimed data storage and "privacy" protection security measures and, at the same time, a showcase of strategies for deterring potential intruders or attackers (from outside or within the company itself).

As video host Stephanie Wong enters the data center site, she acknowledges the presence of guards and cameras as visible actants of surveillance. Then, she proceeds to ask her guide Joe Kava about things she perhaps didn't or couldn't see. If the guards and cameras function as perceptible traces for Google's security measures, they also seem to suggest or imply the co-presence of imperceptible, computational surveillance technologies. Kava affirms Wong's discernment: "Yeah, there's actually a lot of technology and operations going on behind the scene. So from the time that you're on site, we know that you're here, and we're able to do correlation analysis of where you've been" (ibid., 00:01:20–00:01:30). What exactly Kava means by

"Labo VR's Secret Doodle Tools (Elephant Toy-Con)." GameXplain. April 13, 2019. Video, https://youtu.be/IZeoDvouAnQ. Rather than "seamlessly" integrating the player's body in a VR environment, Nintendo Labo's VR goggles plus cardboard elephant mask require them to be held in front of the face with one hand, while the other is used for creating doodles in a VR environment. The set-up quickly becomes physically tiring, calling attention to the inevitability of the body in VR media dispositifs.
Sara Cwynar, *Glass Life*. 2021. https://mubi.com/films/glass-life. An experimental short film assembling digital images, video, and quotes from various theory references that also appear throughout *Post-Cinematic Bodies*.
"The Future Is a Dead Mall – Decentraland and the Metaverse." Folding Ideas. March 27, 2023. Video, https://youtu.be/EiZhdpLXZ8Q. An almost two-hour long video essay about the frustrations of VR and the concept of the Metaverse explored by means of an auto-ethnographic exploration of the platform Decentraland.

"correlation analysis" remains unexplained, and so do the precise 
methods for calculating the facility visitors' previous movements.
Still, the statement implies an omniscience about its visitors'
present and past physical whereabouts that unmistakably
mirrors Google's data-based tracking and probabilistic calculations about Internet users' behavior. Denson's arguments in *Post-
Cinematic Bodies* precisely get at this sense of a barely assessable
bodily implication in, and subjectivation through, computational
regimes. "At stake here," Denson posits,

> is not just an algorithmic enforcement of bias, but an
> implantation of said biases into our embodied relations
> to the world—hence a norming of bodies, minds, and
> societies—with all of the racist, sexist, queer- and trans-
> phobic, and ableist consequences that we might expect.
> (Denson 2023, 34–35 in this volume)

In the virtual tour's following scene, we meet two Black security
guards, Ricky Gordon and Tarik Billingsley, who are also guiding
Wong, herself an Asian-American woman, over the property as
she interviews them. In fact, the video's cast is predominantly
people of color. Wong, Gordon, and Billingsley chat about the
fencing surrounding the premises, as well as night vision and
thermal cameras monitoring the area. On the one hand, Google's
casting signals a sensibility for diversity and the representation
of people of color in their official communications. On the other
hand, when watching the video one can hardly overlook the
fact that the two Black men talking about these surveillance
and security tools belong to a demographic disproportionately
targeted and dehumanized by technologies of datafication
and image recognition. Google's former motto "Don't Be Evil"
(Wikipedia 2005) seems to be reconfigured here in an attempt to
frame technologies of surveillance in a positive, inclusive light,
utilized purely to keep users' data safe.

> Wong: Ricky, Tarik, can you tell me more about what's unique
> about the fencing?

Gordon: This particular fence is an anti-climb fence. It's also equipped with fiber. The technology tells us if someone's near the fence or touches the fence.

Billingsley: So we use thermal cameras and standard cameras. So we're able to see video footage at night just as clearly as we can during the day (Google Cloud Tech 2020, 00:01:40–00:02:02).

As this conversation reveals, some of the technology presented—for example a fence around the perimeter—anticipates the body and its behavior without that body perceiving that it is being perceived. In other words, even if the body is by all appearances located outside of the fenced-off area, it is already included in the medial regime articulated here. This pre-subjective or unconscious inscription of the body in the technological regime of Google's multiple security layers thus regulates and organizes inclusion and exclusion through methods of anticipating, measuring, and evaluating the body and its behavior in unnoticeable but deeply consequential manners. Of course, these regimes can be subsumed under the key phrase "surveillance capitalism" (Zuboff 2019), not least because it is in Google's interest to reassure its business clients and to confirm their confidence in using Google infrastructures. Extending this lens, however, Denson seeks "to expose the ways that *bodies* are subject to unprecedented forces of surveillance, control, and modulation in the age of post-cinematic media" (2023, 227 in this volume; our emphasis). In addition to capitalist surveillance, data acquisition, and data evaluation, then, Google's "smart fence" also, and crucially, operates at the bodily levels of the micro-temporal and the imperceptible: what Denson calls the "metabolic." At stake is the implication and configuration of corporeal processes in these datafication regimes. Denson's work thus constitutes a deep, media philosophical reflection on computational media as much as a valuable reminder that the seemingly abstract processes undergirding them are, in fact, operating on the body at the level of its metabolism. It is crucial to remember that most of these processes of dis/correlation, as  Denson conceptualizes them, happen at the pre-subjective level. Our aforementioned scavenger hunt for materials, inspired as it was by the book's arguments and case studies, was thus also in some strange way a search for that which is imperceptible.

## Mysteries of Formatting Data and Bodies

The exploration of these forms of regulating, configuring, and "norming of bodies" (Denson 2023, 34 in this volume) by means of computational technologies is another crucial throughline of *Post-Cinematic Bodies*. Denson alerts us to the fact that "our formatted environments of digitally designed architectures, objects, and devices work directly on our bodies and materially shape the conditions of our social relations" (ibid., 41). This "formatting of space" (ibid., 70) is not to be taken metaphorically but very literally. Moving from chapter to chapter, it emerges that our bodies themselves are subject to complex, usually pre-cognitive, invisible, and intangible processes of formatting in the post-cinematic regime. Denson describes this difficult, sometimes even troubling reconfiguration in terms of "new forms of visuality and tactility that shape the environment for contemporary life," and further finds that these "operate on speeds and scales that are immune to our perception. They anticipate us, predicting our behavior, pre-visualizing our interactions, and pre-formatting our bodies and brains" (ibid., 227).

Vivian Sobchack, a prominent reference throughout *Post-Cinematic Bodies*, once wrote that "as we subjectively live both our bodies and our images, each not only informs the other, but they also often become significantly confused" (2004 [1999], 36). This observation, which Sobchack makes in relation to cinematic special effects and cosmetic surgery as entangled cultural practices, becomes especially relevant in Denson's exploration of DeepFakes throughout the book. DeepFakes are moving images that in many ways aim to confuse bodies, often in harmful acts that exploit political power to manipulate who said what, or to create non-consensual pornography by digitally stitching together faces and bodies. However, DeepFakes have also become a technology of aspiration: enter Elon Musk's Chinese doppelgänger Yilong Ma. In his viral TikToks, the self-proclaimed "ardent follower and imitator" (Ma 2023) of Musk dresses in a three-piece suit and poses with a Tesla as he recites phrases about tech and money in phonetic English. This displacement of the powerful tech-billionaire, who has repeatedly sought to ban any satirical interpretations of his character (cf. Perrigo 2022; Milmo and Hern 2022), allows for both critical and affirmative interpretations. Hence, Musk somehow did not mind the online presence of Yilong Ma, and via Twitter even offered to meet him "if he is real" (Musk 2022). From the get-go, there has been suspicion about Yilong Ma potentially being a DeepFake, sending his online audiences on frustrating searches for glitches and imperfections in his very Musk-like facial features; or, in Denson's words, for signs of "seamfulness" (2023, 110 in this volume) as opposed to an (ideological) ideal of digitally constructed seamlessness. A rare video interview with a US-American content creator fluent in Yilong Ma's first language Mandarin presents another perspective on his character. Titling his video "Exposing the Chinese Elon Musk," the YouTuber sets out to reveal that Ma is in fact deepfaking his appearance. But when confronted directly, Ma simply responds: "I think it's nice to maintain an air of mystery" (Xiaomanyc小马在纽约 2023, 00:06:45–00:06:50).

Interestingly, this notion of mystery as a quality that is to be maintained also appears in Google's video about the data center's security management: the facility's sixth and final layer, an exclusive space that the fewest may access, is referred to as "mysterious" (Google Cloud Tech 2020, 00:04:30–00:04:33). Here, the cognitive unavailability of computational processes is not framed as a problem but rather as part of the fascination of engaging with the images they create. We learn that this mysterious sixth security layer is dedicated to the destruction of

physical data carriers by means of a human-operated machine. 
Through the transparent top window of the otherwise black
box, we glimpse the culled hardware on a conveyor belt, moving
towards a grinder. The process of data destruction is at once
visible and invisible. What we *can* see is part of an "operational
aesthetic," a term Denson borrows from Neil Harris to describe
the tension between opacity and transparency that makes visual
spectacles possible (2023, 106–113 in this volume). It also pertains
to our experience of DeepFakes:

> DeepFakes also trade essentially on an operational aesthetic,
> or a dispersal of attention between visual surface and the
> algorithmic operation of machine learning. However, the
> post-cinematic processes to whose operation DeepFakes
> refer our attention fundamentally transform the operational
> aesthetic, relocating it from the oscillations of attention that
> we see in the cinema to a deep, pre-attentional level that
> computation taps into with its microtemporal speed. (Ibid.,
> 109)

What is on the line in this specific case, but also in many of
Denson's own case studies, is the making visible of computational
processes otherwise invisible to humans. He assumes that
something important for the understanding of technologies (or
post-cinematic media) is hidden there. What is being secured,
protected, and invisibilized, from whom, and at what/whose
cost? By the end of Google's video, we learn that "getting out of
the data center is arguably even harder than getting in" (Google
Cloud Tech 00:05:33)—a barely veiled metaphor for the computational, post-cinematic regimes implicating and processing
our bodies. All of this may seem troubling and darkly pessimistic;
however, you will find that Denson, throughout his writing, is
dedicated to the position that technologies and techniques of dis/
correlation are not inevitably disempowering, and he frequently
turns to independent artists and critical thinkers to draw out
hopeful perspectives on post-cinematic bodies. His project
is, importantly, "also to ask about the material and aesthetic

18 potentials embedded in these systems to become something else" (Denson 2023, 35 in this volume).

## Did He Really Say "Post-cinematic"?

The fact that a book featuring the term "post-cinematic" in its title is now part of the Configurations of Film book series might raise an eyebrow for those who remember our suggestion to speak of "configurations" of film rather than the post-cinematic (cf. Boguska and Hediger 2019, 11). To some of us, this choice of words suggests that the cinematic dispositif had once been the norm, but no longer is. In *Post-Cinematic Bodies* (as well as his earlier books *Postnaturalism* and *Discorrelated Images*), Denson explicitly engages with the notions of presumed crises, caesuras, or paradigmatic shifts that his terminology might indicate to some readers. While Denson is clear in his position that computational technologies have fundamentally affected the way we (don't) perceive moving image media and art, he states just as clearly that moving images have always had dis/correlative potentials— rather, it is the operations of dis/correlation at work that have shifted (2023, 35 in this volume)—and that post-cinematic media do not occur exclusively outside of the cinema space. In that sense, Denson does not so much oppose oldness and newness, but instead emphasizes relevant continuities while also pointing out discontinuities. The book will oftentimes ask you to consider differences of degree rather than kind: "But within this continuity, there is also a difference to be found in the speed, scope, and degree of operationalization of metabolic processes" (ibid., 32). Although framerates and photochemical reactions might thus constitute imperceptible processes in the cinematic viewing situation, they nevertheless seem more accessible to consciousness than the myriads of microtemporal operations that occur before, during, and after we watch the video tour of Google's Data Center security or scroll through the TikTok and Twitter feeds of Yilong Ma. You might take a look at the relevant advertising categories Google or Meta assign to you in order to catch an indirect glimpse of algorithmic calculations, and perhaps speculate about their  variables. But the actual processes of data collection and evaluation—and thus their operations at the bodily, the metabolic level—are a different matter altogether. For Denson, the relevant threshold is crossed when we try to make sense of these "invisible, microtemporal processes that are categorically outside the window of human perception" (ibid., 30).

So, what exactly happens to the body when film leaves the cinema, and how can film studies account for the migration, transformation, and bodily situation of its viewing/addressed subjects? As the present authors have read, watched, scrolled, searched, scavenged, thought, talked, and wrote, Denson's book continuously urged us to mind our bodies. Indeed, and in contrast with positions that maintain the body's absence from, or even its irrelevance to digital spaces, Denson's meticulous engagement with the body as a site on which computational technologies operate, especially as their object of interpellation and subjectivation processes, further shows that the body is far from being a stable entity. (This it shares with film studies' objects of analysis, as argued in the research program's mission statement.) The body cannot be taken for granted; instead, the body and embodied existence is re/configured all the time, whether we take notice or not. *Post-Cinematic Bodies* makes an astute case and offers media-philosophical tools as well as analytic pathways for thinking through the complicated questions of embodiment in the face of, and posed by, the complicated technologies we casually use.

## References

"Exposing the Chinese Elon Musk." Xiaomanyc小马在纽约. February 23, 2023. Video, https://youtu.be/ZnF4emrEIZQ. Accessed April 20, 2023.

"Google Data Center Security: 6 Layers Deep." Google Cloud Tech. June 18, 2020. Video, https://youtu.be/kd33UVZhnAA. Accessed April, 14 2023.

Boguska, Rebecca, and Vinzenz Hediger. 2019. "Introduction." In John Mowitt, *Tracks from the Crypt*, 7–18. Configurations of Film Series. Lüneburg: meson press.

**20**   Denson, Shane. 2014. *Postnaturalism: Frankenstein, Film, and the Anthropotechnical Interface*. Bielefeld: transcript-Verlag.

Denson, Shane. 2020a. *Discorrelated Images*. Durham: Duke University Press.

Denson, Shane. 2020b. "'Thus isolation is a project.' Notes toward a Phenomenology of Screen-Mediated Life." In *Pandemic Media: Preliminary Notes toward an Inventory*, edited by Philipp Dominik Keidl, Laliv Melamed, Vinzenz Hediger and Antonio Somaini, 315–322. Configurations of Film Series. Lüneburg: meson press.

Denson, Shane. 2023. *Post-Cinematic Bodies*. Configurations of Film Series. Lüneburg: meson press.

Milmo, Dan, and Alex Hern. 2022. "Twitter bans comedian Kathy Griffin for impersonating Elon Musk." *The Guardian*, November 7, 2022. https://www.theguardian.com/technology/2022/nov/07/twitter-will-ban-permanently-suspend-impersonator-accounts-elon-musk-says-as-users-take-his-name. Accessed April 21, 2023.

Musk, Elon (@elonmusk). 2022. "I'd like to meet this guy (if he is real). Hard to tell with deepfakes these days." Twitter, May 9, 2022, 3:28pm. https://twitter.com/elonmusk/status/1523656160699502593.

Perrigo, Billy. 2022. "Twitter Bans Accounts Mocking 'Free Speech Absolutist' Elon Musk." *Time*, November 7, 2022. https://time.com/6229960/twitter-bans-accounts-elon-musk-impersonators/. Accessed April 21, 2023.

Sobchack, Vivian. 2004 [1999]. "Scary Women: Cinema, Surgery, and Special Effects." In *Carnal Thoughts: Embodiment and Moving Image Culture*, 36–52. Berkeley: University of California Press.

Ma, Yilong (@mayilongo). 2023. Twitter biography. https://twitter.com/mayilongo. Accessed April 20, 2023.

Wikipedia. 2005. "Don't Be Evil." Wikimedia Foundation. Last modified March 28, 2023. https://en.wikipedia.org/wiki/Don%27t_be_evil.

Zuboff, Shoshana. 2019. *The Age of Surveillance Capitalism: The Fight for a Human Future at the New Frontier of Power*. New York: Public Affairs.

# Preface

*Post-Cinematic Bodies* is about the making, unmaking, and remaking of embodiment in contemporary media. In this book, I am concerned with a range of new modes of corporeal address: commercial, experimental, mainstream, and deviant alike. I am especially interested in the ways that artistic interventions can shed light on, or make available to embodied experience, the parameters of an emerging but already powerful system by which computational media put bodies in their place, define them, and discipline them. Between such discipline and its disruption, embodiment serves as both subject and object of post-cinematic media—and oftentimes as something else: neither a well-defined subject nor an object *per se*, but the multistable ground of both. It is this embodied substratum of experience that is at stake in—and is in many ways *the fulcrum of*—the shift from cinematic to post-cinematic media; the speed, scale, and fine-grained precision of computational operations enables an unprecedented targeting of the neither-fully-subjective-nor-quite-objective flesh, which is by turns addressed, quantified, reified, formed, deformed, modulated, and worked over in the process of subjectivizing and/or objectifying viewers and users. Aimed at uncovering the aesthetic and political dimensions of these transformations, this is a book about the mediated situation of corporeality today.

But after decades of work on embodiment and new media, as well as the broader trend within film and media studies to valorize the body as a site of resistance and excess, do we really need another book of this sort? In recent years, there has been growing suspicion of such appeals to the body. Coupled with the turn to affect, the turn to embodiment has come to appear all too predictable, hardly the radical gesture that it once seemed to be. Moreover, opposition to this mode of theorizing is fueled not simply by an impatience with scholarly fashions that refuse to die, but by concerns that the appeal to embodiment might in

22   fact stand in the way of other, more pressing issues. If, as some critics have suggested, it is understood as a turn *inward* and *away from ideology*, the corporeal turn threatens to obfuscate politics. If understood as a turn *away from the space of discourse and reason*, the corporeal turn appears as a refusal of critique. And if understood as a turn *toward a supposedly unimpeachable stratum of private experience*, this apolitical and post-critical corporeal turn also provides an easy way to evade the labor of analysis and interpretation, thus rendering the very point of aesthetic inquiry uncertain. Eugenie Brinkema (2014), in *The Forms of the Affects*, provides the most trenchant critique of these tendencies, arguing that the appeal to the body as the supposed seat of the affects effectively neutralizes and disables political and scholarly debate alike. In the place of a "visceral aesthetics," she provocatively offers instead a disembodied affect: "Affect, as I theorize it here, has fully shed the subject [in accordance with a familiar Deleuzean line of thinking], but my argument goes a step further and also loses for affects the body and bodies" (ibid., 25). Against the feeling body, Brinkema "regards any individual affect as a self-folding exteriority that manifests in, as, and with textual form" (ibid., 25). As an exteriority, affect is not private but inherently political and open to debate; and as a textual form, affect demands analysis, interpretation, and critique—all of which the appeal to the body foreclosed.

How, then, does this book's focus on embodiment stand in relation to such arguments? Let me note, first, that I wholeheartedly agree with Brinkema's indictment of the post-critical impulse: for both political and scholarly reasons, we simply cannot give up on close reading and the analytical engagement with aesthetic forms. And it is because of this shared conviction that I also share Brinkema's suspicion of those modes of criticism and theory that valorize the body and its affects as an unproblematic bulwark against discursive power or interpellation. The corporeal excess appealed to there is neither valuable in its own right, nor is it safely outside the space of political strife. In fact, and this marks my divergence from Brinkema, embodiment is a central site of the political conflicts indexed and addressed by aesthetic forms and the scholarly discourses with which we respond to them. If I advocate something like a "visceral aesthetics," it is not because of the flesh's inherent resistance but precisely because of its increased vulnerability to capture and cooptation. Now more than ever, due to the expansion of computational powers to bypass conscious perception and intervene directly on prepersonal embodiment, we are simply not at liberty to ignore the body in our engagements with affective and aesthetic forms.

One task of this book is to elaborate a theory of embodiment and its relations both to sensation and to power that will help us to understand the deeply political stakes of our current media-historical moment. In this endeavor, I believe, the points of agreement far outweigh any points of disagreement between Brinkema and myself. To begin with, Brinkema's opposition to embodiment is rooted in a particular understanding of the relation—what I will theorize as a "correlative" relation—between affect and the body, which I agree needs to be scrutinized, revised, and (as Brinkema puts it) "resisted" (2014, 32). In Brinkema's account of film and media studies' development over the past three decades or so, scholars turned towards embodied affect as an alternative to the supposedly disembodied and textually inscribed subject-positions of the "apparatus theory" of the 1970s. For Brinkema, affect-oriented scholars were united not only by a suspicion of "form and ideology, meaning and sign," but by a fetishization of theorists' *personal* experiences: singular and irrefutable sensations identified with one's own body (ibid., 27, 31). Brinkema foregrounds the way that such personalization, effectively a "solipsism," stands in the way of theoretical generalization and critique (ibid., 31–33). I would add that such an approach also radically simplifies and positivizes embodiment, turning it into *my personal property* rather than the multistable ground that I have gestured towards above: neither subject nor object, but probably on balance more public than private, and hence both the nexus of a nascent, presubjective collectivity and a volatile battleground in the struggle over subjectivation and objectification. My critique of a reductively reified notion of embodiment is in fact a corollary of Brinkema's critique of affect as private, "directional," or "intentional" in the phenomenological sense (ibid., 31). "Affect is taken as always being, in the end, *for us*" (ibid., 31). For theorists who regard affects in this way, as interior states or sense-data that are open to inspection by the theorist and no one else and/or as outwardly expressive signs of the internal lives of others, they function (as Brinkema frames it in a Husserlian vocabulary) as noematic objects bound as the correlates of intending subjects' noetic experiencing (ibid., 33). But this, as Brinkema and I both agree, is a perversion of affect, which is precisely *not* personal or correlative in this sense, but is instead "non-intentional, indifferent, and resists the given-over attributes of a teleological spectatorship with acquirable gains" (ibid., 33).

Against the stabilizing correlation of affect and embodiment, Brinkema chooses to abandon the body and revise affect. She describes "a subjectless affect, bound up in an exteriority, uncoupled from emotion, interiority, expressivity, mimesis, humanism, spectatorship, and bodies" (ibid., 45). In my own view, this "uncoupling" should be read not as a privative or exclusionary non-relation, but as a loosening or undoing of the "directional" idea that affect must necessarily be attached to or correlated with any of these terms; if understood in this way, such that couplings of this sort are optional but not impossible—on the contrary, in fact, that such affective couplings can be effective means of subjectivation and interpellation—then I am ready to endorse every aspect of Brinkema's redescription of affect, *with the exception of its disembodiment*. Both affect *and embodiment*, in my view, are non-obvious and malleable, potentially opaque to subjective experience and therefore demanding of theoretical problematization and interpretive engagement. Brinkema writes of affect, and I would extend this to embodiment as well, that it cannot be reduced to a "model … based in and of individual psychology or phenomenological experience. Rather, it inheres in material objects, takes shape in an exteriority and in formal structures" (ibid., 76). As I will argue later in this book, embodiment is indispensable not because it serves either to stabilize affect or to destabilize discursive power structures, but because it is the multistable ground upon which the binary of interior and exterior itself rests and makes sense—as well as the necessary ground for its deconstruction. To truly undo the coupling of affect with subjective interiority, we will have to undo the coupling of embodiment with private experience as well. And here, I suggest, the recently computerized culture industries are way ahead of us in their targeting and operationalization of embodiment outside the purview of subjective experience.

Brinkema warns against the dangers of "an introspective style" in mobilizations of affect "that attempt to focus on the immediate, visceral, and corporeal" (ibid., 32); in addition to the "classical interiority" that inheres in such accounts, against the wishes of affect theorists' "attempts to reject and move beyond such metaphysical frameworks," Brinkema identifies a very material and political-economic hazard: "Perhaps the greatest danger of this approach is that it emphasizes the successful *consumption* of affect and thus makes theoretical accounts of each private feeling experience complicit with the explicit marketing of feeling from the commercial side of film production" (ibid., 32). Whether this is truly the "greatest danger" is open to debate, but it is indeed worth noting a formal resemblance between the critic who would capture and neutralize affect as the object of their own experience, on the one hand, and an industry that aims to capture bodies and interpellate them as dutifully enthralled consumers on the other. What this points to, I suggest, is the way that affect, far from disrupting the system of "form and ideology, meaning and sign" at the heart of apparatus theory, is actually an integral part of that system. We are dealing, in other words, with an affective apparatus. And if that apparatus was operative already in a cinematic culture, its operation and efficiency is greatly intensified in a post-cinematic one, where sensing bodies are subject to non-stop automated tracking, ubiquitous monitoring, and minute quantification—discreetly inserted into computational feedback loops aimed at engineering an optimal user experience that would leave us feeling good about a life of consumption and the incidental value that it produces for Apple, fitbit, Sony, Peloton, Facebook, or Aetna. Webcams track our every move in department stores, while machine learning systems process our eye movements and scan our images for facial microgestures that would reveal our feelings about various products. Affective computing companies like Affectiva, with their emotion analytics software Affdex, collect and facilitate exchanges of this information to producers of consumer products and online platforms, who use it to optimize their targeting of advertisements.[1] All of this happens on the basis of bodily behavior, taken as the outward sign of interior states that might or might not ever be registered by me as a subject, processed by machines operating imperceptibly at microtemporal speeds to predictively anticipate future behavior and thus mold future subjective states. In this system, the exteriority of embodied affect to subjective experience is the precondition for its effective targeting *as a vehicle for the subjectivizing or interpellating act itself.* The culture industry, we could say, understands very well the multistability of embodiment and knows how to instrumentalize it in its role as the ground and transducer of the interior/exterior divide. We, as critics of culture and aesthetic experience, need to understand it as well.

Theorizing this dimension of embodiment, which is alternately correlated and discorrelated from subjective experience, will take us to the heart of aesthetics and mediality in their sensory, technical, and political dimensions. Against the "introspective

---

1    For an excellent history of affective computing, from cybernetics to Affectiva, see Nagy 2022.

style" that Brinkema rightly impugns as part of the "attempt to focus on the immediate, visceral, and corporeal" (ibid., 32), it will not do simply to insist on the exteriority of affect—though Brinkema's provocation is certainly a step in the right direction; beyond this necessary initial step, we need to theorize the *possibility* of exteriorization as a fact of fleshly multistability, replacing the notion of bodily immediacy with a fundamental *mediality* of the visceral and corporeal. Later, in Chapter 2, I will argue for this originary mediality of the flesh, rooted in its alternating powers of tactile interiority and specular exteriorization, as the (alienable) ground of aesthetics, technicity, and political collectivity alike. The consequence, I suggest, is that Brinkema's dislodging of affect from the body, its exteriorization as a textual and aesthetic form, should be seen as an extension of the flesh; it is possible, in other words, only because embodiment is not and cannot be restricted to the realm of the personal and the private but always stretches affectively and materially out-ward, beyond the empirically determinate or introspectively avail-able body. The ability to take on external form, to separate *from* the body, is very much (owing to) a power *of* the body.

I will fill out this picture later, but first I would like to provide a bit more contextualization for this project, which concludes a trilogy of books, and to explain some of the terms that I use. As someone who uses the prefix "post-" a lot, I am often called upon to account for the apparent caesuras implied in my work and to explain the periodizations entailed therein. My first book, *Postnaturalism*, seemed to some readers to suggest that there was a kind of *before* and *after* with respect to nature, a break marked by technology and our interface with it (what I called the anthropotechnical interface). In fact, I claimed that "we have never been natural" (Denson 2014, 24), and so if there was any such break at all it was a prehistoric one, or one marking the beginning of human history or of hominization itself. Beyond that, my elaboration of postnaturalism posited that the history of human-technological interfacing was in fact full of radical

28 transformations, not so much breaks as transitions, when virtually everything—our whole embodied and enworlded relation to the environment—was up for grabs. But because in these transitional moments the very foundations of our thought are subject to global change, these revolutions remain difficult if not impossible to survey. Traces of them would have to be sought in broadly aesthetic rather than epistemic domains. At stake, ultimately, was less a periodization of such changes than a theory of media as their crux or hinge.

Media, I argued, are "the originary correlators" of experience, where the "correlation" in question here indexes what Edmund Husserl referred to as "the fundamental correlation between noesis and noema," which more recently had come under attack from the speculative realists, under the rubric of "correlationism," as a pernicious form of anthropocentrism infecting Western philosophy more generally.[2] Taking this challenge seriously, I argued that any effort to develop a non-correlationist theory of media would have to account for the special relation that media have to our embodiment, as a prepersonal substrate exceeding our intentional relation to the world but materially informing the shape of intentionality itself.

> As for media in this postnatural perspective, they are no longer thought here from *within* the horizon of correlationism but, we might say, *as* that horizon—as the *very correlators* of the phenomenal, the concrete, and the empirical on the one hand and the noumenal, the abstract, and the transcendental on the other. This means that media are themselves not merely artifactual and instrumental—a correlational view of media *for us*—but are precisely media, that is, milieux *for anthropotechnical historicity* itself. (Ibid., 297)

2    Husserl 2012, 192. On correlationism, see Meillassoux 2008.

This broadly cosmological view of media as the originary correlators of experience lays the basis for much if not all of my subsequent work. But questions of media-historical breaks and periodizations were aggravated when I turned to the concept of "post-cinema" as a new media regime emerging out of computational technologies and their transformation of visual culture and media. In the collection *Post-Cinema*, which I co-edited with Julia Leyda, and in my book *Discorrelated Images*, it might have seemed that I had returned to the idea of a simple break, a before and an after, described now in terms of the "regimes" of cinema and post-cinema (Denson and Leyda 2016; Denson 2020a). To be sure, I asserted that "there is no hard break, no bright line between cinema and post-cinema; the vision of post-cinema advocated here is predicated not on cinema's 'end' but rather on its envelopment within the larger space of an environment that has been thoroughly transformed by the operation of computational processing" (Denson 2020a, 2). Thus, rather than a simple binary, I was again concerned with a media-technical and perceptual transition marked by elements both of continuity and discontinuity. However, if the cinema/post-cinema transition was to be understood as one more episode in the ongoing history of media as the variable correlators of experience, hence as a reshaping of the fundamental correlation between historically and materially situated subjects and their environments, this picture would seem to be complicated by the notion that post-cinematic images and infrastructures are *discorrelated* from our experience.

One might ask—and I have been asked repeatedly—isn't it too simple to describe cinema as a correlative and post-cinema as a discorrelative media regime? There are many versions of this question, and they all bear some relation to the question of continuity and discontinuity. For example, the question might be posed in terms of novelty. Is discorrelation really new? The argument for the novelty of post-cinema, in relation to the broadly cinematic regime from which it is distinguished, rests on the idea that computational images depend on invisible, micro-temporal processes that are categorically outside the window of human perception. These new imaging techniques undercut and to a certain extent undo the phenomenological correlation, or the intentional relation between a perceiving subject and an image object. But while the specific technological processes might be new, we would have to admit that there have been countless techniques for discorrelation throughout the ages: certain forms of meditation, mystical practices, or experimental drug use, for example, are aimed precisely at loosening the bond or even dissolving the difference between self and world. And besides, there have always been multifarious processes subtending our conscious perception, quite independent of whether we are concerned with them as a matter of our ethical or religious practices. Clearly, computers didn't create discorrelation. But they do, I think, create new relations to the universe beyond the correlative suture, bringing this universe to bear directly on images and other objects of our attention and aesthetic interest.

The question can be extended, though: don't plenty of other aesthetic practices also do just this? Hasn't it been a major function of art to discorrelate, to undo the bonds of (conventionalized forms of) human subjectivity? From religious art that communicates the power of the divine, disorients human perspective, and deflates ideas of mastery, to avant-garde practices that look beyond the norms of bourgeois subjectivity, many forms of art seem deserving of the discorrelative title. And the same could be said of cinema: many experimental and avant-garde film-makers have likewise sought to deform and dismantle perceptual norms—or to exteriorize affective forms. And not only that: they have done so by means of material processes—photochemical and mechanical processes—that are every bit as much outside the frame of human perception as the microtemporal operations of digital processing. But here we see that two distinct notions or dimensions of discorrelation are at play. One of them concerns *techniques for* undoing correlation, while the other concerns what

might be called *technologies of* discorrelation. Roughly, this is the 
difference between, on the one hand, practices that aim for whatever reason to expand agencies (of perception, cognition, experience, etc.) beyond the subjective frame and, on the other hand, apparatuses that harness energies and materials that operate outside that frame. The former seeks to create discorrelative states, while the latter simply exploits discorrelated matter.
As I understand it, the transition from cinema to post-cinema concerns both of these dimensions, but it will be useful to hold them apart in order to dispel potential misunderstandings and to clarify relations both of continuity and change.

Let me begin with the idea that post-cinema is defined by *technologies of discorrelation*, operating on materials outside the scope of human relation. What I mean, again, is that the perceptible phenomena (sights, sounds, etc.) generated and transmitted by computational technologies are the product of myriad processes, operating at a variety of ever more finely articulated levels of hardware and software, that are categorically immune to perceptual capture. As I have argued in *Discorrelated Images*, these largely microtemporal processes are best described as "metabolic" processes, in that they are environmental with respect to subjectivity, altering the interactive pathways or ecological exchange routes that define our material existence. Operating on our prepersonal, embodied processing of duration, post-cinematic media are thus involved in a broad, environmental shift in the conditions of life. In this way, post-cinema marks a difference of an existential sort, even though the images we view might in many respects seem continuous with those of cinema. In other words, and this is key, the discorrelative operation of post-cinematic media does not rule out the persistence of more familiar forms of perceptual-phenomenological correlation. And yet the underlying conditions of correlation have shifted, which can hardly be inconsequential from the perspective of our embodied sensibilities.

32    It might be objected, however, that this does not mark an absolute difference: cinema also relies on a number of dis-correlated processes, many of which can be described in terms of "metabolism." For example, the photochemical reactions involved in producing images on celluloid are not only invisible to the spectator, but more importantly these environmental exchanges operate at scales and speeds that are outside of human perception. Indeed, I would be the first to make this argument, and it was in fact already in the context of celluloid-based cinema that, in *Postnaturalism*, I began invoking the metabolic dimensions of media to describe their environmental powers to reshape the correlational bond.[3] But within this continuity, there is also a difference to be found in the speed, scope, and degree of operationalization of metabolic processes. That is, while both cinematic and computational processes harness matter and energy lying beyond the pale of human perception, post-cinema intensifies and accelerates these interventions to an unprecedented extreme. The cinema continues to operate if some of its images are improperly developed, and there is quite a bit of leeway with respect to frame rates and other mechanical operations that more or less imperceptibly enable the appearance of the image on screen. Post-cinematic images, on the other hand, are at all times dependent on a much more finely tuned ensemble of operations, many of which are coordinated in microscopic spatial and temporal intervals, all the way down to commands executed in the nanosecond range. While a few bits out of place here or there may not derail the post-cinematic apparatus altogether, its images are everywhere threatened with glitches and other malfunctions—many of which will *not* be perceived but may still be operative in terms of materially shaping our correlative possibilities.[4]

---

3    The groundwork for the argument is laid, with reference to the Industrial Revolution and the steam engine, in Chapter 5 and extended to the cinema and media more generally in Chapter 6 of *Postnaturalism* (Denson 2014).

4    See, in particular, Chapter 2, "Dividuated Images," in Denson 2020a.

This brings us to the other dimension of discorrelation, the 
*techniques of discorrelation* invoked in aesthetic experiments and other derangements of our sensory relations to the world. Here, too, there are continuities and discontinuities to be noted. Just as various artistic media, including the cinema, could be used for purposes either of bolstering or challenging (normative forms of) subjectivity, so too can post-cinematic media be used for subject-affirming and disorienting purposes alike. In other words, the technological operationalization of discorrelated materials (compression protocols, data caches, machine learning algorithms, whatever) does not dictate a particular perceptual effect—and yet I want to claim that these processes are hardly insignificant aesthetically. Clearly, the new technologies transform aesthetic possibilities, and not only in the sense of expanding them: some new aesthetic forms (for example, those associated with the appearance of digital glitches or the disorientations of digital lens flares or DeepFake videos, to name just a few that I have looked at elsewhere) are made possible, while other older aesthetic forms (for example, the perceptual derangement enacted by the flicker film) are rendered impossible. The difference, therefore, is to be located in the overall redistribution of aesthetic potentials, where the aesthetic is understood to encompass both formal-technical and embodied-sensory dimensions. It is above all in terms of the latter dimensions, those classically referred to under the heading of *aesthesis*, that we can indeed register a potential expansion of discorrelative techniques or possibilities for disarming or neutralizing the individualizing force of subjectivity. For computational processes enable forms of sensing that are radically distributed, both in time and space, picking out signals and patterns at scales ranging from the microscopic to the planetary and thus liberating embodied sensation from the here and now. Significantly, however, post-cinematic media most commonly neither empower nor disorient; rather, their discorrelative potentials are implicated in hegemonic subjectivation processes, whether by interpellating a normative (white cis male heterosexist etc.) subjectivity in blockbuster movies and videogames

or, more subtly, by engineering users' experience via predictive algorithms and the statistical correlations at the heart of big data and AI. Accordingly, as it is deployed in post-cinematic media environments, discorrelation is not primarily an aesthetic effect or form of experience, but rather an invisible operation that can be used for various purposes, both aesthetic and political.

We are beginning, finally, to answer another question sometimes raised about the relations of correlation and discorrelation. Isn't digital discorrelation ultimately a misnomer, or at least a distraction, as it is simply the means for another, possibly more insidious, mode of correlation? In other words, it would seem that digital processes, while operationalizing extraperceptual domains, are not only engaged in engineering perceptual experience—thus forging new correlative bonds—but that they also operate primarily *by means of* correlation. Here we need to disentangle two distinct senses of correlation—statistical correlation versus phenomenological correlation—but holding them apart is only a conceptual, not a practical possibility in the twenty-first century.[5] For effectively, statistical correlations—whether in the form of the statistically normed protocols at the heart of video codecs or the population-scale correlations enshrined in databases exploited by social media for targeted advertisements—are being grafted into the underlying aesthetico-politico-metabolic pathways that define our environments, with the effect of re-engineering the phenomenological correlations of intentionality that are open to us. Thus, while "correlation is not causation," as the mantra goes, we might add that "discorrelation is not *not* causation." At stake here is not just an algorithmic reinforcement of bias, but an implantation of said biases into our embodied relations to the world—hence a norming of bodies, minds, and societies—with all of the racist,

---

5     The story of correlation in this statistical sense is of course longer, and it spans fields of inquiry and activity as diverse as insurance, eugenics, and electrical engineering. Two important recent studies of correlation in this sense are: Chun 2021; Amoore 2020.

sexist, queer- and transphobic, and ableist consequences that we  might expect. To ask, as I do in this book, about "post-cinematic bodies" is thus to ask about how technologies of discorrelation become techniques for correlation. But it is also to ask about the material and aesthetic potentials embedded in these systems to become something else.

Summarizing, then, discorrelation is nothing new, and yet it is implemented in new ways in a post-cinematic media regime. Correlational continuities may exist despite discontinuities wrought by media-technical discorrelation. Every discorrelation, including those effected by computational technologies, inevitably leads to a new form of correlation—a new, seemingly unquestionable alignment of subjects and objects—and these processes may be exacerbated by the calculated confusion of statistical and phenomenological correlations. Ultimately, then, it is incorrect to oppose cinema and post-cinema to one another as, respectively, a correlative versus a discorrelative regime. Rather, each of them, as an instance of media in their role of originary correlators of experience, is radically multistable, alternating between correlative and discorrelative potentials. I will often use the term "dis/correlative" to foreground this fundamental multi-stability, which I seek to elaborate in this book as the basis for a new phenomenological and political aesthetics of embodiment in a world of VR, AI, smartphones, and robots.

# PART ONE: DIS/CORRELATING EMBODIMENT

# Introduction to Part One

*Post-Cinematic Bodies* explores the volatile relations that people have with their bodies in a world of computational media. In this world, embodiment is both an aesthetic and a political matter—a question of deeply contested materiality. In fact, computational technologies render the body even more contestable, that is, open to fine-grained quantification, objectification, and transformation, than perhaps ever before. Many of these processes take place at spatial and temporal scales that are outside of my subjective purview, thus challenging the existential relation that "I" have to "my" body. Clearly, subjective "ownership" of one's body was never a straightforward matter—and the idea of the body as property has been implicated in a whole host of philosophical and political quagmires, from mind/body dualism to the construction of whiteness and its racialized and gendered others.[1] It would be naive to think that the algorithmic processing to which our bodies are everywhere and invisibly subjected today would somehow liberate us from these pernicious forces; if anything, the computational capture, networked collation, and automated processing of biometric data renders our bodies even more vulnerable to categorization and violence. Significantly, though, these sociopolitical effects depend upon interventions in a stratum of fleshly existence that is itself resistant to easy categorization—a multistable stratum of prepersonal affect and embodied aesthesis. The wager of this book is that this stratum, where computation interfaces with flesh, just might—with great

---

1    The literature dealing with these questions is extensive and ranges from feminist, antiracist, and intersectional critiques of the body as property, phenomenological interrogations from Simone de Beauvoir to Frantz Fanon and Sara Ahmed, black feminist thought from bell hooks and Hortense Spillers to Saidiya Hartman, disability theorists like Rosmarie Garland-Thomson, and queer and trans theorists from Judith Butler to Gayle Salamon. See, for example, Beauvoir 1982; Fanon 2008; Ahmed 2006; hooks 1990; Spillers 2003a; Hartman 1997; Garland-Thomson 1997; Butler 1993; Salamon 2010. A useful overview of relevant discussions, including and beyond those noted here, is provided by Lennon 2019.

luck and great effort—become a resource for complicating, if not dismantling, systems of bodily oppression and standardization. Towards this end, I develop a phenomenological and political aesthetics of dis/correlation—foregrounding the multistability of the flesh's correlative and discorrelative powers and potentials—as the basis for rethinking our embodied relations to a computational lifeworld.

As a starting point, we might think about the deep interconnections between aesthetics, politics, and embodied multistability in terms of the following—drastically simplified—account of human-technological relations. Our bodies ground our sensory capacities and hence our aesthetic sensibilities in the world, anchoring our subjectivities in organic matter and environmental processes of exchange. In addition to their subjectively defined purposes, technologies also insert themselves into those underlying circuits, acting materially to modulate the metabolic flows that sustain, transform, and threaten us—thus potentially changing the shapes of our bodies, the forms of our sensation, our reflexive capacities to judge those sensations, and the forms of subjective and collective existence that are available to us. None of this is new. It's a story as old as humanity itself, and in many ways just as indeterminate as that uncertain signifier "humanity."[2] What this materialist story points to, in other words, is the lack of essence, the existential (which is to say, historical and cultural) variability of human subjectivity and collectivity—as well as an openness, via embodiment, to forces of standardization, norming, or typification. The latter forces are exacerbated in our increasingly globalized media and material cultures, especially via computational infrastructures that elude

---

2    A compelling version of this story, which posits technology as co-constitutive of the human, is told by Bernard Stiegler. An interesting complication of Stiegler's version of the story might emerge through an encounter with the Black feminist thought of Sylvia Wynter, who identifies several "genres" of the human and suggests their individuation is linked to technological and artistic practices. See Stiegler 1998; Wynter and McKittrick 2015.

subjectivity altogether and intervene directly in the underlying 
stratum of embodied and environmental metabolisms. Communications networks that span the planet depend for their inter-
operability on standardized protocols; microtemporal processes
outstrip perception, while predictive algorithms anticipate and
pave the way for subjectivities that lag behind; our formatted
environments of digitally designed architectures, objects, and
devices work directly on our bodies and materially shape the conditions of our social relations.[3]

What we see here is an interplay of indeterminacy and determination that complicates some of our usual ways of thinking
about media. On the one hand, media cannot be simple tools
or instruments of subjective determination (the NRA's view in
which "guns don't kill people, people kill people") if those tools
are reshaping the environment and thus the subjectivities
that inhabit it. On the other hand, if "media determine our
situation," as Friedrich Kittler claimed, then they do so by
way of tapping into an indeterminate stratum of existence, a
realm of Bergsonian "indetermination" (Kittler 1999, xxxix).[4]
What we might call *correlative capture*—combining both the
phenomenological and the statistical senses of correlation to
think the norming of subjectivity and collectivity—is effected
via an intervention in the discorrelated matter of prepersonal
embodiment. Political structures are thus seeded in the realm of
affect and aesthesis, which I suggest leaves a margin of indeterminacy from which resistance might be mounted, though it is
hardly guaranteed. In Part Two of this book, I look at some of the

3    An early, pre-computational line of thinking about the standardizing force
of objects and environments, to which I will return often in this book,
stems from Sartre's late, Marxist work. See Sartre 2004. Two thinkers who
have updated this line of thought for our contemporary media environment are McKenzie Wark and Jonathan Crary. See Wark 2021; Crary 2013.
Another essential perspective on the role of protocols in the contemporary
mediation of power is: Galloway 2004.

4    Henri Bergson refers to the body as a "center of indetermination": Bergson
2007.

**42** ways that artists are able to avail themselves of computational techniques in order to disrupt and destabilize their usual effects of normative correlative capture. In particular, I focus on the ways that embodied aesthesis and its dis/correlative multistability is up for grabs in VR, in human-robot choreographies and related interactions with automated agents, and in devices (including EEG interfaces and smart exercise devices) that bypass subjectivity and attach themselves directly to the metabolic processes of brains and bodies.

The chapters of Part One lay the media-philosophical groundwork for these analyses, refining the question and defining the stakes of embodied dis/correlation. Chapter One begins by questioning the place of the body in relation to what I have called discorrelated images. Putting Vivian Sobchack's phenomenological perspective into dialogue with Steven Shaviro's affect-oriented view of the cinematic body, the chapter seeks to reconcile correlative and discorrelative options as twin potentials of embodiment, which are especially key to understanding post-cinematic media in particular. Drawing on resources from Maurice Merleau-Ponty and others, Chapter 2 develops a theory of what I call the originary mediality of the flesh, grounding the aesthetics of dis/correlation that will be explored through concrete objects and artworks in Part Two.

# Bodies, Cinematic and Otherwise

On the screen in front of me, a yellow puddle floats weirdly above
a mostly barren landscape, casting a shadow on the beige ground
a few feet below it. To judge by the size of the humanoid figures
scurrying around it, the puddle is about the size of a smallish
backyard swimming pool. But then again, I can't really be sure if
the creatures I am comparing it to are the size of average human
adults; beyond their general form and bipedal gait, they certainly
don't resemble any humans I know. With somewhat enlarged
heads and vaguely animalistic faces, they tend to flock close
to one another, their behavior quite erratic. Some of them run
excitedly toward some activity off to the side of the visible space.
Others just stand in place for a while, seemingly oblivious. Occasionally, a group of them will kneel around an object, as if wor-
shipfully. It's hard to understand what they are doing or why.

In any case, these humanoid figures (which I later learn are
called Oomen) are rather peripheral figures, both narratively and
optically. The shape-shifting yellow puddle is firmly at the center
of things, driving both the story (if indeed there is one) and the
virtual camera alike. A small bit of the digital puddle separates

[Fig. 1.1] Ian Cheng, (American, born in 1984), *Emissary Sunsets The Self*, 2017. Live simulation and story. Courtesy of the Artist, Pilar Corrias, Gladstone Gallery, Standard (Oslo). Cantor Arts Center, Stanford University. William Alden Campbell and Martha Campbell Art Acquisition Fund, 2019.200. Installation view at the Cantor Arts Center, Stanford University (Photograph by Johnna Arnold).

from the rest, and the camera tracks the liquid's movement with pixel-perfect precision as it floats away and attaches itself to one of the grey pieces of organic matter strewn about the landscape. The latter, so-called Wormleaves, seem to come alive when the liquid comes into contact with them. Then ensues a rambunctious spectacle, accompanied by loud popping noises, whistles, and rustling sounds, as the symbiotic assemblage of yellow liquid and grey matter animatedly steers around the landscape like some kind of otherworldly jalopy or semi-sentient cyborg monster, accruing more grey pieces here and there, growing in size, and knocking things over left and right (fig. 1.1).

The camera follows closely, always keeping the liquid, now sitting at the helm of the growing grey creature, squarely at the center of the screen's isometric view. The humanoid figures flail and squawk around the creature, apparently upset by it. They are hardly characters that I can "identify" with, and neither is the leaf

[Fig. 1.2] Ian Cheng, (American, born in 1984), *Emissary Sunsets The Self*, 2017. Live simulation and story. Courtesy of the Artist, Pilar Corrias, Gladstone Gallery, Standard (Oslo). Cantor Arts Center, Stanford University. William Alden Campbell and Martha Campbell Art Acquisition Fund, 2019.200. Installation view at the Cantor Arts Center, Stanford University (Photograph by Johnna Arnold).

machine. In fact, there is nothing to identify with, and—more importantly—*nowhere to identify from*. The virtual camera's POV floats strangely in its fixation on the moving creature, unsettling the viewer's relation to the computer-generated images. The screen is accordingly not a neutral window onto a world, inviting me to peer into it unseen, as in certain types of filmic works; instead, it is an active interface, its isometric perspective reminiscent of a certain type of videogame—and that is precisely what the CGI graphics signal to me: I am watching a game, one that is perhaps still in beta testing, with somewhat clunky animations, crudely pixelated representations of fire, and apparently unfinished environmental elements provided by the game engine in which it was developed. To judge by the parallel projection method used in rendering the 3D environment, this is a somewhat older game—or more likely a somewhat nostalgic indie production—its camera's perspective, looking down from a vantage fixed at roughly 30° above the horizontal plane, similar to a 1990s *Sims* game before the franchise switched over to a true 3D, quasi "Renaissance-style" perspective projection.[1] Visually, then, I have a feel for the interface, even if the camera movement feels glitchy and alien.

Except that this game is not driven by a player; rather, it plays itself. We might say that the human is thereby taken out of the loop, but this isn't wholly accurate. I am still here, looking. But *where* am I? Physically, I am seated in a gallery space, looking across the room at a large, almost square-shaped screen (extending 12 feet up from the floor and with an unusual aspect ratio of 7:6) at the other end, a little over 20 feet from where I sit (fig. 1.2).[2] But I am also suspended in some indeterminate relation to the images on the screen. I am not engrossed in the images of a prerecorded work of film or video art; instead I attend to the real-time generation of computational images—but my usual modes of interacting with such images, by way of a videogame controller, a keyboard, or a VR headset, have all been denied to me, foregrounding a kind of vertigo that has less to do with the sublime nature of the images (though I won't deny an element of that)[3] and more to do with the unresolved place of my body, which is seemingly called upon to act, or interact, but cannot. The insistent centering of the yellow liquid suggests that this *would be* my point of interface, that my task would be to control its movement. But since I cannot, I feel more like *it* is controlling

1    A useful exploration of perspective versus parallel projection in videogames can be found in Larochelle (2013).

2    My encounter with this work occurred in July 2022 at the Iris & B. Gerald Cantor Center for Visual Arts at Stanford University.

3    Interestingly, the artist's installation guide for the piece specifies: "The installation, whether using projection or using LED, should feel awe-some, in the way that a vista or view of a landscape feels awe-some. The scale of the image should convey a relative higher status to the viewer, so that the viewer feels like a witness to something vaster than himself." Maggie Dethloff (Assistant Curator of Photography and New Media, Cantor Arts Center, Stanford University), personal email communication, September 9, 2022.

*me*, or at least controlling my visual access to the scene, giving the images and their motion a distinctly inhuman feel.

Indeed, the displacement of agency and the general disorientation I have been describing is not accidental. Media artist Ian Cheng's *Emissary Sunsets the Self* (2017) is a "live simulation"— an open-ended evolutionary system driven by AI agents interacting with environmental rules encoded in the physical properties of objects and their reactive potentials.[4] Produced in the popular Unity game engine (or game-authoring environment), the work is highly self-reflexive, framed in accompanying lore as an enigmatic story about a futuristic artificial intelligence, MotherAI, bored of its own disembodied existence and driven to experiment with taking on material form.[5] The yellow liquid is the AI's emissary to the biotic realm, through which it is able to "drone" or take possession of the Wormleaf fauna in "an attempt to feel the sensations of incarnated life."[6] Thus, a real AI plays a diegetic AI, and the videogame plays itself, thereby usurping the role of the human player now left feeling sidelined and strangely disembodied. The perspective of the viewing subject is thus defined by a virtual amputation of their interactive potential. My presence seems optional before a system that might go on forever, through endless cycles of virtual daylight and nighttime, through

4    This is the third piece in a trilogy of "live simulation" works by Cheng, following *Emissary of the Squat Gods* (2015) and *Emissary Forks at Perfection* (2015–16).

5    As detailed in Cheng's *Emissaries Guide to Worlding*, which elaborates the narrative lore behind the work, as well as the artistic process and rationale, the *Emissaries* trilogy depicts, in its first episode, the birth of human consciousness about 3000 years ago (*Emissary of the Squat Gods*); then an AI simulation operating on the last remaining "Original Human Matter" about 200 years in the future, around the 23rd century CE (*Emissary Forks at Perfection*); and finally the bored AI seeking embodiment as one last experiment before extinguishing itself about 250 years later, around the 25th or 26th century CE (*Emissary Sunsets the Self*). This timeline is recounted in Cheng's interview with curator Hans Ulrich Obrist, in Cheng 2018, 286.

6    Ian Cheng 2018, 47. This narrative background is also communicated in more compressed form through exhibition wall text.

 all the seasons, the AI never tiring of sending out probes, the camera always following its adventures in vicarious embodiment before resetting its gaze—over and over again but never twice the same—on the big yellow puddle at the center of it all. Where do I stand in relation to this system? Cheng's generative artwork poses this question forcefully, its ambiguous non/interactivity calling upon us to rethink our phenomenological relations to a variety of contemporary images. Above all, it asks us to reassess the place of the perceiving body today.[7]

As I argued in *Discorrelated Images*, the invisible computational processing at the heart of contemporary digital images like those in Cheng's artwork erodes the perceptual bond or correlation between viewers and the images they see. In the era of

---

7    For Cheng, the trilogy of works is more about the evolution of consciousness than a problematization of embodiment. Yet his approach, which draws on recent cognitive science, is one that sees these dimensions in necessary interconnection. Hence, this piece's focus on the question of what would happen if AI became embodied, rather than the usual sci-fi scenario of AI becoming sentient, can be seen also as a speculative narrativization of the dis/correlative destabilization of embodiment in post-cinematic media. Also of note is Cheng's focus on the interplay between goal-oriented narrative and open-ended simulation, which he describes as a struggle between "deterministic" and "non-deterministic" forces that he pits against one another (2018, 285). These forces are already at work in the creative process, which Cheng describes as a battle between the assertion of "a reliably humanistic vision" (ibid., 285) and the attempt to overthrow "an all-too-human agenda" (ibid., 137). These conflicting impulses are then given free reign in the final, unpredictable work, which operates independently of its author: "Creating complexity, and living with the indeterminacy inherent in complexity, begins to feel like working a muscle that has always been there. As I write these words, versions of the *Emissaries* trilogy are humming along in multiple parallel instances on multiple computers on multiple continents" (ibid., 203). The ultimate optionality of the author (or viewer) and the "deliberate incompleteness" of the work (ibid., 205) point towards a discorrelative trajectory that is balanced, however, by the deterministic trajectory of narrative, which would serve to correlate the viewer's perception of events within an ongoing arc. Cheng's multilayered probing of multistability should not be cordoned off, I suggest, from the probing of embodiment the work initiates, both diegetically and materially.

celluloid-based cinema, that correlation had been theorized 
in a variety of ways—for example, as a psychoanalytic bond
of "suture," whereby the spectator is imaginatively inserted or
inscribed into narrative and ideological structures (Dayan 1974,
22–31). In a different vein, phenomenologically oriented theorists
like Vivian Sobchack argued convincingly that any such cognitive
bond had to be anchored in a material, bodily relation between
the viewer and the cinematic apparatus (Sobchack 1992). But if,
as I believe, the post-cinematic apparatus is characterized by a
discorrelation between human perception and computational
processing, where does that leave the body? Cheng's work, by
simultaneously proposing and withholding an embodied (interactive) relation, suggests that the answer might lie in a multistable give-and-take between correlative and discorrelative
trajectories. As we shall see, these issues are not restricted to
intentionally disorienting works like Cheng's; indeed, the question of the body and its relation both to images and to infrastructures is a pressing one even in relation to mainstream and
mundane media experiences, including videogames, virtual
reality, and digital exercise machines. Looking at these and other
sites, including a range of artistic interventions that, like Cheng's,
disrupt our taken-for-granted relations, I hope to account
more generally for the ways in which viewing bodies are implicated today in the automated and data-intensive production
and reception of images—and to shed light, ultimately, on the
place of the body in a post-filmic visual culture. Before I take up
these digital media objects and address the underlying question
of post-cinematic bodies directly, however, it will be useful to
establish a baseline of comparison by way of two different conceptions of embodiment and the role that it plays in our experience of cinematic (that is, pre-digital and non-televisual) moving-
image media.

# Cinematic Bodies and Beyond

Writing at roughly the same time, in the early 1990s, both Vivian Sobchack and Steven Shaviro turned to the body in order to offer alternatives to the still dominant psychoanalytic film theory of the day. But their accounts of embodiment and the attendant experiences of the filmic image that they describe are very different from one another: Sobchack draws on existential phenomenology and is inspired particularly by Maurice Merleau-Ponty's reflections on the body as the active base of perception, while Shaviro draws on Gilles Deleuze's work on the cinema and his ultimately Bergsonian theory of affect to theorize a passive viewing body enthralled by the image (Sobchack 1992; Shaviro 1993). Sobchack theorizes a subjective, temporal, and ultimately ethical bond of correlation between the embodied viewer and film's unfolding of visual experience, while Shaviro celebrates cinema's potential to dissolve the subject in experiences of excess and abjection. These differences—between an active and a passive body, between a perceptual or an affective body, or between the body as the seat of the subject or as the site of the abject—are hardly inconsequential, but I want to foreground first of all the common recourse to corporeality, which both thinkers take to be a basic material fact of our existence and the key to understanding our relations to and experiences of cinematic moving images. Later, I will suggest that there is a more fundamental, though often overlooked, philosophical common ground between these positions as well, and that it can help us to think about post-cinematic bodies in particular.

Accordingly, it is not my intention either to downplay or to exaggerate the differences between these conceptions of the cinematic body, nor even really to reconcile them. Both Sobchack and Shaviro have been and remain huge influences on my own thinking, and I am grateful to have learned from

both of them over the years.[8] For me, at least, there is simply no **51**
competition between these two thinkers, as they each articulate
something necessary about our embodied relations to images.
In fact, I think the necessity of *both* points of view becomes fully
apparent—perhaps for the first time—when our images enter
into computational systems, when they start to lose the sensuous
qualities that had defined images as self-evidently visual objects
up until then, and when they thus begin their discorrelation from
human perception.

For the moment, however, we are focused on the cinema in
its pre-digital form. For Sobchack, cinematic experience is
defined in terms of a phenomenological correlation between the
viewer's subjective perception and the objective presentation
on screen of a perceptual act. At the heart of this conception
lies a dynamization of static photographic images, through
which the cinema distinguishes itself from all previous media
and simultaneously effects a momentous shift in embodied
and perceptual relations. Photography had already effected a
revolution of sorts, making available "images of the world with an
exactitude previously rivaled only by the human eye" (Sobchack
2016, 96). Thereby demoting human vision, the photograph nevertheless empowered human seers by offering *"the material control,
containment, and objective possession of time and experience"* (ibid.,
96). But this came at the cost of isolating a moment, snatching it
from the flow of time, and rendering it an inert physical object—
offering only an arrested view of a frozen past that "cannot be
inhabited" in the present (ibid., 99). The cinema reversed this
trend, setting photographic traces of the past back in motion and
making them habitable again by subjects experiencing them *now*.

Sobchack writes: "Through its objectively visible spatialization of
a frozen point of view into dynamic and intentional trajectories
of *self-displacing vision* and through its subjectively experienced

---

8    Accordingly, I could not have been more thrilled to have endorsements on
the back of *Discorrelated Images* from both Sobchack and Shaviro!

temporalization of an essential moment into *lived momentum*, the cinematic radically reconstitutes the photographic" (ibid., 99). This is to say that film, when actualized as a spatiotemporal phenomenon through projection, fills the intentional consciousness of the viewer, unfurling an ongoing experiential content that exceeds the inert objectivity of the photograph. Thus, "[c]inematic technology *animates* the photographic and reconstitutes its materiality, visibility, and perceptual similitude in a difference not of degree but of kind. The *moving picture* is a visible representation not of activity finished or past but of activity coming into being and being" (ibid., 101). As a temporal object in Husserl's sense, the time of the film is identical with the time of my consciousness of it.[9] Furthermore, and this is the key, the moving picture is not *just* a representation: "the moving picture not only visibly represents moving objects but also—and simultaneously—presents *the very movement of vision itself*" (ibid., 101). In the cinema, we see the process of seeing itself:

> In its pre-electronic state and original materiality ..., the cinema mechanically projected and made visible *for the very first time* not just the objective world but the very structure and process of subjective, embodied vision—hitherto only directly available to human beings as an invisible and private structure that each of us experiences as "our own." (Ibid., 104)

Even stronger, the cinema presents itself "as the *subject of its own vision*, as well as an *object for our vision*" (ibid., 104).

But subjective perception, in the existential phenomenological tradition to which Sobchack belongs, presupposes embodiment—it relies on the rich, intentional form of embodiment that, following Merleau-Ponty, exceeds the merely physiological body as a condition of worldly perception and action (Merleau-Ponty 2002). Our perception is always anchored in a "lived body" that

---

9   On temporal objects, see Husserl 1964; for a media-theoretical extension, see Stiegler 2011.

encompasses our practical abilities and disabilities, our material
and technical interests and entanglements with the world. If
cinema presents its own form of subjectivity, then film must also
have a body of its own. And, as Sobchack argues at length in *The
Address of the Eye*, though film's body is not identical with ours, it
is homologous with it in certain respects.[10] With "the camera its
perceptive organ, the projector its expressive organ, the screen
its discrete and material center of meaningful experience," what
Sobchack calls "the cinematic lived body" is able to perambulate,
perceive, and express "a concrete habitable *world*" that is commensurate with our own lifeworld (Sobchack 2016, 108, 107). And
thus, the perceptual correlation between viewer and film rests
on an underlying bodily correlation, where "[t]he correlation and
materiality of both human subjects and their objective artifacts
… suggests some commensurability and possibilities of confusion, exchange, and reversibility between them" (ibid., 94). The
cinematic image, on this basis, constitutes itself as "an anonymous, mobile, embodied, and ethically invested *subject* of worldly
space" (ibid., 102).

But this correlation, according to Sobchack, begins to break down
with cinema's transformation through electronic and digital
technologies, which radically call into question the homology
between the infrastructures of visual experience (human
embodiment) and those of visible images (the cinematic lived
body). Because of the dependence of the perceptual on the
material, the technological reorganization of the post-cinematic
image challenges, in Sobchack's view, the medium's moral gravity
and its ability to engage us in an exploration of the lifeworld.
The "electronic world incorporates the spectator/user uniquely
in a spatially decentered, weakly temporalized and quasi-dis-
embodied (or diffusely embodied) state" (ibid., 109–110). This is
because, according to Sobchack,

10   See Sobchack 1992, particularly chapter 3: "Film's Body," 164–259.

54

the electronic is phenomenologically experienced not
as a discrete, intentional, body-centered mediation and
projection in space but rather as a simultaneous, dispersed,
and insubstantial transmission across a network or web that
is constituted spatially more as a materially flimsy lattice-
work of nodal points than as the stable ground of embodied
experience. (Ibid., 110–111)

In this environment, "subjectivity and affect free-float or free-fall
or free-flow across a horizontal/vertical grid or, as is the case with
all our electronic pocket communication devices, disappear into
thin air. Subjectivity is at once decentered, dispersed, and completely extroverted" (ibid., 116).

Compare now Shaviro, who in *The Cinematic Body* celebrates
precisely this dissolution, which he already finds at work in
the cinema, independent of the shift to electronic or digital
mediation. Advocating for a "thoroughly postmodern sensibility"
that foregrounds "inescapable ambivalences and affective intensities," Shaviro revels in the cinema's ability to "dissolv[e] any
notion of fixed personal identity or of an integral and self-con-
tained subject" (1993, vii, viii). But rather than a weakening of
embodiment, Shaviro credits the dissolution of subjectivity to a
heightening of bodily experience in "visceral, affective responses
to film," or what he identifies as "prereflective responses" and
"corporeal reactions of desire and fear, pleasure and disgust, fascination and shame" (ibid., viii). Thus, Shaviro no less
than Sobchack is interested in material relations that exceed
the purely representational and define a space of axiological
significance and struggle: "Power works in the depths and on
the surfaces of the body, and not just in the disembodied realm
of 'representation' or of 'discourse.' It is in the flesh first of all,
far more than on some level of supposed ideological reflection,
that the political is personal and the personal political" (ibid.,
viii). By activating this "involuntary, presubjective realm of
visual fascination" and foregrounding "the materiality of affect
and sensation," according to Shaviro, the cinema helps us to

understand the ways that power is materially, corporeally con-
densed in normative subject formations, or "to discover the
conflicting forces, the 'molecular' movements, that subtend and
invest—and often contradict—the global, 'molar' order of phallic
representation" (ibid., 19, 15, 23).

Opening up Deleuzean "lines of flight" away from a purely cognitive relation to images, the cinema collapses the distance
between subjects and objects, plunging them into the space of
affect as defined by Henri Bergson: a space that is in between
our capacities for perception and for action, "an irreducible gap
between stimulus and response" that is prior to the articulation
of the subject (Shaviro 1993, 51). It is in this sense that Shaviro
claims "[t]he experience of watching a film remains stubbornly
concrete, immanent, and prereflective: it is devoid of depth and
interiority" (ibid., 32). Subjective registration, on this model, is
an afterthought: "I have already been touched and altered by
these sensations, even before I have had the chance to become
conscious of them" (ibid., 46). To recuperate this presubjective
realm, which theory tends to occlude and obstruct through its
assertion of critical distance, Shaviro asks us to submit to a "radical passivity" which negates "the realm of traditional subject/
object dualism, but also of phenomenological intentionality" as
we give in to "a forced, ecstatic abjection before the image" (ibid.,
48, 47, 49).

Clearly, Sobchack's and Shaviro's accounts of embodiment and its
relation to the cinema are in many ways diametrically opposed.
But as I stated before, my goal here is not to adjudicate between
their positions. In fact, I do not even see a need to reconcile
them (though I will, in a sense, do just that in a moment). Taken
together, Sobchack's and Shaviro's approaches suggest that a
spectrum of embodied relations exists, neither indifferent to nor
unilaterally determined by media as technological and cultural
forces. Sobchack argues that the cinema lends itself to a new
perceptual relation (that of subjectively seeing subjective seeing),
but she also insists that the embodied subject of perception is

informed and reshaped by technologies and culture alike—that (in terms she borrows from philosopher of technology Don Ihde) the "microperceptual" level of immediate bodily sensation is inextricable from the "macroperceptual" level of linguistic and cultural hermeneutics (Sobchack 2016, 92–93). So there is no guarantee that the relations described by her will actually obtain in any given situation, even if the materiality of the cinematic apparatus in its relation to human embodiment strongly suggests them. Meanwhile, Shaviro's focus is neither on the micro- nor the macroperceptual level, as he seeks to open something that might more properly be labeled the *nanoperceptual* domain of prepersonal affect. Between Sobchack and Shaviro we thus find differences of method and of focus, but there is no ontological conflict: the lived body of phenomenology is not free-floating or without an infrastructure, so to speak; and its infrastructure includes not just anatomy and physiology, but also the realm of presubjective awareness or environmental responsiveness that we share in common with animals and even plants. This molecular or, as I prefer to call it, metabolic level is a constant companion to perceptual subjectivity, even if it largely remains unseen (for the simple fact that it subtends the seeing subject as a material condition of subjectivity and visuality alike). As Shaviro shows us, however, it too is an option for the sensing body at the cinema.

But there is more at stake in these conceptions than just ontology. As we have seen, Shaviro locates hope for a more liberatory politics in cinema's affective option, which would unyoke experience from the constraining force of normative subjectivities. Sobchack, on the other hand, sees cinema's embodied correlation as an ethical matter, and she warns that the perceptual, subjective option for cinematic experience is being displaced, due to the material dispersion of the image in the infrastructures of electronic and digital media. Interestingly, Deleuze would seem to concur, despite his usual championing of the presubjective; in his analysis of the so-called control

society, we find him warning that the forces of "dividuation"—
or the de-individualizing powers of blackboxed computing,
packet-switching, networked communications, and big data, for
example—operationalize (perhaps even weaponize) the infra-
or nanoperceptual level (Deleuze 1992, 3–7). So while Shaviro's
appeal to affect is offered as a means to challenge normative
subjectivities and the binary formations that undergird them, the
dissolution of the subject can also lead to a more radical policing
and regulation of political agencies, as the predictive operations
of algorithmic culture are granted the ability to anticipate us in
advance and actively modulate the process of subjectivation.

I will be returning to these political ambivalences and multistabilities, which enable either the dismantling or reinforcement
of normative forms and forces of embodiment, such as those
of cisheterosexist and binaristic gendering and racialization,
throughout the chapters of this book. But before I get too
far ahead of myself, it is important to emphasize that what
Sobchack and Shaviro together demonstrate is *that cinema both
exercises a correlative force and holds a discorrelative potential*; it is
marked both by an integrative force that consolidates subjective
perception into a body and a dissipative potential that multiplies
or dis-integrates the body into a jumble of affective intensities.
Recognizing that there may be contentious political and ethical
consequences attached to either one of the alternatives, we can
regard these first of all as cinema's twin *aesthetic options*—not in
a superficial sense of "aesthetics," e.g. concerning which option
we might prefer or find more pleasing, but in a deeper sense of
embodied *aesthesis*; in other words, these are correlative and
discorrelative options with respect to the way our bodies are
sensorially attuned to the image. However, this way of framing
the issue suggests we are dealing with an image that is visual and
available to sensation in the first place, while it is precisely this
visuality and sense-ability that is in question in a post-cinematic
media regime. Artist Trevor Paglen (2016) has put the point most
provocatively with his notion of "invisible images"—images

 produced by machines for other machines, never seen by human eyes. For example, automated drones and self-driving cars process millions of unseen images in order to detect objects and navigate in space. As I have argued in *Discorrelated Images*, similar processes are at work in the computational pre-processing also of the images that we *do* see, whether through motion-estimation processes in digital coding and decoding of digital video, real-time upscaling, or motion smoothing, among other things.[11] Through these processes, images are subject to dividuation or dis-integration just like the subjectivities that Deleuze describes. And in this discorrelation or severing of the image from our perception, it is our consciousness or sensation that becomes the immediate target of dividuation.

But in order to evaluate the place of the body in post-cinema, we need to keep both Sobchack's correlative and Shaviro's discorrelative aesthetic options in mind. For computational discorrelation is largely a matter of micro- or nanotemporal operations that subtend *and enable* the subjective perception of images, sounds, and narratives. Each level, the subjective and the subperceptual, is operative simultaneously, though the temporal relations between them are hardly linear due to the incom-mensurability between the time-scales of computer processing and of human perception. My point, as I have already stated, is that we need to account for both scales, and hence both the correlative and the discorrelative operations, if we are to come to terms with post-cinematic embodiment. And this is where it is imperative to uncover what I have referred to as the often over-looked philosophical common ground between Sobchack's sub-jective, phenomenological body and Shaviro's affective body.

This common ground is articulated by Merleau-Ponty in *The Phenomenology of Perception* in terms of what he calls a *"pre-objective view"* that characterizes the primordial (and equally pre-subjective) state of embodiment, which he elaborates as follows:

11    See, in particular, Denson 2020a, chapter 2, "Dividuated Images," 51-72.

"Prior to stimuli and sensory contents, we must recognize a kind of inner diaphragm which determines, infinitely more than they do, what our reflexes and perceptions will be able to aim at in the world, the area of our possible operations, the scope of our life" (2002, 92). This "inner diaphragm," operative prior to the articulation of subject and object, is in no way opposed to the active, intentional body of phenomenology; rather, the latter, the lived body, supervenes on the former, which always remains operative alongside perceptual and motile subjectivity. Anticipating his later conception of the "flesh of the world" by a good decade and a half, Merleau-Ponty's "inner diaphragm" corresponds almost exactly to Bergson's conception of affect, which is similarly located prior to perception and action or stimulus and response as "that part or aspect of the inside of our bodies which mix with the image of external bodies."[12] In both cases, we are dealing with a presubjective core that can *either* give rise to a correlative relation between subject and object *or* enable blurring, confusion, or material indistinction.

As for why this common ground is so often overlooked, I place the blame with Deleuze, who in his *Cinema* books strategically exaggerates the differences between phenomenology and Bergsonian metaphysics. There, Deleuze presents a sharp alternative between phenomenological intentionality, summarized in the phrase "all consciousness is consciousness *of* something," and Bergsonian thought, which he glosses as "all consciousness *is* something" (Deleuze 1986, 60). The suggestion is that this is an unbreachable gap, and that phenomenology is categorically unable to account for prepersonal intensities and other realities that are not the objects of subjective perception. But in addition to erasing the non-referential nature of the inner diaphragm (as well as other subperceptual processes invoked by thinkers in the phenomenological tradition), Deleuze's focus on

12    Bergson 2007, 60. On Merleau-Ponty's concept of "the flesh of the world," see his posthumously published *The Visible and the Invisible* (Merleau-Ponty 1968b).

consciousness comes at the expense of the body, and he thus overlooks or suppresses the common ground of preconscious embodiment at the root of both philosophies.

When we restore this ground of the "inner diaphragm," which acts *alongside* the subjectivized body, we are better able to account for a range of phenomena, both cinematic and otherwise. Etymologically, a diaphragm refers to a "partition-wall" or "barrier," but rather than simply dividing an inside and an outside, it is itself characterized by an internal division. Even in its anatomical sense, according to which it refers to the septum dividing the thoracic from the abdominal cavities in mammals, the diaphragm is internally divided as "partly muscular, partly tendinous."[13] In the subanatomical sense invoked by Merleau-Ponty, the inner diaphragm epitomizes this self-division by bridging stimulus and response, subject and object, in such a way as to enable reversals (such as in Merleau-Ponty's famous example of two hands touching, each of which can reversibly be touched or do the touching (1968a, 130–155)). In other words, this inner diaphragm is not a simple barrier between the subjective and objective, or between those and the presubjective, but is, more fundamentally, the multistable ground that divides itself into perceptually correlative and discorrelative forms of embodiment. Accordingly, we might rebrand this the dis/correlative diaphragm, in order to foreground its multistability (and to deemphasize the misleading binary suggested by the term *inner diaphragm*, which lacks any straightforward *outer* or external counterpart). The utility of this concept is that it enables us to account for, without resolving, the aesthetic duality of the cinema as an arena for embodied experience—a duality that is exacerbated in computational media. Most importantly, with respect to post-cinematic experience, the dis/correlative diaphragm provides a mechanism by which to explain the impact

13    "diaphragm, n." Oxford English Dictionary Online, June 2022 (Oxford University Press): https://www.oed.com/view/Entry/52038.

of computational processes that operate largely outside our perception but nevertheless exercise a material force on our bodies and our experience. In *Discorrelated Images*, I argued along these lines that digital video compression, which can give rise to perceptual objects such as compression artifacts and glitches that make us momentarily aware of its otherwise invisible operations, also and more fundamentally continues to exert such a force on our bodies *even when it remains invisible*.[14] This it does by way of microtemporal operations affecting the nanoperceptual sensitivities of the dis/correlative diaphragm, which though they escape conscious notice may nevertheless reshape our embodied habits and eventually also our higher-order perceptual sensitivities. For example, as Jordan Schonig has argued, we may become unconsciously (or nonconsciously) attuned to scenes that are computationally more challenging to process—for instance, high-bitrate scenes with lots of quick, detailed motion, which are thus more likely to produce a glitch when they encounter a processing bottleneck during their translation from encoded data to screen event.[15] This attunement, which is not to say awareness, is an affective, embodied relation that accompanies and does not preclude a more intentional, subjective relation with the objects depicted *in* the images.

In the next chapter, I will further develop this dis/correlative aesthetic framework in terms of the flesh's self-division, or what Merleau-Ponty calls the *écart* or fission between tactility and specularity, that initiates what I call the originary mediality of the flesh. This will put us in a better position to understand the various modalities according to which post-cinematic media play on our multistable sensitivities and transform our bodies through intertwined processes of dis/correlation. First, however, let us stay with the issue, broached here several times, of the visual image and its shifting relation to invisibility.

14    I make the argument in chapter 2, "Dividuated Images," particularly 56–72.
15    See Schonig 2022, especially chapter 6, "Bleeding Pixels," 149–178.

# Visuality Beyond Vision

Earlier, I referenced Trevor Paglen's notion of computation's "invisible images." This provocative concept is invaluable for any attempt to understand the transition from cinema to post-cinema and the increasing operationalization of discorrelated materials, and I have appealed to it elsewhere to argue that we are now living in what is essentially a post-visual culture (for example Denson 2020a, 67–72). But as I have been emphasizing the multistable coexistence of dis/correlative options, it is important that we also look at invisibility's flipside and ask: what becomes of the image's visuality and its correlative potentials for vision today? As we shall see, this question has significant bearing on the question of embodiment.

In his book *Uncomputable*, Alexander Galloway offers a path forward with his distinction between photographic and computational "contracts" of visuality (2021, 52). Essentially, these contracts describe the correlative potentials of different image types, framed in terms of the geometric configurations that they suggest for perceiving subjects and perceived images.

> The photographic version of the contract, if it were drawn as a diagram, would resemble a cone splayed outward from an origin point, like a horn. Something of great importance occupies the spot at the tip of the horn, something important like a lens or an aperture or an eyeball or a subject. Starting at the focal point, photographic vision fans out into the world, locating objects in proximal relation to the origin. (Ibid., 52)

According to Galloway, the photographic contract is thus a subject-centric or ocularcentric correlation, which is significantly challenged by computational media and its very different geometry. As he puts it,

> computational media has finally impoverished the eye …. Indeed, computational vision is also conical, but inverted,

more like a funnel with the tip facing away. Here the perceiving subject is not focused into a dense, rich point at the center but diffuses itself outward toward the edge of the space .... The object, by contrast, lies at the point of the funnel, receiving all the many inputs issued to it from the perimeter. Thus, if the photographic eye is, as it were, *convex*, then the computational eye is *concave*, flanking and encompassing the world from the fringe. (Ibid., 53)

In these alternatives of concentration or densification and diffusion, we hear echoes of the correlative and discorrelative potentials outlined by Sobchack and Shaviro. Provocatively, though, in posing them as visual (and geometrically visualizable) contracts, Galloway challenges us to see both of them in terms of their correlative possibilities, each as the inverse of the other.

At the heart of this topological inversion from the photographic to the computational lies an architectural rather than optical perspective, one that emphasizes a volumetric rather than planar conception of the image: "The condition is simple: assume that objects and worlds will be viewable and manipulable from all sides in multiple dimensions" (ibid, 53). As Jacob Gaboury (2021) details in his definitive history of computer graphics, computational images are first of all modeled objects, only subsequently rendered as flat, quasi-photographic images. There is a pipeline that goes from ingesting real objects via digitization (some historically significant objects include a Volkswagen Beetle, a Melitta teapot, a man's hands, and several women's faces), abstracting them into computationally manipulable models, and then rendering them visually in a graphical interface. But beyond just pixelating our visual culture, these image objects are actively reshaping our world through the computer-aided design and standardization of new material objects and architectures, with far-reaching ramifications for our embodied relations to lived space.[16] Thus, the bulk of our images are no longer flat; instead, they occupy and indeed format space whether simulated or real. Interestingly, in this context, the isometric visuals we encountered in Ian Cheng's *Emissary Sunsets the Self*, which were characteristic of an earlier moment in videogame history, represent a kind of technical compromise between the fully volumetric and the strictly planar: in arcade games from the early 1980s, for example, 2D sprites and tiles were made to look like 3D objects through parallel projection, a visualization technique that keeps objects the same size on screen regardless of their depth, thus sidestepping the complex recalculations that would be required to simulate visual perspective. Because such images are neither completely volumetric nor perspectival, they entail a significantly volatile perceptual compromise, the multistability of which Cheng's work exploits for dis/correlative purposes.

Clearly, then, the inversion of photographic visuality is not just a technical matter; the shift to visuality as a question of modeling, rather than representing, is a matter of fundamental philosophical importance. But are philosophers even aware of this momentous inversion masquerading as the mundane reality of computer modeling? "Plato, sure; Husserl, probably not," Galloway (2021, 53) quips. That is, Husserl regards the world via the subject-centric photographic contract, whereas Plato approaches things from the perspective of computational visuality, attempting to assume the role of a concave eye that wraps around all that can be seen. Such a perspective would involve a strange self-displacement, as even the philosopher's visible body would become an object of this all-seeing eye—thus turning itself and the world into a weird volumetric ouroboros. But that must be what it feels like to picture oneself from

16    Gaboury discusses several compelling instances of such standardizing effects, including "Boeing Man," a computer model of a human body used for the ergonomic design of aircraft cockpits (2021, 12–17), but also more mundane objects, like Ikea furniture, that begin their life as image objects and while radically shaping the built environment (ibid., 191–202).

the standpoint of the eternal Forms: focused and punctually embodied vision dissolves into total, environmental visuality. Rather than Platonism in any strict sense, what this inversion points to is therefore the emphatic environmentality of contemporary images: "Computational vision takes it as a given that *point of view is not necessary for seeing*" (ibid., 53).

If this seems like hyperbole, consider that it is in fact a dominant vision in today's tech world, as evidenced by the imagery at play in the names of prominent Silicon Valley companies. The data analytics and surveillance company Palantir, as is well known, takes its name from the "seeing stones" that, in J. R. R. Tolkien's *The Lord of the Rings*, allowed their users (notably, the evil wizard Sauron) to see events taking place at great distances, including those in the past and future. Another company, self-driving car systems company Argo AI, derives its name from the *Argo*, the magical ship of the Argonauts, built by Argus, son of Arestor, who happens to share a name with Argus Panoptes, an all-seeing giant with a hundred eyes; although humanists might insist on the importance of disambiguating these figures, the confusion is strategic for a company whose magical self-driving car technologies rely centrally on a system of AI-powered cameras and LIDAR sensors that encircle the vehicle, modeling the environment from all angles in real time. If there is any doubt about how central this new visuality is to the tech industry, consider that countless other companies have adopted the name Argus to signal their strengths in surveillance, imaging, and the increasingly ubiquitous commodity called "insight": Argus HD provides live streaming and video production, including VR and 360-degree video[17]; Argus Cyber Security uses the new visuality to protect smart cars against cyberattacks[18]; Argus Advisory, a predictive analytics and data modeling company, caters to financial institutions and promises to "uncover insights that others can't"[19];

17    See https://argushd.com.
18    See https://argus-sec.com.
19    Quoted from https://www.argusinformation.com.

and Argus Media, billing itself as the "leading independent provider of energy and commodity price benchmarks," similarly offers "exclusive prices and insight" to help companies navigate the coming energy transition (or exploit climate catastrophe for profit).[20] The message, in all of these cases and countless others, is clear: in today's world, you need more than eyes to see what's going on; you need nothing less than an all-seeing vision machine, capable of illuminating things (objects, images, data, environments, worlds) from all sides at once.

Somewhat jarringly, when seen in the crassly commercial (and militaristic) context of Silicon Valley, Galloway characterizes this new visual regime as an "'ethical' visuality," explaining that "the ethical is the mode in which all points and positions dissolve in favor of a single, generic claim: 'all is love'; or, here, 'there is no point of view.' Photography says *here is a view*, but computer vision says there is no point of view because *here are all of them*" (2021, 56). I suspect the provocation is intentional, and that part of Galloway's point is to highlight the way this ethics, based in the generic universal, serves to suppress or neutralize the realm of political contestation and difference. Bypassing the camera obscura and Renaissance perspective, this new visuality denies "situated knowledges" and asserts a god's eye view from everywhere and nowhere (Haraway 1988, 575–599). Nevertheless, while the singular, ocularcentric point of view disappears, Galloway asserts that "[v]isuality does not vanish. On the contrary, visuality goes metastable, appearing at any place and any time under the aegis of the 'virtual camera'" (2021, 56). This is an important point, as it foregrounds flexibility, portability, and modularity as key to the exercise of power in this new regime, but it also raises a central question: how can this paradoxical visuality, for which Plato stands fittingly as the philosophical patron saint, be a correlative option at all—and one that challenges the "correlationism" of the Husserlian-photographic alternative? I agree with Galloway

20    Quoted from https://www.argusmedia.com/en.

that the answer is to be found in an interface that "goes metastable." Only such an interface can mediate between the Platonic and Husserlian options and establish the possibility of what is essentially a *non-correlationist correlation*. The latter is a topic that I have broached elsewhere as one of central concern for the definition of media (Denson 2014, 279–350). I believe the present context—particularly, the question of how environmental visuality can be made commensurate with embodied existence—calls for some expansion, if not modification, of my previous account.

In *Postnaturalism*, I argued that the speculative realists' anti-correlationism (their challenge to what they perceive as the refusal, in thinkers like Kant and Husserl, to think beyond "the correlation between thinking and being") comes up against a limit in media, which *as media* necessarily implicate humans (ibid., 279-350). But rather than acquiesce to a narrowly anthropocentric view of media, I posited a non-correlationist alternative: what is first required is a dissociation of media from their narrow connections to perception, cognition, and communication, allowing us to conceive of them, instead, in their broader materiality and function of mediating between embodied experience and the material environment—interceding at a metabolic level as well as the more familiar subjective one. Essentially, the non-correlationist option is to locate the very mediality of media in their function as the "originary correlators" of experience (ibid., 282-298). The philosophical payoff is not only that the abstraction of "the human" is decentered, but radical change and variation in the shape of phenomenological correlation (concretely: historical, cultural, and embodied differences) become thinkable, and it is precisely media in their metastability that are able to articulate these shifts.[21]

---

21    My argument that media articulate deformations in the "shape" of correlation might be compared to Sara Ahmed's argument that the material situations, objects, and environments that uphold social and familial arrangements have a similar role with regard to the "orientation" of correlation, including keeping it "straight" or "queering" it. See Ahmed 2006.

Already in my earlier account, this metastability was connected to embodiment, but the massive expansion of the computational visual contract requires some additional focus on the way that the flesh is operationalized as a mechanism of political control. As the complement to the originary correlative function of media, there is an originary mediality of the flesh that, as I will argue at greater length in the next chapter, concerns the body in both its specular and its tactile powers, its powers of vision and of touch. The transformation of the visual contract, which dissolves ocularcentric individualism only to replace it with a generically universal ethics of imaging, therefore also implies a transformation of the body's felt relation to space and spatiality. As we have seen, the Platonism of computational vision imposes a total environmental view and formats space in advance of our embodied habitation of it. This universal formatting leaves just as little room for argument, just as little tolerance for deviation from the norm, as the transcendental individualism of Husserlian photographic visuality. What is missing in both visual contracts is room for collectivity and difference, which are neutralized by the absolute separation of seeing subjects from one another in the photographic contract and by the total pre-visualization and design of space in the computational contract.

The shift between these contracts occurs on the basis of what I have termed the dis/correlative diaphragm, adapting Merleau-Ponty, whose conception of the flesh actually locates a nascent sociality, and hence a basic political stratum, precisely at this presubjective level where visuality and tactility begin to divide. Briefly, in anticipation of a fuller treatment later, the self-division of the flesh into a tactile here-body and a specular there-body that exceeds the skin is grounded in a transpositional reversibility of inside and outside, self and other, that ties the very possibility of subjective identity to the body's tactile and visual presence to others. The fleshly body, according to Merleau-Ponty, is never simply "mine," as collectivity precedes subjectivation. Any intervention in the prepersonal flesh is therefore a political act. It is precisely here that power comes into play in the establishment of the new visual-tactile contract of computation. Computational visuality seeks to capture tactile spatiality itself, standardizing it from all possible angles and for all possible viewpoints; in the process it instrumentalizes the dis/correlative diaphragm for the strategic confusion of statistical and phenomenological correlation that I alluded to in the preface: statistical norms get implanted directly into the flesh, thus setting the stage for a standardization of subjective-phenomenological correlative options. To see how this process of correlative capture works, it will be useful to turn to a key site where visuality and tactility are being put to work today: in motion capture.

## Motility Beyond Motion

In the course of examining the two visual contracts, Galloway briefly invokes Donna Haraway's suggestion, in the "Cyborg Manifesto," that "our best machines are made of sunshine; they are all light and clean because they are nothing but signals, electromagnetic waves, a section of a spectrum" (Haraway 2016, 13; quoted in Galloway 2021, 54). Galloway credits Haraway with capturing "the essence of computation," elaborating on her statement:

> Computers are made of sunshine because they include things like fiber optic cables and photon switches. They are made of sunshine in a looser sense too because they consist of energy moving through matter. Furthermore, the discipline of computer modeling strives to simulate the behavior of light using mathematical equations, and thus is a kind of "sunshine simulator." (Galloway 2021, 56)

Of course, we know that these machines, while increasingly light, are far from clean; witness the environmental impact of Bitcoin mining, in which GPUs—sunshine simulators *par excellence*— are appropriated for the very non-optical task of solving cryptographic problems, turning electricity into money and in the process producing emissions that cloud the skies and dim the sunlight. Moreover, as Haraway also knew, processing sunshine creates social burdens that are unequally distributed; right after the lines quoted by Galloway, her text continues: "these machines are eminently portable, mobile—a matter of immense human pain in Detroit and Singapore. People are nowhere so fluid, being both material and opaque" (Haraway 2016, 13). Here Haraway points to the hidden physicality of computation and to a fundamental discrepancy between its flexible modeling of light and the relative inflexibility of the human body. Computational visuality, in short, makes demands on bodies that can stretch them to the breaking point.

Galloway begins to outline the mechanisms by which sunshine simulators exert their effects on human bodies. He writes:

> After all, vision is just a variable for the computer, a variable like anything else. And the typical elevations and sections inherited from architectural drafting are now as fungible as any other kind of input. Such unbridled freedom itself breeds a secondary form of regularization in which the infinity of possible views reduces to a short list of common ones. Thus architecture, the art of space and volume, is also the profession that has most efficiently disciplined vision into elevation, section, and plan. (Galloway 2021, 56)

The key terms here are fungibility, secondary regularization, and discipline. What's at stake is the formatting of space, which when transferred from the drafting program to the built environment translates into the standardization and constraint of embodied motion. This is all the more obvious when we move from the architectural bureau to the factory floor or the Amazon fulfillment station, where bodily motion is continuously monitored, optimized, and disciplined with an array of machine learning, video, and biosensing technologies.[22] Welcome to the sunshine factory.

22　There are countless journalistic accounts detailing Amazon's internal surveillance systems. Particularly revealing are the documents recently

[Fig. 1.3] Hito Steyerl, *Factory of the Sun*, 2015; Single-channel HD video, environment, LE grid, beach chairs on Screen and Truss; Collection of San José Museum of Art. Purchased jointly by San José Museum of Art with funds provided by the Lipman Family Foundation, Museum of Contemporary Art Chicago with funds provided by Albert A. Robin by exchange, and Hammer Museum, Los Angeles, through the Board of Overseers Acquisitions Fund, 2017.08.; Installation view from San José Museum Art, 2021. Courtesy of the Artist and Andrew Kreps Gallery, New York (Photography by J. Arnold, Impart Photography).

In her video installation *Factory of the Sun*, German media artist Hito Steyerl mounts a powerful visual-narrative critique of this new fungibility of movement, showing how its entwinement with computational visuality has far-reaching political consequences for embodied subjects around the world—consequences that by far exceed those remarked by Haraway in 1985, as they are generalized today from the factory worker to more or less every consumer of digital imagery. Steyerl focuses in particular on motion capture technology, which makes possible

obtained by *Vice* and published as: Gurley 2022. It has also been revealed that Amazon is marketing machine-learning–enabled surveillance systems to other companies: Morse 2020.

the abstraction, modeling, and transfer of concretely embodied movement from one body to another. Such transfers, as she shows, are not frictionless, despite the promise of "light and clean" technology; they leave marks on bodies, and on the basis of these marks, such transfers of computationally visualized and modeled movement can be converted into lucrative financial exchanges—as well as sites of potential resistance.

The installation is set in a black box gallery marked out on all six sides—floor, ceiling, and walls—with a grid pattern of thin blue luminescent lines (fig. 1.3). There are comfy lawn chairs strewn about the darkened space and a large screen before us, enframed by a metallic construction and loudspeakers on either side.[23] Upon entering, there's not much to see, just a grey screen with a subtle oval gradient effect, lighter at the center of the screen, darker around the edges. There's a countdown underway in the top right corner: NEXT ROUND IN 01:37…01:36…01:35… It feels like one of those nondescript digital "waiting rooms" that one might encounter before a scheduled telemedicine appointment. Then: A MESSAGE FROM THE SPONSOR appears, with a smaller video window (about half the size of the screen, centered vertically and offset to the left) opening up against the grey background. A digitally rendered Deutsche Bank logo assembles itself out of blocky pixels, vaguely reminiscent of Michael Bay's visualizations of Transformers doing their robotic thing. Below the logo, a digital Earth rotates slowly, and a label appears, punctuated by CGI lens flares: "Deutsche Advanced Execution Services."[24]

23     I encountered the work at the San Jose Museum of Art in November 2021. It was shown in similar configurations at the 2015 German Pavilion at the Venice Biennale, where it debuted, and at the Museum of Contemporary Art in Los Angeles, where it had its US premiere in 2016.

24     I have written at length about the subtle phenomenological disorientations effected by digital lens flares, as well as in the hyperinformatic transformations displayed in Michael Bay's *Transformers* movies. See, in particular, Denson 2020a, 21-50. See also Chapter 6, "Post-Cinema after Extinction," 206-236, on the significance of (digital) images of the Earth in post-cinema, including Bay's movies. Though I will not dwell on these aspects here, they

Then, another Transformers-like animation spells out "A STUPID BRAND INFOMERCIAL" in a transparent glass-styled font before a gradient blue background. The letters rearrange themselves again, spinning out and readjusting to form the question, "FASTER THAN LIGHT?"

Inane techno music starts playing, and the Deutsche Bank logo reappears in the top right corner of the window. A stubble-bearded, blonde-haired, blue-eyed man in a suit starts running his mouth and gesticulating before a green-screened digital background: a computer-generated space with blue grid lines and an animation showing a relatively simplistic architectural model, illuminated blue from within. Over the man's shoulder, we can briefly see the name Teufelsberg—"Devil's Mountain" in German—identifying the model as a rendering of the complex of buildings that sit atop a man-made hill in the Grunewald area of Berlin. Something weird is going on here. Teufelsberg is a non-natural hill made of rubble and debris that covers the Nazi-era Wehrtechnische Fakultät, an unfinished military academy designed by Albert Speer. After WWII, so the story goes, Allied forces were unable to destroy the academy with explosives and thus found it easier just to bury it and build on top of it. In 1963 the American NSA erected a listening station there, complete with antenna radomes arranged in a somewhat phallic configuration, two round structures on the roof of the building, another one sitting high atop a thick column between them.

What does this fast-talking bank executive have to do with Teufelsberg? The man speaks a giddy Hochdeutsch, while sparse English subtitles appear below: "The speed of light. A big question. Can we match or even accelerate the speed of light?" Actually, a lot of the affective and even informational content has

are significant also in Steyerl's piece, as the lens flares subtly dislocate the diegetic/extradiegetic membrane, while the planetary imagery signals the global generalization of the exploitative processes detailed in the video, which depend on the confusion of spaces previously encapsulated as either diegetic or not.

 been stripped from the German, which has him saying, roughly, "The speed of light. A big question! We ask it all the time: is it somehow possible, ever so gradually, just *almost* to approach it? Or even to reach it? Or—who knows?—to surpass it?" The man's image glitches momentarily, flickering transparent and glowing blue like the background. An animated fly-through of the architectural model commences, a virtual drone shot foregrounding the phallic structure in particular and the Deutsche Bank logo on a nearby wall. A "Skip Ad" button has appeared at the bottom of the window, but there's no way to click it, unfortunately; the man, who seems to have snorted a bunch of coke or adderal just before going on camera, is more annoying by the second. (As in Cheng's work, but for different reasons, the suggestion of interactivity coupled with its impossibility makes itself felt as a painful amputation of embodied interface potentials.) Increasingly excited, the man tells us that someone has in fact already managed to reach the speed of light: at CERN, where a particle was accelerated and sent from Switzerland to Italy. As he says this, a bright light appears in his hand, which he throws in imitation of the particle at CERN. The ball of digital light flies quickly out of the smaller video frame and circles around the larger grey background (are we staring at a computer desktop?), where the countdown is still running in the top right corner: NEXT ROUND IN 00:40...00:39...00:38... Digital lens flares bounce around the digital space, as the light particle re-enters the smaller video window and exits again before disappearing altogether from the screen. While this spectacle takes place within the span of just a few seconds, spatiality has been throughly deconstructed. The suited man's glitchy figure/ground reversals with the digital animation behind him, and the light particle's violation of its diegetic framing as it crosses the threshold of the window and creates lens flares outside of it in the empty grey space of computation—these visual phenomena unsettle any stable perspectival relation we might have with the space, revealing it as the product of a thoroughly computational visuality.

It would seem, in fact, that this computational space extends beyond the screen, and that I have been sitting in it all along. I notice that the grid behind the architectural model of Teufelsberg exactly replicates that of the physical installation space. My body is both situated and deeply unsettled by the perceptual reversals and confusions between the various screen spaces (the nested windows) and now between the video screen as a whole and the installation space around it.

At long last, the aufgeregter Bankkaufmann is done with his Spiel, and his video window disappears from the screen. Now, at the center of the grey background, a larger digital countdown appears: 00:20…00:19…00:18… When we finally reach zero, a digitally animated laptop appears in the farthest recesses of the grey digital non-space. Slowly moving towards us, we can also make out some text floating in front of it: FACTORY OF THE SUN. We hear a woman's voice, speaking Chinese, and the subtitles indicate variations on Haraway: "Our machines are made of pure sunlight. Electromagnetic frequencies. Light pumping through glass cables. The sun is our factory." Digital lens flares again spread across the screen, as the animated laptop arrives. The computer is recognizable as a metallic MacBook Pro, but its screen is completely transparent to the space behind it, as if it were simply a plane of glass with no internal components or outer lid to obscure the view. What looks like the sun begins to shine, either on the laptop screen, or through it, before it bursts forth and countless animated lightbulbs tumble out towards us. These opaque but highly reflective golden bulbs swirl around while the laptop rotates, the bright sun still shining through. Swift movements of the virtual camera to the back of the laptop reveal that its screen is in fact transparent, both front and back.

Another woman's voice, now in English, begins riffing on the Haraway theme, mashing it up with the *Communist Manifesto* and reflections on digital image rendering: "Our machines are made of pure sunlight. Electromagnetic frequency. Light pumping through fibre glass cables. All that was work has melted into sunshine. Sunshine is our factory." The laptop dissolves into a cloud of particles, then reappears. "All that was work has melted into sunshine. Into deadly transparency." The objects become liquid. "All that was work has melted into sunshine." The laptop repeatedly dissolves into a swarm of particles and reorganizes, the lightbulbs swirling around the digital space, sometimes closer and sometimes farther from the virtual camera. A conic wireframe figure appears—a "Cone Radius manipulator," as it is known in the Autodesk Maya 3D computer graphics application, where it is used "to change the angle of a spot light's beam."[25] "This is an image," the woman's voice instructs as a giant golden lightbulb appears in the foreground, overlaid with the Cone Radius manipulator. "An image made of light. An image moving through fiberglass cables." The images reflected in the lightbulbs are now easier to make out, depicting what looks like an empty parking lot, black asphalt with white lines under a blue sky. "Electropolitical frequency. Our machines are made of pure sunlight. Sunshine is our factory. All photons are created equal." As the virtual camera slowly pulls back, a metallic structure identical to the one surrounding the screen before us in the installation space moves into view. Florescent lighting appears above and gridlines on the floor. "Our machines are made of pure sunlight. All that was work has melted into sunshine. Sunshine is our factory." Slowly the figure of a black-clad dancer comes into view, his body covered in light-emitting ping-pong balls. "All that was work has melted into sunshine." The dancer wears a Che Guevara-style beret. "Into deadly transparency. Our machines are made of pure sunlight."

Cut to a woman seated before a laptop computer, her reflective golden suit mirroring the golden digital lightbulbs still swarming behind her. A computer-synthesized voice introduces herself as Yulia and informs us that she is "coding a game called *Factory of*

25    Autodesk details the tool here: https://download.autodesk.com/global/docs/
        maya2014/en_us/index.html?url=files/BoL_Move_the_Cone_Radius_of_a_
        spot_light.htm,topicNumber=d30e607533

*the Sun*. But you will not be able to play this game. It will play you." 
The dancer now appears on a rooftop, in video shot at Teufelsberg, while onscreen graphics inform us that "THIS IS NOT A
GAME. THIS IS REALITY." Tumbling further and further into this
mise en abyme, I am again reminded of Ian Cheng's non/interactive unsettling of embodiment. And now, after a quick cut to
to a black screen where a progress bar loads and a heartbeat
dominates the soundtrack, it becomes clear what computer
graphics and the non-space of computational visuality have to
do with the politics of embodied movement: "This is your mission: You start off as a forced laborer in a motion capture studio.
Every movement you make will be captured and converted into
sunshine." And of course it is now clear that the installation space
*is* this motion capture studio. Am I being held captive? Before I
have time to ponder this, breaking news interrupts to distract
me. Video clips show what are described as "global uprisings,"
reporting that "a spokesman for Deutsche Bank denied using
drones to kill protestors." Splitscreen video shows a drone
hovering near one of the satellite radomes at Teufelsberg, firing
a light particle across the screen and into the crowd in the other
windowed video, the location of which can be identified as the
Millbank Tower in London—apparently, this is video shot at the
2010 occupation of the building by students protesting against
the recent increase of tuition fees. Once more, the violation of
medial boundaries—the weaponized light particle, itself just a
digital image, passing between windows showing video from
different locations—unsettles spatial orientation, but now this
phenomenological disorientation is put into an explicitly global
political framework.

A sort of tutorial level for the game commences, and we see
interface options being selected for difficulty levels and other
parameters (including choices for "Idealism," "Materialism,"
"Realism," and "Reality Beta"). Coder Yulia now appears within
the game environment and instructs how to use the available
weapons, demonstrating by shooting at golden digital lightbulbs

and metallic heads, including that of Stalin. During the demonstration, she also recounts her family history, including their many international relocations in response to world-historical changes and political turmoil. The environment shifts and flickers between various renderings of (more and less realistic) spaces and their digital infrastructures, including, again, the gridlines that quantify space in motion capture environments and in graphics design applications alike. The merging of spaces is total, but far from seamless.

Cut back to the motion capture studio, where we see our dancer performing a "dying scene," simulating his fall to the ground upon being shot, so that his embodied motions can be abstracted from his body and ported into the game where they will be available for the simulation of countless other deaths. Yulia directs him from behind her laptop, specifying that his motion should correspond to being shot from a drone hovering overhead.

"And this is where the dancing thing starts to happen." A laptop displays a golden suited dancer on Youtube, while the Che Guevara lookalike dances in the motion capture studio in the background. Yulia's brother started Internet dancing in the family basement in Edmonton, Canada, and the videos went viral, making him a star—and making his moves the basis for an economy of motility abstracted from embodied motion.[26] Various avatars, some realistic and some stylized as anime figures, are shown performing the same moves in unison. Yulia introduces each of the characters and their typical moves, as they perform in front of a digital building, marked "Factory." Drone footage of the Teufelsberg compound focuses the phallic structures again, the radomes in disrepair and the building covered in graffiti.

26    Apparently, there is some factual basis for this. "The story is based on an actual YouTube phenomenon (a studio assistant's brother whose viral homemade dance videos were used as a model for Japanese anime characters)," according to an announcement for the exhibition at San Jose Museum of Art (2021). The labor of motion capture also fuels a burgeoning industry around virtual influencers in China; see Tobin and Zhou (2022).

Graphical elements on screen indicate that this will be a site of gameplay, and we see a group of dancers superimposed on the rooftop, where the player is instructed that they can "Press A for Total Capture," "Press Y to Leak Light," or "Press B to Shoot Light Ball at NSA Domes." We again hear the woman's voice. "Our machines are made of pure sunlight." And interspersed with her, we hear the Deutsche Bank executive as well: "Schneller als Licht. Ein Platz an der Sonne."[27] Onscreen text directs us to rotate the joystick on our nonexistent gaming controller in order to "Accelerate Speed of Light." But the game starts mocking us, teasing us for our impotence in the face of the missing interface: "Oh, is it not working? But YOU are working! own3d!" The scene dissolves into particles, and a news report butts in with more breaking news: the architectural model of Teufelsberg is shown on screen and identified as Deutsche Bank's "Sunshine Campus," where a person was killed during experiments to accelerate the speed of light "to improve high-frequency trading."

Shortly thereafter, we see the game's various avatars dancing while they introduce themselves in voiceover. One of them, speaking with a British accent, notes he was killed in the London student protests but respawned with the ability to "bend light in a Lobachevsky hyperbolic" or turn it into music. Echoing Haraway's remarks that "light and clean" technologies can also be "a matter of intense human pain," the digital avatar notes that "light is deep entertainment—and destruction. A matter of intense human pain." Another avatar, speaking Russian, says he was killed in the 2018 Singapore uprisings after he and his comrades "occupied the free port art storage and turned it into a render farm cooperative." A third avatar, speaking Chinese, recalls being

27    The latter phrase, which translates as "a place in the sun," is well-known to Germans as the slogan from 2003 until 2012 for the Deutsche Fernsehlotterie, a long-running lottery show in which winning numbers are drawn live on the main public television station ARD. The phrase has a more sinister and apparently lesser-known historical background connected to the German Kaiserreich's colonial pursuits in China and Africa—sunshine thus long being linked to global power.

"killed twice in Kobani fighting with Kurdish forces against IS," while a fourth, speaking Spanish, "was killed fighting Deutsche Bank High Frequency Trade Bots." A final voice announces, from offscreen, "We got killed in the future. We crowd your games and applications. We're nonplayable characters. We cannot be played."

Suddenly, a new game level starts in the uncertain digital space. We see Steyerl directing the actors behind the scenes. But the scene of production is wrapped uncertainly into the diegesis. Yulia, offscreen, explains that in this level you are unable to play any of the characters, and because she "didn't have enough time to program all of the environments," it turns out that "actually the game is real." Yulia explains that her brother the YouTube star "was part of a research group where they focused on the way in which light interacts with explosive material. You see this was for developing airport security. There was a lot of concern about homeland security at the time." Soon thereafter the game ends, and we see the avatars dancing in her brother's Edmonton basement while a leaderboard is displayed at the bottom of the screen. Donna Summer's 1989 late disco song "This Time I Know It's for Real" plays in celebration, before fading out. We are then back in the digital waiting room, the timer again counting down: NEXT ROUND IN 02:58...02:57...02:56. At some point, however, the platform is "hacked" and "The Bot Manifesto" appears against a black background. It reads:

> All photons are created equal!
> No photon should be accelerated at the expense of others!
> Resist total capture!
> Be a non-playable character!
> Sunshine belongs to everyone!
>
> Dunk Zombie Marxism!
> And Zombie Formalism!

All politics are proxy politics!
Mez! Dazzle! Shine!

At once playful and deadly serious, Steyerl's *Factory of the Sun* offers important lessons for contemporary processes of correlative capture. By dismantling boundaries between diegetic and extradiegetic spaces, as well as between video and installation spaces, Steyerl disrupts the subject-centric orientation of visual perception and instead makes *felt* the power and politics at stake not only in motion capture, but in the larger framework of computational visuality. A tactile relation to images is foregrounded by the amputated interface that the piece shares with Ian Cheng's *Emissary Sunsets the Self*, such that the interface "goes metastable" and the shift from Galloway's (Husserlian) photographic contract to the (Platonic) computational visuality is made available to sensation—not as an object of focused perception, but as a diffuse and globally distributed force that takes *our bodies as its objects*. As Galloway has argued, computational visuality challenges optical vision by abstracting and modeling objects that can be seen and manipulated from all sides. Steyerl's work insists that this applies also to our bodies, both as visual and as motile objects; in its political and commercial deployments, computation aims at the total fungibility of motion, the ability to abstract motility from concrete individual bodies and motions and render it into general schemas transferable to other bodies—in the process standardizing and disciplining them and their correlative potentials. How are we to resist the gamification and financialization of fleshly motility? Artists like Cheng and Steyerl point the way by activating both correlative and discorrelative potentials of embodiment, playing on the multistability of experience and its mediation, and focusing the tactile roots of aesthesis as the site of struggle. Following their lead, the answer to our problems will not be found in a simple hardening of the self or reassertion of correlative stability in the face of discorrelative technologies. Rather, if we are to "resist total capture" and "be non-playable characters," we will need to delve deeper into the dis/correlative potentials that make us vulnerable so that we might cultivate aesthetic powers for liberation.

# On the Originary Mediality of the Flesh

Setting out from the question of embodied orientation and relation to visual media, as raised by Sobchack's and Shaviro's divergent perception-oriented and affect-oriented approaches to the cinema, we were led to consider the coexistence of two basic aesthetic options. The latter, tending respectively towards correlative and discorrelative potentials, were then traced to a multistable and presubjective level of embodied being, taking us far afield of the usual frames of reference within which film studies is conducted. In this space where correlative and dis-correlative forces converge, or *from whence they diverge*, we can no longer (or not yet) speak of "the image" or "the cinema" as a clearly delineated media object, for the simple reason that we cannot yet speak of a subject. Galloway's refocusing of photographic and computational "contracts" of visuality, outlining two mutually opposed correlative options, helped to envision how such a presubjective materiality can nevertheless have a bearing on the political organization of subjective life. And his reflections on computation, in particular, provided a necessary framework for thinking about the ways that post-cinematic media target and discipline our bodies. Meanwhile, it has been the media artists, Ian Cheng and Hito Steyerl, who have provided the key phenomenological insights and experiences that point the way to resistance.

Some readers might be troubled by my proposal of an aesthetic remedy to political problems. I hope that it is clear, however, that I am not pursuing the "aestheticization of politics" that Walter Benjamin (2006, 122) warned against as one of the methods of fascism. But nor do I think that the "politicization of art" that he urged in the name of socialism operates today in clear opposition. This is because of computation's increasingly intensive operationalization of the flesh, I contend, which changes the terrain of both art and politics. That is, post-cinematic technologies take aim at a stratum of embodiment where the distinction between the aesthetic and the political is itself not clear-cut, and where transpositions and blurrings are to be expected. The flesh is emphatically not apolitical. I do not believe that it is universal and undifferentiated; rather, it is the bearer of bodies' differential access to the world, of the impositions of racial and gendered typification, and of differences in the correlative potentials that we have with respect to ourselves and others. The flesh is thus deeply political, but it is inseparable from the aesthetic, and it is this inseparability that enables what I have called the correlative capture of embodied experience: post-cinematic media make appeals to our sensory perception and our aesthetic sensibilities more broadly construed, only then to open up our presubjective flesh and to implant there conventions and norms derived from statistical correlations. If we are to find strategies for resistance that can reverse these tendencies, we will have to probe deeper into the aesthetic operations that make us vulnerable in the first place.

In this chapter, I aim to carry this cause forward by way of asking some fundamental questions about mediality. My investigation here pertains both to the mediality of media like cinema and its post-cinematic successors, but it also pertains, first and foremost, to the body itself. What I hope to show is that there  is a complementarity between media technologies and the presubjective flesh, each in a sense answering the other—a not always harmonious complementarity that underwrites the multistabilities of dis/correlation and enables media to act transformatively on the shape of the subjective and collective correlations through which we experience the world. This line of inquiry necessarily takes us away from the art and into a philosophical terrain, in particular the philosophy of media. But the broadly aesthetic reorientation to be effected here will enable us to return to artistic interventions with a greater sensitivity for their political relevance in resisting some of the more insidious techniques by which our bodies are targeted today.

## Towards a Philosophy of Mediality: Transcendence and Negativity

To ask about the mediality of media is to engage in a paradigmatically philosophical mode of theorizing, one that takes us well beyond conventional ways of doing *media studies*—a field that, though variously defined and practiced, tends toward some combination of the following: interpreting mediated contents, interrogating the cultural contexts of media, or inquiring about the effects or consequences of particular forms or contents of mediation. Of course, the particularity attaching to such modes of investigation—the particularity of content, context, or consequence as the object of media studies investigation—is called into question by various forms of *media theory* that aim to theorize more generally about media in their relation to history, perception, art, culture, or meaning. The degree of generality, however, and its relation to particular cases that are marshaled to illustrate or illuminate the more general properties and relational influences of media can vary wildly among different media theoretical approaches and practices. Some of the latter restrict themselves to a particular historical moment or study the political consequences of a given media innovation or transformation, for example, while others broach a larger philosophical terrain and ask about the relations of media to epistemology or theorize the ontology of a given medium or media.

Thus, the borders between media theory and media philosophy are hardly fixed or impervious. But some questions, such as that about *mediality per se*, must be seen as properly philosophical questions that seek to transcend the particularity of any and all specific media (or contexts or implementations thereof). This is a question of essence, the quiddity or "whatness" of any and all media, as opposed to the positive "thisness" or haecceity that adheres not only to specific media but even, in a sense, to the desideratum of the ontological question *"What is a medium?"* For the latter, while clearly a philosophical question, presupposes that a medium is defined by its substantial objecthood or thingness, an ontic positivity (what it "is"), while the question of mediality leaves this open and declines to define media in advance as a positive, delimited presence with respect to a perceiving subject. Perhaps even more radically, to take up the question of mediality is to refuse from the outset a strictly *empirical* approach to media, along with all the particularities (of content, context, and consequence) that characterize the empirical realm, and instead to open up what might be called a *transcendental* space of interrogation.

In Dieter Mersch's (2006) "negative media theory," for example, the decision to ask about mediality qua essence rather than media as empirical objects derives from the insight that media are not only or even foremost objects of empirical attention but may instead function as conditions of apparition and revelation—conditions of phenomenal appearance or phenomenality itself. They cannot, therefore, be treated positively—or positivistically—as data given within sensory experience; at least, to treat them as such is to forego the question of mediality as it pertains to a transcendental or quasi-transcendental function. And yet, precisely to the extent that it pertains to such a function, the question of mediality cannot be completely divorced from sensory experience either; the mediality of media refers, in other words, to what we might call (following Luce Irigaray (1993) and, in her wake, Mark Hansen (2006)) a *sensible-transcendental* nexus or interface.

Mersch's aesthetic framing of the question is significant and illuminating in this respect. He foregrounds the origins of the concept "medium" in connection with that of *aesthesis*—where the latter term signified sensory experience itself prior to the modern narrowing of "aesthetics" to the domain of artistic judgment and value; in the broader context, "medium" designated a "hybrid concept" that "oscillates among formative element [*Konstituens*], dispositif, and indeterminacy" in referring to a "materiality that, eluding perception, originarily [*allererst*] makes perception possible" (2006, 219). In this sense:

> Media "mediate" [*vermitteln*] without themselves being "immediate" [*unmittelbar*]. As figures of the middle, moreover, they occupy an "in-between space" [*Zwischenraum*], through which something comes to appearance, through which representations [*Darstellungen*] are given, relations [*Bezüge*] established, and meanings brought forth. (ibid., 219)

But, explains Mersch, this concept, which was still dominant into the nineteenth century, was subsequently replaced by narrower conceptions of media: language, as the "medium of all *Darstellungen*" (which might refer variously to representations, presentations, or depictions across various contexts), established itself as a "meta-medium," while it became clear in the meantime that the "triumph of technical media could no longer be denied" (ibid., 219). This double transformation in conceptions and configurations of media leads eventually to a technological understanding: "Since then the medium concept has alternated between linguistic *a priori* and technical *a priori*, which through the linguistic modelling of technology and the technical modelling of language finally converge and find their completion in the medium of the computer" (ibid., 219).

 It is against this reduction, and as a "critique of technicism," that Mersch seeks to revive the notion of mediality latent in its broadly aesthetic origins—and for which purpose he returns to aesthetics in its narrower sense, in terms of the "medial paradoxes" or aporia that artistic practice is able to reveal: the glitch-like "interferences [*Eingriffe*], malfunctions [*Störungen*], obstructions [*Hindernisse*], contrary configurations" that constitute the "*strategies of difference*" by means of which artists and their works are able to reach back to the originary conditions of mediality as a sensible-transcendental space of the in-between (ibid., 226). Such "negative practices" are self-reflexive methods by which the artwork qua positive entity recedes behind the paradoxes it opens up in order to reveal its own conditions of expression, representation, and being (ibid., 226). As such, these interventions enable the viewer (or auditor, reader, user, etc.) of the work

> to occupy positions of distance without a localizable other. They therefore blast the immanence of the medial out of its immanence, as it were. Accordingly, they meet with no *discursive* justification, no foundation in objectifiable [*objektivierbaren*] criteria, but rather satisfy themselves in the interminability [*Unabschließbarket*] of the artistic experiment. Medial reflexivity [*Medienreflexion*] requires such maneuvers, just as, conversely, where they are lacking the mediality of the medium remains magically obscured. (ibid., 227)

In this interplay between concrete artistic practices and artworks, on the one hand, and the material and formal conditions of *aesthesis*, on the other, Mersch's negative media theory helps to elucidate the interrelation between the sensible or empirical and the (quasi-)transcendental as they present themselves with respect to the mediality of media.

It is important, however, to clarify that the aesthetic framing of mediality, as a "critique of technicism," should not be taken as a repetition of the ground-clearing operation whereby philosophical aesthetics in the eighteenth century drove a wedge  between art and technology (formerly undifferentiated in both the Latin *ars* and the Greek *techne*).[1] On the contrary, rather than limiting the scope of our investigations to art's ability to reveal its sensible-transcendental conditions, the aesthetic or "negative" reframing has much broader consequences, including brokering a reconception of technicity—which alongside aesthesis should be seen as an "originary" power of medial revealing. To see it as such requires that we set aside positivistic notions of technology, as empirically evident tools or prostheses, for example. The critique of technicism lays bare sensible-transcendental conditions of technicity, such that our understanding of technical media should benefit as much as our understanding of art from this widening of aesthetic scope via mediality. Ultimately, I suggest, the critique of technicism enables us to restore an awareness and appreciation of the aesthetic dimensions of technicity, and of the technical dimensions of aesthesis, both of which have been amputated by the reduction of *ars* and *techne*—the purification of "fine arts" and their separation from "applied arts"—which gave rise to the philosophically impoverished, positivistic notion of media in the first place. This suggestion might seem vaguely Heideggerian (recalling arguments made in essays ranging from "The Question Concerning Technology," "Building Dwelling Thinking," or "The Thing" (Heidegger 1977, 1971a, 1971b); and to that extent it is in accordance with Mersch's appeal to Heidegger (and Derrida in his wake) in order to rethink mediality via the transcendental functions of language (or of *arche-écriture*), which reveal themselves through self-reflexive modifications and fractures. Here I would like to follow a different tack, however, and re-situate aesthesis and technicity within embodiment, as twinned originary powers of the body in human lived experience as it is articulated in a corporeal phenomenological understanding of fleshly existence. For ultimately, I argue, to adopt a non-technicist

1    For the most famous, but also perhaps significant instance of this tendency, see Kant 2007.

 conception of technicity and its entwinement with aesthesis requires that we understand, and lay bare, the embodied basis of mediality itself.

## Aesthetico-Technical Transduction

What, precisely, is at stake in the *critique* of technicism? With respect to critique, I suggest that we understand this not as a simple "criticism," but very much in the spirit of Kantian critique—as a reflexive effort to lay bare the underlying conditions of possibility for a phenomenon. In this case, as I have suggested, the reductively empiricist or positivistic technicism in question is possible only on the basis of a more fundamental, "negative" technicity of human existence. We shall return to this conception of technicity in a moment, but first we need to understand what its obverse, "technicism," entails. The latter, I suggest, might be seen as a fetishization or reification of technological apparatuses and operations—which is to say an objectification of them as separate (or separable)—and thus a disavowal of their constitutive entanglement with human existence and experience. My point is not just to reassert the role of human agency against the bogeyman of "technological determinism." Most such gestures overshoot the mark by putting (at least some) human subjects back in control, and situating technologies as tools that, while they may have unintended consequences, can still be seen as extensions of their designers' (or corporate owners', if not also their end-users') wills—or else as exterior obstacles to them. Against the impasse of technological determinism and the reassertion of human autonomy, the entanglement that I have in mind, that which is disavowed in the technicist attitude, is of a transductive nature—which is to say that the interrelated elements, in this case humans and technologies, are constitutively and originarily related; the relation between them is fundamental to their existence, and they are thus inseparable from one another.[2] Thus,

2    On transduction, see Simondon 2020; Simondon 2017.

we can no more speak of technology determining human beings than we can of humans determining (the telic development or effects of) technology; as a transductive relation, the question of causality is complicated by feedback loop–like interactions that are anything but unidirectional. The human, as Bernard Stiegler (1998) has argued, is originarily technical, our temporal subjectivity inseparably bound to the concretized memory and futural structures embodied in and enabled by technical objects; and since the birth of human subjectivity/technicity, our evolution has no longer been purely biological but henceforth a matter of co-evolution with technics. As we shall see, it is this transductive logic that originarily connects aesthesis and technicity—and that, correlatively, explains why a theory of mediality necessarily pits aesthetics against a reductive technicism.

Technicism's disavowal of the technicity-aesthesis transduction is epitomized by Kittler's (1999, 1) refusal of the interface as so much "eyewash," as a distraction from the underlying operations of computational processing. This is a refusal of the aesthetic or sensory itself in favor of a technical infrastructure divorced from sensation. Aesthesis, for Kittler, is thus secondary to technology, which dictates sensation's parameters or limits; media constitute for him a media-technical *a priori*. This is tied to Kittler's understanding and appropriation of Foucauldian archaeology, according to which a "historical *a priori*" permits and proscribes that which is expressible under a given discursive formation or episteme (Foucault 1972, 126–131). The paradoxical formulation of the historical *a priori*, for Foucault, challenges the atemporality of what he calls "formal *a prioris*," against which he positions "[a]n *a priori* not of truths that might never be said, or really given to experience; but the *a priori* of a history that is given, since it is that of things actually said" (ibid., 128, 127). Open, therefore, to elements of contingency, chance, and change, the historical *a priori* gives rise to a historically, culturally, and epistemically specific "archive" that defines "the system of discursivity" and "the enunciative possibilities and impossibilities that it lays down.

The archive is first the law of what can be said, the system that governs the appearance of statements as unique events" (ibid., 129). It should be noted that for Foucault himself, the archive functions similarly to the in-between space of mediality:

> Between the *language* (*langue*) that defines the system of constructing possible sentences, and the *corpus* that passively collects the words that are spoken, the *archive* defines a particular level: that of a practice that causes a multiplicity of statements to emerge as so many regular events, as so many things to be dealt with and manipulated. (ibid., 130)

In other words, the archive is neither absolutely transcendent nor is it positively empirical; rather, it is a sensible-transcendental condition. But, in contrast to the broad scope of mediality in the light of *aesthesis*, this archival mediality is limited in scope and pertains foremost to the realm of linguistic or discursive appearance. Hence Kittler's broadening of it to other forms of mediation, such that it is no longer the condition only of the sayable but also the condition of the sensible itself across its various modalities. But ultimately this marriage of linguistic and technical *a prioris* is consummated in a doubly reductive outcome, as Mersch suggests is typical of media theories that favor media over mediality: the convergence of discursive and media-technical *a prioris*, now subject to Foucault's qualification of them as historical, quickly and paradoxically gives way to an apocalyptic end of history in the computer. The latter effaces the sensible dimension of the sensible-transcendental membrane at the heart of mediality; the "eyewash" of the interface notwithstanding, the computer destroys the aesthetic dimension altogether, thus dislodging technology from its underlying transduction with human existence—at least, that is, if we are to believe Kittler's telling of the story.

Suffice it to say that I do not fully buy into this narrative, which undoes the constitutive entanglement of what I have elsewhere called the "anthropotechnical interface" (Denson 2014).

The latter refuses to be dissolved into separate (or separable) elements, with the human on one side and technology on the other. As I have suggested, the transductive relation between them implicates both aesthesis and technicity, both of which are powers of embodiment and its material involvement in the world—which is ultimately a question of mediality. It is this picture of the originary mediality of the flesh that I would now like to develop, but in so doing I want to hold onto Foucault's idea of the historical *a priori*, which as we have seen opened a sensible-transcendental space of the in-between that, though restricted to discursive appearance or enunciation, offers a promising model by which to account for the historically variable forms, conditions, or possibilities of mediality—and ultimately to recognize the originary mediality of the flesh as the locus of anthropotechnical co-evolution. Is it possible, then, to generalize the historical *a priori* for the mediality of non-discursive media, including technical media, without falling into the trap of technicism?

## Negative Media Theory in the Flesh

In fact, there is a use of the concept of the historical *a priori* that predates Foucault's by two and a half decades, and it provides an opening onto an alternative, anti-technicist and embodied notion of medial aesthesis and technicity. Had this earlier usage provided the basis for Kittler's media archaeology, rather than Foucault's archive, the course of (German) media theory might have taken a radically different trajectory. In his 1945 magnum opus, *Phenomenology of Perception*, Merleau-Ponty invokes the concept following an extended discussion of phantom pain and its philosophical implications—above all, its undoing of mind/body dualism and its resituation of psyche and physiology with respect to a hybrid *"pre-objective view"* that is that of embodied being-in-the-world (2002, 92). He writes: "just as clothing, jewellery and love transfigure the biological needs from which they arise, in the same way within the cultural world the historical *a priori* is constant only for a given phase and provided that

the balance of *forces* allows the same *forms* to remain" (ibid.,
101). In this somewhat enigmatic passage, Merleau-Ponty is
seeking to mediate between the relative unfreedom of the physiological, which is beyond our determination and thus binds us
to the material world, and the relative freedom of the psychic,
which is the realm of subjective deliberation and our partial
transcendence with respect to the world. In Merleau-Ponty's
corporeal phenomenology, however, these domains must be
"reintegrated into existence," and when they are, "they are no
longer distinguishable respectively as the order of the *in-itself*,
and that of the *for-itself*," but rather "they are both directed
towards an intentional pole or towards a world" (ibid., 101). As
such, the lived body, now an *intentional* body, exceeds the merely
biological—a fact which enables the incorporation of prostheses
(such as Merleau-Ponty's famous examples of the blind man's
cane, the woman's feathered hat, or the car whose extension we
incorporate into and *feel* as an extension of our body (ibid., 164–
167)). But this extendibility of the body, as a hybrid psychic-phys-
iological mode of being-in-the-world, is not without limitation;
the very fact of embodiment's modulation, its contraction and
expansion, implies our material and spatial finitude. Beyond this,
our embodiment, and hence our intentional subjectivity, is inseparable from the material objects which happen to be present
in the environment and with which we come into contact; quite
simply, we could not experience prosthetic extension by means of
an automobile or a feathered hat in a culture or an era that lacked
such objects. Merleau-Ponty's mention of clothing and jewelry
in the above passage is therefore not insignificant: the technical
objects of our material cultures, which "transfigure the biological
needs from which they arise," constitute for us a historical *a priori*
by enabling and disabling the possible field of perception, action,
and subjectivity.

In this view, aesthesis and technicity are constitutively entwined
with one another. So far, however, I have not distinguished the
"negative" notion of technicity from the "positive" concept of

technical objects, and this is necessary to complete the argument 
for the originary mediality of embodiment. Towards this end, we
should note that, though Merleau-Ponty is largely concerned in
his early work with what might be seen as a positive (but hardly
positivistic) notion of embodied experience—which by way of
the primacy accorded to perception situates the body as active
and infused with subjectivity, and hence extendible by way of
prosthetic objects—his appeal to the historical *a priori* comes
just several pages after he has outlined what might be called a
properly "negative" notion of embodiment implicit in his notion of
the "inner diaphragm," which I explored in the previous chapter.
Again, this is Merleau-Ponty's term for a presubjective stratum of
embodied sensibility, which acts and reacts prior to the individuation of noetic objects: "Prior to stimuli and sensory contents,
we must recognize a kind of inner diaphragm which determines,
infinitely more than they do, what our reflexes and perceptions
will be able to aim at in the world, the area of our possible
operations, the scope of our life" (2002, 92). Operative prior to the
articulation of subject and object—and hence negatively "sub-
tracted" from them—this diaphragm, as I have argued, provides
the basis for thinking the multistable options of dis/correlation.
It articulates the common ground between and can give rise
either to perceptual correlations of subject and object or affective
discorrelation and indistinction. More importantly, in terms of
understanding media changes such as the replacement of a
photographic contract of visuality by a computational one, this
dis/correlative diaphragm designates the stratum of embodiment
where such change takes place—a space of material transition
between shifting correlative potentials. Embodiment itself begins
to take on the contours of the sensible-transcendental condition
of mediality.

But it is only in Merleau-Ponty's (1968b) late work, above all in
the unfinished and posthumously published *The Visible and the
Invisible*, that this conception comes to full fruition in the chiasmic
"flesh of the world." And it is here that we are able to discern a

"negative" technicity that is essentially and transductively entangled with aesthesis. If the early work looked at technics primarily in the form of prosthetic extension, the late work inverts this perspective through an implicit "critique of technicism" to derive the underlying condition of extension and exteriorization—and in the process shows it to be inseparable from the interiorizing aesthesis of tactility. Significantly, the chiasmic paradoxes detailed in Merleau-Ponty's working notes outline the basis for this transduction in terms that mirror the "negative practices" or *strategies of difference* that, for Mersch (2006, 226), reveal "medial paradoxes" at the heart of artistic self-reflexivity. For example:

> I do not entirely succeed in touching myself touching, in seeing myself seeing, the experience I have of myself perceiving does not go beyond a sort of *imminence*, it terminates in the invisible, simply this invisible is *its* invisible, i.e., the reverse of *its* specular perception, of the concrete vision I have of my body in the mirror. (Merleau-Ponty 1968, 249)

Like the glitches that can be marshaled in an artwork to reveal the underlying sensible-transcendental space of aesthetic mediality, the body here experiences a glitch of its own: it fails to reach full positivity, which always remains imminent, and thereby foregrounds the body's noncoincidence with itself.

> To touch and to touch oneself (to touch oneself = touched–touching) They do not coincide in the body: the touching is never exactly the touched. This does not mean that they coincide 'in the mind' or at the level of 'consciousness.' Something else than the body is needed for the junction to be made: it takes place in the *untouchable*. That of the other which I will never touch. (Ibid., 254)

Negatively, therefore, the medial ground of the flesh is only made apparent through a self-modifying intervention, which necessarily fails to produce objective positivity. Moreover, the noncoincidence of the seeing/seen and feeling/felt body is negatively revealed as the ground of an interplay between interior tactility  and exterior specularity *by way of—and as the invisible reverse of— the technical object, the mirror.* What this means is that the flesh itself involves a negative, pre-objective technicity to which the technical object answers in correspondence with subjective self-awareness; the flesh, however, which is revealed negatively as the presubjective ground of embodiment, knows no subject or object and thus outlines an originarily de-objectified technics.

We are approaching what Merleau-Ponty refers to as the *écart,* the schism or fission of the senses, the separation of the visual from the tactile, which Mark Hansen has argued is "essentially technical" in serving as *"the sensible-transcendental ground for exteriorization as such"* (2006, 60, 61). This fission, which points to the originary mediality of the flesh as simultaneously aesthetic and technical, is especially apparent in Merleau-Ponty's commentary on Lacan's "mirror stage." Here, specularity is seen as derivative of a primary tactility that at once links inside and outside, self and other, by projecting the interior outward and incorporating technicity within, as the mirror answers the body's essential and prepersonal desire to be consummated by technology. In "The Child's Relation with Others," Merleau-Ponty writes:

> It is a problem first of understanding that the visual image of his body which he sees over there in the mirror is not himself, since he is not in the mirror but here, where he feels himself; and second, he must understand that, not being located there, in the mirror, but rather where he feels himself interoceptively, he can nonetheless be seen by an external witness *at the very place at which he feels himself to be* and with the same visual appearance that he has from the mirror. In short, he must displace the mirror image, bringing it from the apparent or virtual place it occupies in the depth of the mirror back to himself, whom he identifies at a distance with his interoceptive body. (Merleau-Ponty 1964, 129)

There is thus a doubling of the body between the interoceptive and specular that, as Hansen puts it, "marks the advent of a more complex self-relation … and compels a massive spatial extension of the body's primary tactility" (2006, 56). What is required is not, as many psychoanalytic interpretations would have it, "a wholesale displacement of identification from the interoceptive to the specular self" in the consolidation of a unified body image, but instead "a bodily occupation of the visible, a 'touching' across an essential distance" (ibid., 56). This exteriorization *of tactility* via specularity anchors technicity as an essential power of the flesh; it is the precondition of technological extension such as we see instanced but not exhausted in the prosthetic extension of intentional subjectivity. The prosthetic extension does not exhaust such technicity precisely because the latter remains inseparably entwined with primary tactility as the presubjective ground of fleshly self-affection. Hence the originary transduction of aesthesis and technicity—which transduction is nothing other than the originary mediality of the flesh as the sensible-transcendental ground for any and all appearance.

## The Politics of Embodied Mediality

This is emphatically not to say that the body is "a medium." Against such a positivization, I assert the essentially negative mediality of the flesh. On this ground alone is mediation in its more particular forms possible. And by tracing the transduction of aesthesis and technicity back to the *écart*, or the separation of self-affective tactility and outward-oriented specularity from within the flesh as the ground of mediality, we now have a comprehensive answer to technicism. Against Kittler's apocalyptic end of (media) history in the computational convergence of data streams, we can now assert that the medial transduction of the anthropotechnical interface cannot be dissolved so long as we remain in and of the flesh. The "eyewash" of the interface is therefore ineradicable, and (media) history continues. And thus, though one might worry that this rooting of mediality in the

flesh serves to dehistoricize and universalize mediated relations 
under the umbrella of a suspiciously unmarked (and therefore
presumably white, male, cis-heterosexist) form of embodiment, I
suggest that it actually serves to strengthen the concrete material
force of the historical *a priori* and points to specifically embodied
differences such as might pertain to gendered and racialized
being—differences that themselves appear on the ground of the
flesh. Before going on to consider the relevance of the foregoing
argument for post-cinematic media, I would therefore like to gesture briefly towards several avenues of thinking that suggest the
usefulness of a negative media theory of the flesh for antiracist
and feminist projects. These will also help outline the stakes and
the potentials of the artistic interventions to which I return in Part
Two.

One way that a negative media theory of the flesh could be of
use, politically, would be in terms of elaborating on Iris Marion
Young's argument that gender, far from being an "essence" that
is given by physiology, is nevertheless a materially (and not
just discursively) constructed category: a "seriality" in Jean-
Paul Sartre's terminology (Young 1994, 713–738). The latter,
as developed in his late, Marxist work, *Critique of Dialectical
Reason*, is Sartre's term for the loose and mutually alienated
forms of collectivity that characterize urban modernity—such
as the accidental assemblage of people waiting in line for the
bus (Sartre 2004, 256–269). These people are united merely by
the force of the common infrastructures of the built environment (the bus stop, the roads, and the city itself), their common
relation to commodities and technologies (centrally, here, the
bus as an instrument for getting to work or to go shopping)—
they are united negatively, that is, by what Sartre calls "worked
matter" or the "practico-inert" in recognition of the way built
structures and technologies store human praxis, or past living
labor, while condensing it into inert objective form. Around these
objects, increasingly standardized through industrial capitalism's
serialized production processes, are arrayed alienated and

 impotent social collectives of interchangeable, fungible subjects. The negative collective of the "seriality" is thereby opposed to the "group," which is united by a common and unified praxis. The appeal of this conception for a feminist politics, according to Young, is that it enables us to identify the category of "women" as one that is neither essentialistic nor voluntaristic, but that could serve as the foundation for collective action on behalf of women in general. According to Young, "the series of women … is a passive unity, one that does not arise from the individuals called women but rather positions them through the material organization of social relations as enabled and constrained by the structural relations of enforced heterosexuality and the sexual division of labor" (1994, 733). Like all serialities, in line with Sartre's notion of the practico-inert, gender as a seriality is "unified passively by the objects around which [its members'] actions are oriented or by the objectified results of the material effects of the actions of others," materialities that define "routine practices and habits," such that "[t]he unity of the series derives from the way that individuals pursue their own individual ends with respect to the same objects conditioned by a continuous material environment, in response to structures that have been created by the unintended collective result of past actions" (ibid., 724). For women, these practico-inert realities include but are not limited to or rooted exclusively in "physical facts of … female bodies" (ibid., 729); equally crucial are "[s]ocial objects [that] are not merely physical but also inscribed by and the products of past practices," such as "the social rules of menstruation, along with the material objects associated with menstrual practices," but also pronouns, "[v]erbal and visual representations," and the "gender codes" attached to "[c]lothes …[,] cosmetics, tools, even in some cases furniture and spaces" such as gender-specific bathrooms or dorms (ibid., 729–730). These practico-inert objects "constitute the gendered series women through structures like enforced heterosexuality and the sexual division of labor," such that inclusion in the series depends neither on a natural essence nor on subjective identification: "being positioned by these

structures in the series women does not itself designate attributes that attach to the person in the series, nor does it define her
identity" (ibid., 730). That is, the historically and culturally specific
social formation of gender categories, which is an emphatically
negative determination, is produced by the mingling of originary
technicity and aesthesis that marks the flesh as the ground of
mediality.

Furthermore, as Gayle Salamon (2010) has shown in her appropriation of Merleau-Ponty for the theorization of transgender
embodiment, this essentially negative grounding of gender in
the flesh is far from a biologization of the same. In her reading
of Merleau-Ponty's notion of the "sexual schema," Salamon foregrounds the role of desire and the "transposition" of desiring
subject and desired object, according to which a "complicated
interplay between interiority and exteriority" can be discovered
(2010, 23). For Merleau-Ponty, "sexuality, without being the object
of any intended act of consciousness, can underlie and guide
specified forms of my experience. Taken in this way, as an ambiguous atmosphere, sexuality is co-extensive with life. In other
words, ambiguity is of the essence of human existence" (2002,
195–196; qtd. in Salamon 2010, 50–51). As an *atmospheric* reality,
sexuality permeates embodied intentionality, or the directed-
ness of perception and agency, which is suffused with desire.
Rather than attaching to a particular body part, it is prepersonal
or generic—not yet empirically "specified." Seen thus desire, as
Salamon puts it, is "embodied but—importantly—not located"
(ibid., 51). Recall, in this connection, how the medially reflexive
artwork, for Mersch, allows the viewer to "occupy positions of
distance without a localizable other" (2006, 227). For Salamon,
desire's atmospheric nature "performs an unyoking of bodily
parts from bodily pleasures," thus de-positivizing the body in
its mediality (2010, 51). Significantly, in her elucidation of this
process Salamon implicitly opens the door for an understanding
of a prepersonal interface with technology: "The join between
desire and the body is the location of sexuality, and that join

  may be a penis, or some other phallus, or some other body part, or a region of the body that is not individuated into a part, or a bodily auxiliary that is not organically attached to the body" (ibid., 51). Transposition, the "general function" that enables this variable erotogenization of "parts," can do so because it exceeds all partial determination; in its excess of the empirical body, it can therefore also incorporate prostheses ("bodily auxiliaries") and interface directly with objects outside the body. In this way, the prediscursive materiality of embodied gender is also originarily technical. As a result, the question of mediality becomes centrally relevant for an antinormative conception (and politics) of gender, as embodied gender and technicity are inextricably entwined in the flesh.

The question of mediality as explored here might also be taken up in a rethinking of the embodied aesthetico-technical processes and politics of racialization. Alexander Weheliye, in his book *Habeas Viscus*, draws on Hortense Spillers's distinction between flesh and body, which deserves careful comparison with Merleau-Ponty's similar distinction, alongside Sylvia Wynter's notion of the various "genres" of the human—an idea that suggests that race is produced technically, by means of a biological implantation of an extra-biological sociogenic principle (following and building on Frantz Fanon)—thus defining the flesh as a global battleground where power is exerted and resistance might be mounted (Weheliye 2014; Spillers 2003b; Wynter and McKittrick 2015). Weheliye's titular concept of *habeas viscus*—"You shall have the flesh"—is offered as a counterconcept to the juridical *habeas corpus*—which reduces the body to an empirical object, a living corpse; the viscerality of *habeas viscus* serves "to signal how violent political domination activates a fleshly surplus that simultaneously sustains and disfigures said brutality, and, on the other hand, to reclaim the atrocity of flesh as a pivotal arena for the politics emanating from different traditions of the oppressed" (2014, 2). Out of the "fleshly surplus" over against the empirical body—which is to say: out of the sensible-transcendental ground

of embodied mediality—the question becomes: "How might we 
go about thinking and living enfleshment otherwise so as to usher
in different genres of the human ...?" (ibid., 2–3). Since race and
racialization are enacted on the flesh by means that are both aesthetic (i.e. sensory) and technical—"via institutions, discourses,
practices, desires, infrastructures, languages, technologies,
sciences, economies, dreams, and cultural artifacts" (ibid., 3)—a
transformation of these practices will have to be addressed at
their root, in the domain of embodied mediality. Weheliye con-
cedes that

> habeas viscus is but one modality of imagining the relational
> ontological totality of the human. Yet in order to consider
> habeas viscus as an object of knowledge in the service of
> producing new forms of humanity, we must venture past the
> perimeters of bare life and biopolitics and the juridical his-
> tory of habeas corpus, because neither sufficiently addresses
> how deeply anchored racialization is in the somatic field of
> the human. (ibid., 4)

The flesh at stake here is not *natural*: "Habeas viscus suggests a
technological assemblage of humanity, technology circumscribed
here in the broadest sense as the application of knowledge to
the practical aims of life or to changing and manipulating the
human environment" (ibid., 12). This racialized flesh is therefore
a medial pivot between an objectifying technicism and a presubjective technicity, and it demands a deeply somatic politics that
is simultaneously technical and aesthetic: "alternative critical,
political, *and poetic* assemblages." (ibid., 2, emphasis added)

Finally, this line of thinking will be crucial, in the context of a post-
cinematic media regime and its politics of the body, for the way it
helps us conceive the intersectionally racial and gendered stakes
of a desubjectified visuality—or the presubjective specularity
invoked by Merleau-Ponty, seemingly without attention to such
matters. Let us follow Weheliye's provocative but undeveloped
suggestion that Spillers's body/flesh distinction bears comparison

 with Merleau-Ponty's. For Spillers, the distinction between body and flesh, or between subjectively correlated versus desubjectified or discorrelated corporeality, is "the central [distinction] between captive and liberated subject-positions. In that sense, before the 'body' there is 'flesh,' that zero degree of social conceptualization that does not escape concealment under the brush of discourse or the reflexes of iconography" (Spillers 2003b, 206). Accordingly, "European hegemonies stole bodies," but in the course of the slave trade they committed "high crimes against the *flesh*," which was subjected to "the tortures and instruments of captivity" (ibid., 206): "iron, whips, chains, knives, the canine patrol, the bullet" (ibid., 207). "These undecipherable markings on the captive body render a kind of hieroglyphics of the flesh whose severe disjunctures come to be hidden to the cultural seeing by skin color" (ibid., 207). This provides a dark mirror image of Merleau-Ponty's mutable flesh, which responded, in his elucidation of the historical *a priori*, to a culture's "clothing, jewelry, and love" (2002, 101). Against this, the hieroglyphics of the flesh "create[s] the distance between what [Spillers calls] a cultural *vestibularity* and *culture*" (Spillers 2003b, 207). Spillers describes this "vestibule (or 'pre-view')," as she says—strangely recalling Merleau-Ponty's "pre-objective view" of the body—as the site of a fleshly politics that "ungenders" captive bodies, rendering them subject to the "interiorized violation of body and mind," as in rape, as well as the "*externalized* acts of torture and prostration" (ibid., 207), including what she calls "pornotroping" (ibid., 206).

Ungendering is thus associated with desubjectification, a forced reversion from the subjectively and socially coded body to the underlying flesh, the multistability of which is hardly liberating but rather constitutes a target of opportunity for the oppressor. As for its association with the pre-cultural *vestibule*, puzzlingly identified with a *pre-view*, I would like to suggest that it is here that the presubjective visuality that I mentioned above—and that is crucial to discorrelated, computational imaging—enters into the picture. A vestibule is an antechamber, a *Vorraum*, or (in

Italian) an *anticamera*. While the *camera* in question here is mod-  
eled on a architectural space, a metaphorical room or chamber,
the *camera obscura* that precedes the photographic camera
would seem to be implicated as well in the increasingly *"specular
categories"* of racialized "personhood" (ibid., 212). The idea of a
vestibular *anticamera* therefore suggests something that both
precedes and in some ways resists the subjective "view" of the
camera—hence, Spillers's "vestibule (or 'pre-view')" suggestively
illuminates also the non- or pre-visual processing of computer
graphics, which as we shall see shortly is also a multistable vector
of racial (un)gendering. Thus, while neither Spillers nor Merleau-
Ponty is writing about computational imaging processes, the
picture they give us of desubjectified or discorrelated visuality—
splayed across pictures alternately suggesting an empowered or
a radically vulnerable flesh—will be of great use in gauging post-
cinema's transformative powers with respect to embodiment.[3]

As these examples of gendered, transgendered, and racialized
embodiment demonstrate, to assert the originary mediality of
the flesh, defined in terms of the originary transduction of aesthesis and technicity, is far from an apolitical—or worse: uni-
versalizing/marginalizing—gesture. Rather, it foregrounds the
embodied and collective stakes of mediality itself. Ultimately, we
might hope, this originary mediality of the flesh, as a thoroughly
political reality, might come to serve as the aesthetico-technical
ground and vehicle of resistance to the atrocities and injustices of
this world.

---

3    For a powerful exploration of vestibularity in Spillers's sense, which
     connects the flesh to a concept of "black aesthesis" and to mediality in ways
     that resonate with my argument here, see Bradley 2023.

# On the Embodied Phenomenology of DeepFakes

Let us now see how this theory of fleshly mediality helps to illuminate post-cinematic media's transformative powers with respect to embodied existence. Machine learning–enabled face swapping videos, so-called DeepFakes, will serve here as an example. DeepFakes pose significant challenges to conventional modes of viewing; indeed, the use of machine learning algorithms in these videos' production complicates not only traditional forms of moving-image media but also deeply anchored phenomenological categories and structures. By paying close attention to the exchange of energies around these videos, especially the investment of energy on the part of the viewer struggling to discern the provenance and veracity of such images, we discover a mode of viewing that both recalls pre-cinematic forms of fascination while relocating them in a decisively post-cinematic field—thus leveraging a shift in correlative potentials. This media-historically anchored transformation, which recalls the shift from Galloway's photographic to computational contracts of visuality, depends on a partial undoing of constituted subjectivity; the human perceiver, as we shall see, no longer stands clearly opposite the image object but instead interfaces with the spectacle at a pre-subjective level that approximates the nonhuman processing of visual information known as machine vision. While the *depth* referenced in the name "deep fake" is that of "deep learning," the aesthetic engagement with these videos implicates an intervention in the depths of embodied sensibility—at the level of the inner diaphragm's self-displacement into the fleshly *écart* between visuality and tactility. The result is a recoding of the complementary powers of technicity and aesthesis, enabling the insertion of a new "program" into the flesh. While the overt visual thematics of these videos is often highly gendered (their most prominent examples being so-called "involuntary synthetic pornography" targeting mostly

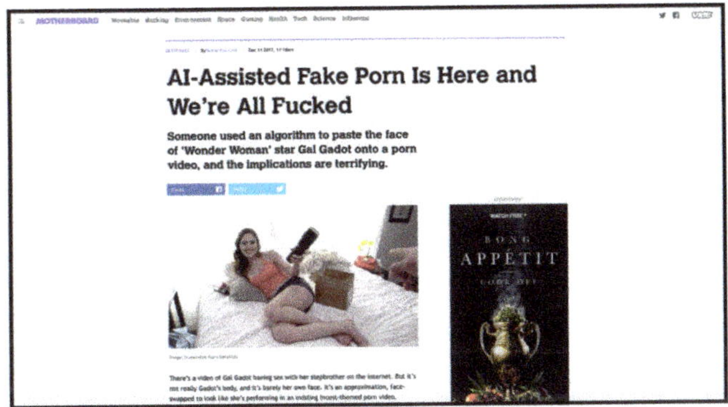


[Fig. 2.1] The online article widely credited with making the DeepFake phenomenon known to a wider public in December 2017 (Screenshot by the author)

women), viewers are also subject to affective syntheses and pre-subjective blurrings that, beyond the level of representation, open their bodies to fleshly "ungenderings" (Spillers 2003b, 207) and re-typifications with far-reaching consequences for both race and gender.

How does this work? First, let us note that DeepFake videos trade crucially on the incommensurable scales and temporalities of computational processing and its ability to defy capture as the object of human perception. To be sure, DeepFakes still present to us something that is recognizable as an image. But in them, perception has become something of a by-product, a precipitate form or supplement to the invisible operations that occur in and through them. We can get a glimpse of such discorrelation by noticing how such images fail to conform or settle into stable forms or patterns, how they resist their own condensation into integral perceptual objects—for example, the way that they blur figure/ground distinctions. The article widely credited with making the DeepFake phenomenon known to a wider public in December 2017 (fig. 2.1) notes with regard to a fake porn video featuring the likeness of Gal Gadot: "a box occasionally appeared around her face where the original image peeks through, and her mouth and eyes don't quite line up to the words the actress is saying—but if you squint a little and suspend your belief, it might as well be Gadot" (Cole 2017). There's something telling about the formulation, which hinges the success of the DeepFake not on a suspension of disbelief—a suppression of active resistance—but on a suspension of *belief*—seemingly, a more casual form of affirmation—whereby the flickering reversals of figure and ground, or of subject and object, are flattened out into a smooth indifference.

In this regard, DeepFake videos are worth comparing to another type of multistable image: the digital lens flare, which is both to-be-looked-at (as a virtuosic display of technical achievement) and to-be-overlooked (after all, the height of such images' technical achievement is reached when they can appear as transparently naturalized simulations of a physical camera's optical properties).[4] The tension between opacity and transparency, or objecthood and invisibility, is never fully resolved, thus undermining a clear distinction between diegetic and medial or material levels of reality. Is the virtual camera that registers the simulated lens flare to be seen as part of the world represented on screen, or as part of the machinery responsible for revealing it to us? The answer, it seems, must be *both*. And in this, such images embody something like what Neil Harris termed the "operational aesthetic" that characterized nineteenth-century science and technology expos, magic shows, and early cinema alike; in these contexts, spectatorial attention oscillated between the surface phenomenon, the visual spectacle of a machine or a magician in motion, and the hidden operations that made the spectacle possible (Harris 1973, 59–89). It was such a dual or split attention that powered early film as a "cinema of attractions," where viewers came to see the Cinématographe in action, as much as or more than they came to see images of workers leaving

---

4    I have written about the phenomenological paradoxes inherent in CGI lens flares in Denson 2020a, especially 27–30.

the factory or a train arriving at the station (Gunning 1986, 63–70). 
And it is in light of this operational aesthetic that spectators
found themselves focusing on the wind rustling in the trees or the
waves lapping at the rocks—phenomena supposedly marginal
to the main objects of visual interest.[5] DeepFakes also trade
essentially on an operational aesthetic, or a dispersal of attention
between visual surface and the algorithmic operation of machine
learning. However, the post-cinematic processes to whose
operation DeepFakes refer our attention fundamentally transform the operational aesthetic, relocating it from the oscillations
of attention that we see in the cinema to a deep, pre-attentional
level that computation taps into with its microtemporal speed.

Consider the way digital glitches undo figure/ground distinctions.
Whereas the cinematic image offered viewers opportunities to
shift their attention from one figure to another and from these
figures to the ground of the screen and projector enabling them,
the digital glitch refuses to settle into the role either of figure
or of ground. It is, simply, both—it stands out, figurally, as the
pixely appearance of the substratal ground itself. Even more
fundamentally, though, it points to the inadequacy, which is
not to say dispensibility, of human perception and attention
with respect to algorithmic processing. While the glitch's visual
appearance effects a deformation of the spatial categories of
figure and ground, it does so on the basis of a temporal mis-
match between human perception and algorithmic processing.
The latter, operating at a scale measured in nanoseconds, by far
outstrips the window of perception and subjectivity, so that by
the time the subject shows up to perceive the glitch, the "object"
(so to speak) has already acted upon our presubjective sensibilities and moved on. This is why glitches, compression artifacts,
and other discorrelated images are not even bound to appear
to us as visual phenomena in the first place in order to exert a

---

5    As recounted, in 1896, by Maxim Gorky. See Gorky 1960, 407-409. See also
Jordan Schonig's video essay (2020).

 material force on us.[6] Another way to account for this is to say that the visually-subjectively delineated distinction between figure and ground itself depends on the deeper ground of pre-subjective embodiment, and it is the latter that defines for us our spatial situations and temporal potentialities. DeepFakes, like other images produced by discorrelative technologies, are able to dis-integrate coherent spatial forms so radically because they undercut the temporal window within which visual perception occurs. The operation at the heart of their operational aesthetic is itself an operationalization of the flesh, prior to its delineation into subjective and objective forms of corporeality. The seamful-ness of DeepFakes—their occasional glitchy appearance or just the threat or presentiment that they might announce themselves as such—points to our fleshly imbrication with technical images today, which is to say: to the recoding not only of aesthetic form but of embodied aesthesis itself.[7]

In other words: especially and as long as they still routinely fail to cohere as seamless suturings of viewing subjects together with visible objects, but instead retain their potential to fall apart at the seams and thus still require a suspension of belief, DeepFake videos are capable of calling attention to the ways that attention itself is bypassed, providing aesthetic form to the substratal interface between contemporary technics and embodied aesthesis. To be clear, and lest there be any mistake about it, I in no way wish to celebrate DeepFakes as a liberating media technology, the way that the disruption of narrative by cinematic self-reflexivity was sometimes celebrated as opening a space where structuring ideologies gave way to an experi-ence of materiality and the dissolution of the subject-positions inscribed and interpellated by the apparatus. No amount of glitchy seamfulness will undo the gendered violence inflicted, mostly upon women, in involuntary synthetic pornography. Not

6    This is a central argument in Denson 2020a. See also Hansen 2016, 785-816.
7    I introduced the concept of "seamfulness" in Chapter 4 of Denson 2020a.

only that, but the pleasure taken by viewers in consuming this 111
violence seems to depend, at least in part, precisely on the failure
or incompleteness of the spectacle: what such viewers desire is
not to be tricked into actually believing that it is Gal Gadot or their
ex-girlfriend that they are seeing on the screen, but precisely
that it is a fake likeness or simulation, still open to glitches, upon
which the operational aesthetic depends.

Nevertheless, we should not look away from the paradoxical
opening signaled by these viewers' suspension of belief. The
fact that they have to "squint a little" to complete the gendered
fantasy of domination also means that they have to compromise,
at least to a certain degree or for a short duration, their subjective mastery of the visual object, that they have to abdicate
their own subjective ownership of their bodies as the bearers
of experience. Though it is hard to believe that any trace of
conscious awareness of it remains, much less that viewers will
be reformed or repent as a result of the experience, it seems
reasonable to believe that viewers of DeepFake videos must
experience at least an inkling of their own undoing as their de-
subjectivized vision interfaces with the ahuman operation of
machine vision.

What I am saying, then, and I am trying to be careful about how
I say it, is that DeepFake videos open the door, experientially, to
a highly problematic but multistable space in which our predictive technologies participate in processes of subjectivation by
outpacing us, anticipating us, and intervening materially in the
pre-personal realm of the flesh, out of which subjectivized and
socially "typified" bodies emerge. It is here that a re-engineering
of correlative potentials is made possible, where tactility is
captured by the new visuality, and where Sartre's "worked
matter" of the "practico-inert" is set to work on the flesh, with
the effect, as Young has argued, that bodies are gendered by
being "positioned," "oriented," and entrained with new "routine
practices and habits" (1994, 730, 724)—thus reorganizing the
social substrates around which gender and race are configured

 and imposed on the body. If it was difficult to perceive these social standardization processes in an industrial-cinematic lifeworld, then it is all the more difficult in our post-cinematic one. For the worked matter at issue now is a *microscopically* worked matter, operating *microtemporally* and *predictively*, well in advance of subjective regard or resistance; the standardization and typification processes I just mentioned are more fine-grained, more "personalized" or targeted than was previously possible. Moreover, the neural nets at the heart of DeepFakes' production are black-boxed entities that are neither directly pro-grammable nor transparent to retrospective analysis. Operating without direct human control or insight, they have been trained on large data sets to produce outputs that statistically resemble their inputs, for example reproducing stylistic traits or "typical" bodily motions. As Hannes Bajohr writes, "repetition is in the very nature of neural nets" (2022, 219); and it is by way of this repetition that DeepFakes discipline and typify bodies—both those on screen and those in front of the monitor.

That DeepFakes nevertheless provide a glimpse, however fleeting, of these processes is thus no small feat; it points us to an important margin of multistability, where the new visuality might be felt as the powerful force that it is. That is, the flattening of subjectivity, the suspension of belief and depersonalization of vision in DeepFake videos, provides limited aesthetic access to the contemporary "ungendering" of the flesh that marks a pre-liminary step in the computational intensification of racialized and gendered subjectivation. This is a truly insidious aesthetics of the flesh, and one that must be combatted vehemently. However, it suggests the possibility that alternative aesthetic options might exist or be forged, that it might be possible to seize the multi-stable margin, to reverse engineer the algorithms of statistical correlation and control, and to appropriate post-cinematic media

in order to recode our fleshly mediality for a less awful world.[8]     **113**
Perhaps the artists can show us the way.

8    Compare Galloway on recoding the black box. Galloway 2021, 215-245.

# PART TWO: POST-CINEMATIC BODY GENRES

# Introduction to Part Two

In Part 2, I aim to refocus the discussion of the flesh's originary mediality, in which aesthetic and technological capacities are transductively entwined, by turning to several sites of intensive transformation of embodied existence. I am especially interested here in the ways that artistic interventions are able to disrupt some of the more pernicious political effects of discorrelative technologies by foregrounding and amplifying their multistable potentials. Holding both the correlative and the discorrelative powers of contemporary media together, the artists whose work stands at the center of the following chapters help us to assess the situation of the body in a post-cinematic media regime and, hopefully, to intuit more ameliorative ways of subjective and collective being.

In order to frame these efforts, I would like to call to mind Linda Williams's famous study of cinematic "body genres"—those "low" genres of horror, melodrama, and pornography, that take aim at the viewer's bodily reactions (1991, 2–13). In fact, these genres already articulated something like the correlative/discorrelative split in that they simultaneously present perceptual contents that we consciously, subjectively perceive while also bypassing consciousness and affecting the body directly through visceral disgust, bodily sympathy to the point of tears, or sexual arousal. Taking Williams's insight here as my cue, my investigations in the following chapters are guided by the question of what new body genres are articulated within a post-cinematic media regime, and how they address bodies that are at once intentional and intensive. Adapting Williams's concept for specifically digital/com-putational media devices, systems, and platforms, we have to pay especial attention to the ways that the user/viewer's body is inter-pellated and imagined, constructed or deconstructed, engrossed or expelled—how, in other words, post-cinematic bodies are subjected to the push and pull of correlative and discorrelative tendencies and forces.

 I should start by recognizing that the older body genres identified by Williams—horror, melodrama, and pornography—are by no means a thing of the past. Horror, as I have argued in recent publications, has found new forms that exploit and/or question the attunement of our bodies to digital cameras, screens, and environments (Denson 2020b).[1] Meanwhile, melodrama continues to thrive in long-running serial formats on television and streaming video platforms—in prime-time serials, daytime soaps, telenovelas, and web series, among others. And pornography, of course, has proliferated on the Internet at a scale that would have been unimaginable at the time Williams (1999) wrote *Hard Core*, her seminal book on the subject. In the following, however, I would like to look at the ways that new devices, platforms, or apparatuses create their own new modes or "genres"—using this term in a capacious sense—that simultaneously question previous forms of the image while by turns addressing, recentering, dividuating, datafying, and modulating their users' bodies.

Chapter 3 questions what I term the "body replacement program" at the heart of virtual reality—i.e. the fantasy, often frustrated, that the user's real body can be temporarily subsumed, engrossed, erased, or forgotten and supplanted by a virtualized body in the immersive virtual environment. VR is in many ways a paradigmatic post-cinematic technology that sets the stage and establishes frameworks for other modes of contemporary imaging (in AR, videogames, and beyond), and it is therefore important to take a close look at it as a genre of visceral interpellation that operationalizes the flesh in what I have referred to as its originary mediality. Because variations of this operationalization, transposed into different spatial and temporal configurations, will reappear and be reimagined in the other post-cinematic body genres treated in this book, this chapter can be seen as foundational to the others and weaves between broad theoretical considerations and a focus on concrete

1    Expanded as Chapter 5 of Denson 2020a.

objects, scenarios, and artworks. In particular, virtual mirrors, which invite experimentation along the lines of Merleau-Ponty's phenomenological investigations while crucially modifying the parameters of tactility and specularity, will be especially important for thinking about the oscillating pulls and potentials of embodied dis/correlation.

Under the generic heading of the "dance," Chapter 4 traces a number of ways that users and artists engage in embodied negotiations with automated agents. Some of these, like artist Catie Cuan's choreographies for industrial robots and their human dance partners, take these negotiations—in this case, literal dances—out of VR's virtual environments and put them back into the real world of muscles, bones, and metal, now augmented with algorithmic control mechanisms acting and reacting in real time. Others, like the machine learning–powered Deep-Fake videos we looked at in Chapter 2, place their viewers back in a more conventional relation to the space of the screen; but far from a passive projection surface, these screens serve as a dynamic interface for perceptual and subperceptual trans-actions between bodies, both onscreen and off, and machines' invisible calculations. Still other scenarios, like using Snapchat's real-time AR filters on a smartphone, split the difference: they return us to the embodied dance, now reconfigured as a real-time improv between users and their handheld screens, react-ing to one another in a complex and delicate circuit of haptics and electronics that has the potential to reshape deep-seated aesthetic senses. Especially in this latter scenario, where the viewer views their own augmented image on the screen, we find echoes of the virtual mirror; but whereas in VR such mirrors are still relatively marginal and troublesome figures due to the challenges they pose for correlative self-recognition, in these playful interactions (as well as in their professional-life coun-terparts such as automated appearance "touch-ups" on the Zoom videoconferencing platform) the virtual or hybrid mirror becomes increasingly banal and taken-for-granted. As a result, the habituated flesh is opened up to radical transformation—or to the algorithmic entrenchment of racial and gendered stereotypes (the original "body genres").

Finally, Chapter 5 focuses on a genre of images that are generated in direct feedback with the user/viewer's embodied metabolism. Whereas the previous chapters looked at the body as an object of replacement/virtualization or as a potential dance partner in real and/or hybrid spaces, the genre under consideration here is one that tends to see the body as an object of "training" and that places the screen as an interface between body and brain—between involuntary metabolic processes and subjective efforts to transform them. As examples of this post-cinematic genre, the chapter looks primarily at several cases where the body's metabolism serves as a resource for the real-time generation of screen events, including so-called "smart" exercise machines that respond directly to the user's physical exertion while laying the groundwork for a new metabolic capitalism. Against this regime, which marshals the forces of algorithmic standardization in real-time feedback loops of interpellation, I consider also a number of experimental and artistic works that avail themselves of EEG and ECG devices, among others, to reveal the scope and reach of post-cinema's operationalization of the flesh and to recuperate political agency in the face of correlative capture.

Of course, the following chapters can hardly do justice to the manifold ways that embodiment is targeted and modulated in a post-cinematic media regime, and this is clearly not an exhaustive list of post-cinematic body genres. Nevertheless, it is my hope that the discussion of these three genres or modes can shed light on the broader dynamics of dis/correlation and provide a foundation for further thinking about the ways that our bodies are now at stake in visual and post-visual media.

# 3

# Virtual Reality and the Body Replacement Program

Virtual reality involves what is perhaps the most obvious re-centering of the post-cinematic viewing body, but it also represents the very height of discorrelation. Putting on VR goggles, a set of lenses is held at a constant distance from the lenses of our eyes. The apparatic lenses disappear and magnify two tiny screens, the stereoscopic images of which fill our field of vision, erasing the frame and turning the screen into a total environment. The screens retain what Stanley Cavell (1979) identified as the duality of both revealing a world and screening or blocking us from it, but this is a radically changed world, due both to spatial and temporal transformations. Unlike in the cinema, we are not screening a world of the past, immune to our interventions, but we are actively involved in generating that world right now. Turning your head left or right, up or down, will reveal different aspects of the scene, which due to its dynamic three-dimensionality is never given fully but only "adumbratively," to adopt a Husserlian term; that is, visual objects have hidden but discoverable computationally generated back-sides and volumetric densities that may be revealed experimentally, by changing one's perspective.[1] As a result of this relational spatiality, it is theoretically possible that you might even catch a glimpse of things from a completely new angle, never before actualized in anyone else's headset-mediated engagement with the simulated world. Active rather than passive, these screens are therefore cameras, generating their images in real time and in direct response to the user's movement. The camera is now an extension of my embodied perception—or vice versa: perhaps I am now an extension of it?

In any case, what I have called the correlative force of the image is in full effect. Importantly, however, this post-cinematic suture is not based in continuity editing and effected via carefully timed cuts and precise eyeline matches; rather, it is based in seamless, real-time, full-body immersion.[2] Rather than inscribing the spectator discursively and obliquely into a disjunctively articulated space via montage, the VR scenario paradigmatically invites the viewer to explore its space directly and from within. Indeed, the viewer's prosthetic embodiment of the camera, alluded to above, ensures that I am always at the center of the space I navigate, just as I am in real life, and that my relation to it remains centered *here*, where I am. At the same time, discorrelation is heightened as well. The image is generated out of the computational dividuation of visual information, combined with the dividuation of my own body and behavior as data.[3] My subjective, integral body is first dissolved into numbers in order that it may subsequently be re-correlated by way of replacement in the virtual world. Only, this process is altogether absent from my awareness; the gap between initial discorrelation and

1   For Husserl's use of "adumbration" (*Abschattung*), see Husserl 2012, sections 41, 44, 97, and 98.
2   Accordingly, it stands in marked contrast to the cinematic suture described in Dayan 1974.
3   In chapter 2 of Denson 2020a, I position the dividuation of the image as a vector in what Deleuze calls the dividuation of the subject in the control society. See Deleuze 1992. See also Gaboury 2021, which shows that computer graphics are not integral images at all.

subsequent re-correlation is not perceived or felt *per se*. If it is **123**
technically correct to say that my body is *first* decomposed into
data and *subsequently* reconstituted as an intentional-relational
unit, it is important to note that *subsequently* here feels like
*immediately*; or, more accurately, it feels like *nothing at all*—at
least, not so long as everything is working properly. The temporal
gap between discorrelation and re-correlation is one that is too
minuscule to be registered phenomenologically. And this is the
source of VR's power to replace—for all humanly possible intents
and purposes—my body and the subjectivity that inhabits it, and
to establish itself as a powerful *correlative* medium.

Assuming that everything is running smoothly (and this is, after
all, a nontrivial assumption), the correlation cannot be denied; it
is perceptually apodictic—regardless of whether or not the virtual
world is (photo)realistically depicted or whether I *believe* that I
am truly in it.[4] This is a perceptual rather than cognitive relation,
and I can confirm it instantly by simply moving my head and
observing the change. The important point is that I experience,
immediately and seamlessly, the relation between the world
and my body—though the latter may be different than what I am
used to thinking of as *my* body. Just as the object-world has been
replaced with a simulated environment generated in real time, so
too has my body been replaced by an environmentally relational
configuration—a correlation more than an avatar—that channels
what and how I see and feel. It is no exaggeration to say, then,
that "I" am reconstituted on this basis as a differently embodied
subject in relation to a different object-world.

This elaborate program of body replacement is often described in
terms of "presence," and upon it rest numerous, often grand and
somewhat dubious claims about the medium's power to make
us "identify" with others and their situations. For example, VR is

4    On apodicticity, referring to a seeing-as rather than belief, see Ihde 2012, 48.

 touted as an empathy machine.[5] We are encouraged to walk in the shoes of a refugee, or to feel what it's like to be the victim of racial violence or sexual harassment. Or, somewhat differently, the correlative force of the medium is foregrounded in VR porn experiences, which invite users to "live" their fantasies, even going so far as to incorporate various prosthetics, teledildonics, or Bluetooth-enabled "smart" sex toys that further solidify the bodily identification of the user with their virtual role. Evidently, this is the very apotheosis of Williams's pornographic body genre. Understandably, however, what is *not* foregrounded in these fantasies is the infrastructural discorrelation required for such immersive experiences: the microtemporal operations that enable real-time feedback and the data capture taking place on various temporal scales, both immediate and longer term, which enable a profiling of the user and serve predictive purposes that aim in part to generate and fulfill the user's future desires and thus contribute to their ongoing subjectivation. It is important to emphasize that in these networks, which are very much anchored in the *real* (as opposed to simulated) world, the body that is subject to replacement or modulation is itself not just a virtual body (qua representation, simulation, or image) but the very real body of the subject. For the latter, seen from a particular phenomenological altitude, simply *is* a correlational configuration; this is why I have suggested that the question of the avatar and of identification more generally are of secondary importance to the question of virtual embodiment: because *all* embodiment is at least in part virtual embodiment, or a question of relations that exceed the actual, including its actual appearance or "skin," whether physical or digital.

As Sartre puts it in *Being and Nothingness*, "my body indicates my possibilities in the world" (Sartre 1984, 403), which is to say that

5    VR director Chris Milk popularized the idea of VR as "the ultimate empathy machine" in his 2015 TED talk (2015). In the meantime, a Google search for "VR empathy machine" brings up far more articles that are critical of the concept.

it is bound up with the instrumentalities of the technical objects and systems that, following Heidegger and his famous tool-analysis in *Being and Time*, structure and reveal the world to me (1962, 91–119). Accordingly, the way in which I am *here* in the world is precisely as being *out there*, in the instrumental relations that offer themselves to me as an embodied being. Rather than an objectively bounded body occupying Euclidean space, my body's dimensionality, spatiality, and location are radically ambiguous: "The space which is originally revealed to me is hodological space; it is furrowed with paths and highways; it is instrumental and it is the *location* of tools" (Sartre 1984, 424). And thus the whole notion of "presence" is ambiguously non-local:

> I *live* my body in danger as regards menacing machines as for manageable instruments. My body is everywhere: the bomb which destroys *my* house also damages my body in so far as the house was already an indication of my body. This is why my body always extends across the tool which it utilizes: It is at the end of the cane on which I lean and against the earth; it is at the end of the telescope which shows me the stars; it is on the chair, in the whole house; for it is my adaptation to these tools. (ibid., 428)

And yet this dispersal of embodiment, its non-punctual pres-ence as co-extension (or co-extendibility) with the instrumentally defined world, is still strictly correlational: indeed, on this view, "the world" appears precisely "as the correlate of the possibilities which I *am*" (ibid., 425). "What counts," then, for this correlation, as Merleau-Ponty puts it succinctly, "is not my body as it in fact is, as a thing in objective space, but as a system of possible actions, a virtual body with its phenomenal 'place' defined by its task and situation. My body is wherever there is something to be done" (2002, 291).

Thus, if the body itself is always already virtual as a condition of its being real, then virtual reality, with its real-time tracking and multisensory feedback, does not simply replace the user's empirical body with a different image, shape, or visual form within the simulated world (though such such representational strategies are hardly inconsequential, as we shall see). More fundamentally, VR is directly involved in a re-engineering of the user's embodied possibilities, desires, behaviors, and intentionalities—a re-engineering that might or might not be extended, in conjunction with a comprehensive surveillance capitalist apparatus, into a more targeted shaping of who one will be (or what one will attend to) when one removes the headset.[6] And even if such longer term effects are deemed implausible (or simply economically-computationally impractical), the re-engineering of bodily comportment towards the immediate future is certainly in effect so long as one remains immersed in the virtual environment. For as Sartre puts it:

> the world as the correlate of the possibilities that I *am* appears from the moment of my upsurge as the enormous skeletal outline of all my possible actions. Perception is naturally surpassed toward action; better yet, it can be revealed only in and through projects of action. The world is revealed as an "always future hollow," for we are always future to ourselves. (1984, 425)

In other words, the temporal corollary of embodiment's dispersal into the non-Euclidean "hodological" space of an instrumentally given world is that we never exist in a punctual present, *now*, but always within the flux of a becoming that is defined and continually redefined by the shifting horizons of possibility, hope, and desire (always against the backdrop, of course, of what has already come and gone).[7]

6    The concept of "surveillance capitalism" has been most thoroughly elaborated in Shoshana Zuboff 2019.

7    Sartre borrows the concept of "hodological space," which combines the Greek *hodos* (path) + *logos* from German-American psychologist Kurt Lewin. See Lewin 1934.

What this implies, in the context of VR, is that the microtemporal moment of discorrelation is continually *folded into* the embodied infrastructure of a vanishing present (or presence) at the heart of correlation. That is, it is not just the case that computationally generated images replace the perceptual objects of vision or even one's own body-image (or the objectively perceived image of one's own perceiving body), as if this were to take place within a static or temporally neutral space of subject-object relations; rather, because perception naturally precedes and gives way to action, while action is also the (retroactive and anticipatory) precondition for the solidification or congealment of perception, then VR's achievement of perceptual correlation necessarily involves a replacement of the retentional-protentional circuits that define our being-in-time. These shifting relations between perception and action point us to the central, enabling role played by affect and its relation to duration in Bergson's metaphysics; as I argued earlier, this role is isomorphic with that played by Merleau-Ponty's "internal diaphragm," which logically or ontologically precedes the spatial and temporal distinctions of stimulus and response—and thus underwrites and enables the empirical or subjective experience of causal temporal relations: of "before" and "after" and "because." It is here, in this presubjective/affective interval of the diaphragm, that computational discorrelation intervenes *prior to* the Sartrean "upsurge" of the perceptual/actional realm of subjective correlation within the simulated world. VR's body replacement program, when successfully executed, is therefore total; at least as long as the viewer is hooked into the virtual world, and as long as the correlation is apodictically confirmed to subjective and motile experience, this replacement pertains to nothing less than the user's real body as the locus of lived spatio-temporal relationality.

As should be clear by now, and as I hope to bear out in the rest of this brief foray into VR as a "genre" of post-cinematic body modulation, this is hardly a simple media-effects argument that positions VR as the "hypodermic" medium par excellence. The transductive relationality of subject and object, or of aesthetic tactility and specular technicity, as explored in the previous chapter, undermines any such simple stimulus-response model of causality. But, as I have been suggesting here, the conclusion to be drawn is *not* that we can simply draw a line between the real and the virtual and bracket off one from the other. For what's at stake, when looked at from this perspective, is a modulation of prepersonal and preperceptual embodied relation to the world itself, according to which virtual reality has to be seen as a "mixed reality" in a strong sense.[8] VR takes aim at the material seat of our open-ended processing of time and space—most proximally, the microtemporal circuit of retention and protention that is necessary for perception and action alike and that provides the phenomenal glue that makes meaningful action possible in the world. The result of such modulation is the apodictically correlative experience of "presence" in the virtual world, but its operative substrate is a computational interface with the physical body in the real world. Bracketing off one from the other is simply not possible, since what is at stake is precisely the originary mediality of the flesh.

## Mixed Realities

For decades now, VR enthusiasts, philosophers, and others have speculated about the possible extent of virtual "presence"—the realistic illusion of *being there* in a digital simulation—while computer scientists and other technologists have continually worked to push the illusion's boundaries. The question, therefore, has often been posed, in both quasi-phenomenological and technological terms, as a matter of whether, and to what extent, a user could be made to *feel* that the simulated world was real and/or that their body was really there. For the most

8    "Mixed reality" has emerged as a conceptual framework for thinking about thinking about the merging of real and virtual worlds. I am inspired here by Mark Hansen's claim that "*all* reality is mixed reality" (2006, 5).

part, the illusion of presence has been recognized as just that: 
an illusion; and it has been seen as dependent on a "suspension
of disbelief," hence of the order of feeling and/or affect rather
than belief and/or knowledge. Arguably, however, undue weight
has nevertheless been given to articulated senses such as
sight (above all) and hearing, which are closely associated with
epistemic justification, and thus virtual presence has tacitly been
judged from a primarily cognitive standpoint. So while research
into tactility, proprioception, and haptic feedback have been
absolutely essential to the development of VR and its ability to
create a feeling of presence, oftentimes their contributions have
been judged in terms of a counterfactual subjectivism: granted
that I know *I am not in the virtual world* I see before me, *could I
nevertheless believe*, in principle, that I am in that world? Here, "in
principle" means, simply, "on the basis of the sensory evidence
presented to me." Essentially, presence is judged on the basis
of a phenomenological epoché, where what is bracketed is my
taken-for-granted knowledge of my *actual* situation, as a user
interfacing with a computational system. The bracketing of real
and virtual worlds is thus baked into how one approaches the
success (or not) of simulation. But even more important: despite
the recognition of the importance of affect (or the *feeling* of presence), which might be taken to broach a presubjective stratum
of existence, the identity of the subject of sensation is not called
into question. Note how, in the counterfactual criterion posed
above, the already individuated subject is taken as fully expli-
cated, pre-existent, and identical across real and virtual spaces:
I (in the real world) know that I am here, not there (in the virtual
world), but presence will be achieved if I can nevertheless believe
(or suspend disbelief) in the sensory contents presented to *me*
(a subject-position that is ambiguously located both in the real
world and the virtual one).

The ambiguity of this subject-position is, I contend, not simply an
analytical confusion but rather an existential indistinction that is
essential to virtual reality as such. This is because, as I argue in

 this section, it is the prepersonal flesh, prior to and as the condition of correlation and discorrelation, that is the primary site of VR's modulation of embodiment. But in order fully to grasp the implications of this fact, we have to take a step back from our discrete senses and their objects, and rethink presence as rooted in preperceptual relations in the process of their attunement and separation—in other words, we need to think about presence in terms of a liminal space in between an unconditioned viscerality and an articulated subjectivity. In short, we need to see the achievement of presence as an act of subjectivation, a shaping and molding of a fluid but not altogether indeterminate embodied subjectivity, the fixity of which cannot be assumed but must be forged.

Let us consider Don Ihde's phenomenological discussion of VR and its relation to what he terms "embodiment" and "disembodiment," which will help to clarify some of the fundamental issues at stake in considering VR in terms of the aforementioned in/distinctions of sense and subjectivity. Written several decades ago, when VR technologies and their cultural presence were mediated through the lens of movies like *Lawnmower Man* (1992) and *The Matrix* (1999), Ihde's discussion responds to the "postmodern hype" of the day, and specifically to the question: "is virtual reality b*etter than* and *substitutable for* real reality?" (2002, 127). While today the question may strike us as hopelessly hyperbolic, and we may therefore suspect that Ihde is setting up a strawman that will easily be knocked over, we should not forget that in the 1990s VR was commonly approached in similar terms not only by Hollywood, but by technologists and philosophers as well. For example, philosopher Michael Heim (who, like Ihde, drew heavily from the phenomenological tradition) claimed in 1993 that "[t]he ontological shift through digital symbols became in VR a full-fledged, aggressive, surrogate reality" (1993, xiii). For Ihde, the question of VR's substitution of reality, and the underlying "technofantasy" of body replacement to which it gives voice, was seen to be enabled by the body's "polymorphically ambiguous"

and multistable nature—its real and imagined extendibility 
beyond the borders of the skin (2002, 6). It is this plasticity
and ambiguity of embodiment that allows for the body to slip
between subjective and objective positions within our active and
perceptual relations to the world and that allow us to imagine
ourselves either from a first-person or a third-person point of
view.

Ihde illustrates this point in terms of the ways different people
imagine what it would be like to jump out of an airplane: when
asked, some people report seeing this imagined scenario through
their own eyes, while others see their body from above or below
as it exits the plane, descends in free fall, and slows with the
opening of the parachute. While there may be all sorts of cultural
and technological factors contributing to this choice of a first-
person or third-person perspective, both perceptual-imaginative
alternatives are live possibilities—a fact that each of us can
confirm by imagining a variety of situations.[9] I can either imagine
myself undergoing a "full sensory embodiment perspective,"
which Ihde identifies as the "here-body" of immediate or real-life
(RL) experience, or I can picture myself, in a kind of third-person
perspective, via "the quasi-otherness of [a] disembodied perspective that nevertheless is a possible perspective that has its
own advantages" (2002, 5). This perspectival ambiguity opens
what Ihde calls "a sliding perspective from the multidimensional experience of my here-body toward the image-body
perspectives" of third-person self-imaginings (ibid., 6). For Ihde,
however, this sliding scale is highly conditional and limited, and
this has consequences for VR's body replacement program: "the

9    Regarding the question of cultural and media-technical influences, Ihde
revisits the parachuting scenario in a later text and reports a shift he
has observed in his students when polled about how they envisioned
themselves: whereas only a minority initially saw themselves from a third-
person perspective, over the course of several decades the proportion of
first- to third-person perspectives had roughly equalized (2012, 137). Here
and elsewhere, Ihde seems to suggest that media-technological changes,
including the rise of videogames, might be in part responsible for the shift.

 dialectic is weighted with sensory richness given to and within the here-body perspective, which I shall associate with the RL body. The partially disembodied or body as quasi-other perspective is already a kind of virtual body in a nontechnological projection. This form of virtuality is an image-body" (ibid., 5).

The question of virtual presence, in other words, trades on capacities of the body that precede any technical development of VR devices or virtual environments, and which can be seen as the enabling conditions for an interplay between "embodiment" and "disembodiment" more generally, including as they might be invoked in cinematic and post-cinematic dispositifs (through forms of suture, interpellation, immersion, estrangement, or alienation effects). It should be clear by now that these capacities of the body are precisely those transductively related powers of aesthesis and technicity discussed in the previous chapter. And because, as we saw, the interiorizing power of fleshly tactility is foundational with respect to the secondary specularity upon which technical exteriorization (or "projection") depends, we can agree with Ihde that the "here-body" is primary with respect to the objectified "image-body." But for Ihde, this already decides the question of the body's replaceability by a virtual body: despite what he recognizes as the significant advances that VR marks, in the history of audiovisual media, towards a more immersive involvement of the experiencing body in the perceptual spectacle of sensory stimuli, it will quite simply never be able to overcome the primacy of the here-body and the reduction and focusing of "full bodily sensory awareness" that is entailed by (prosthetic) extension (Ihde 2002, 7), never be able to do away fully with the "framing" that marks off any and all mediated images from the visual phenomena of directly experienced RL objects and environments (ibid., 10). This is so, according to Ihde, even at the limit of a full-body, haptic, and fully interactive VR dispositif: "The mini-TVs directly in front of the eyes, the body-suit, the wired gloves, all enclose the participant in the up close environment of the technologically encased envelope from the

RL world. This enclosure, however, is neither neutral nor transparent—its vestigial presence may produce a sense of both unreality and disorientation" (ibid., 11). Hence, "phenomenologically, the VR cage remains simply a different degree of virtuality of the open but framed version in the video game"; far from replacing reality, in a *Matrix*-like scenario, "[i]t remains VR theater"—even if it is "a very special kind of theater" (ibid., 11).

Ultimately, for Ihde, "VR bodies are thin and never attain the thickness of flesh. The fantasy that says we can simultaneously have the powers and capacities of the technologizing medium without its ambiguous limitations, so thoroughly incorporated into ourselves that it becomes living body, is a fantasy of desire" (ibid., 15). As with all technological extensions, there are tradeoffs involved that point to VR's inability to fully absorb the here-body into a virtual body and efface the seams between virtual and RL worlds. However, while we might be sympathetic to Ihde's conclusion, we might nevertheless ask if he is responding to the right question. Does virtual presence actually require the total effacement of "framing," or the eradication of all awareness of mediation? More recently, Jay David Bolter, Maria Engberg, and Blair MacIntyre have suggested that

> [t]here is another way to think of presence. Instead of an *as if* feeling, it is a feeling of *both and*; that is, the experience is *both* mediated *and* immediate at the same time. We never entirely forget that we are having a VR experience, but we find ourselves in the threshold of forgetting. Being on that threshold is an uncanny feeling, a sense of presence in a reality medium. (Bolter 2021, 72)

This stands in opposition to "presence [as] a kind of absence, the absence of mediation" or "the user's forgetting that the medium is there" (ibid., 75). Clearly, this introduces a very different perspective than that of the turn-of-the-millennium technofantasies to which Ihde was responding, potentially getting us closer to understanding VR, as I suggested earlier, as an inherently "mixed reality" medium.

Nevertheless, the lasting value of Ihde's discussion lies in the framing distinction between the "here-body" and the "image-body," which prompts us to probe deeper into the interrelations between embodied tactility and technological extension at the heart of presence. In fact, I would argue, this unsettled question becomes more urgent than ever once people *stop believing* the "postmodern hype" that VR can simply replace RL. When the fantasy of replacement fades and VR becomes a more mundane (though still, for now, spectacular) object—a toy or a platform for entertainment, work, or social interaction—it is then that bodily transformations by way of technologies such as VR can become a real force in the experiential and political life of RL. As Ihde himself says, "both RL and VR are a part of the lifeworld, and VR is thus both 'real' as a positive presence and a part of RL" (2002, 13). But to take this seriously means to re-open the "sliding perspective from the multidimensional experience of my here-body toward the image-body" and to re-evaluate Ihde's equation of the richly "embodied" here-body with RL and of the relatively "disembodied" image-body with VR (Ihde 2002, 6). The "sliding perspective" itself speaks to a multistability that undermines these simple equations and reminds us that the RL body itself is always both "here" and "there," subject to oscillations that are inextricable from subjective agency. As we saw in Merleau-Ponty's comments on the mirror stage, to be an embodied subject positively requires that I am simultaneously an image, and the "here-body" and the "image-body" are equally essential to correlative experience. Thus, presence in RL and in VR are equally rooted in the flesh's originary mediality, in the *écart* between primary tactility and specularity. This does not mean that VR is somehow equivalent, logically or phenomenologically, with RL, but it suggests that it will not do simply to cordon them off and comfort ourselves with an image of the insular artifice of VR. For even if, and perhaps especially if, we are not convinced of

the "reality" of technically mediated simulations, VR positively 
changes RL by way of tapping into the transduction of aesthesis
and technicity, into the mediating power of the flesh itself, which
is opened to computational modulation at the subpersonal level
and at the infraperceptual speed of metabolism itself.

## Post/Cinematic Interpellations

It is already clear, on the basis of the foregoing, that there is
no way to approach the body in VR without thinking both the
correlative and the discorrelative, with Merleau-Ponty's "inner
diaphragm" mediating between them and connecting human
sensation and computational processing. How, then, are we to
understand these fleshly interrelations?

In her discussion of Google Earth VR, Brooke Belisle describes the
conjuncture of aesthetic and algorithmic mediations, which put
human vision in touch with machine vision and enact a "visceral
interpellation" that challenges the very terms of visuality (2020,
115). As she writes:

> The visual data in Earth Engine … is not necessarily visible
> in itself, and does not add up to any coherent view. To glean
> what could be grasped from its petabytes of data requires
> active correlation and coordination. This takes place as a
> collaboration between algorithmic techniques and human
> operators—computational processes for consolidating
> "aspects" of information, and aesthetic strategies for making
> these sensible for human perceivers. (ibid., 127–128)

This correlation "relies on a dynamic feedback loop between the
way users proprioceptively sense their body in actual space and
the way a virtual space appears to cohere as navigable" (ibid.,
123). And, lest the illusion fall apart, all of this must happen prior
to subjective awareness; the virtual world has to be generated
dynamically in a microtemporal interval both "in response to—
and anticipating—the user" (ibid., 117). Thus, as Belisle argues,

"embodied processes that are always already underway, and largely involuntary, become the framework through which the model's virtual dimensions are constructed as sensible" (ibid., 118). An interface has to be forged, beneath the threshold of perception, between computational processes and involuntary processes, and this, I argue, involves nothing less than the operationalization of affective or metabolic embodiment.

VR experiences are not all alike, of course, and there are accordingly a variety of different modes in which they take aim at their users' embodied metabolisms. It will therefore be necessary to consider a number of variations, which will hopefully lead us to a more complete picture of the push and pull between correlation and discorrelation in the embodied interface with VR (and post-cinematic media more generally). Belisle's use of the term "visceral interpellation" invites a comparison between VR and cinema, where the term "interpellation" was often invoked alongside that of "suture" in the Marxist-psychoanalytic framework of the so-called apparatus theory of the 1970s.[10] This comparison is also relevant with regard to Ihde's claim that an ineradicable awareness of VR's "framing" stands in the way of complete presence; the *frame* is of course a central problematic within cinematic mediation, and recognizing the variable relations that may obtain between it and cinematic spectators—a variability that is precisely at stake in questions of interpellation and suture—can help us to reopen the "sliding perspective" or scale between Ihde's here-body and image-body and, in this way, to arrive at a better understanding of VR's instantiation of post-cinematic embodiment.

How, then, does interpellation compare across these media? Though she does not make this claim explicitly, Belisle's

10    The concept of interpellation was made popular by Louis Althusser in the early 1970s before being taken up by film theorists like Jean-Louis Baudry. Its influence is widely felt in the British theory associated with *Screen* journal, such as Laura Mulvey, who gives it a feminist twist. See Althusser 1971; Baudry 1974, 39–47; Mulvey 1975, 6–18.

terminology suggests a broad distinction between VR's visceral 
interpellation and a primarily visual form that would be proper
to cinema. However, Shaviro's theorization of the visceral-dis-
correlative potentials of cinema, as outlined in Chapter 1 of this
book, should caution us against any overhasty generalizations
in this regard. And since what is at stake here is the re-correlation of virtual body-world constellations, we will anyway need
to consider viscerality in relation to visual-perceptual environments and the bodies—both avatars and physical bodies—that
inhabit them. In any case, the first thing to note, with respect
to Belisle's analysis, which centers on Google Earth VR, is that
here the virtual body is in fact missing or invisible, i.e. there is
no visible avatar through which the user navigates the Google
Earth space, so this ends up being more of a body effacement
or *displacement* program as opposed to a straightforward visual
body replacement. This might be taken as confirmation, again,
that the avatar as visual object, and visuality itself, is secondary
to the primary role of tactility. Be that as it may, if we restrict our
attention for the moment only to the visual, there are two further
things worth noting here. On the one hand, the apodictically
confirmable correlation with Google Earth's virtual environment
seems to mark a total break with the mechanisms of cinematic
interpellation. As theorized by the apparatus theorists, cinematic
suture served to hail and position its subject through perspective and continuity editing; shot-countershot configurations,
eyeline matches, and similar techniques worked together to
build a coherent diegetic space that, by directing attention and
focus, involved and inscribed the spectator into an imaginary
spectating-position with respect to the text.[11] But here, in Google
Earth, the viewing subject is free to look wherever they want;
their gaze is not directed or yoked by the external forces of lens
length or the succession of shots; and thus VR directors have a

11    Compare Dayan 1974.

  hard time *directing* users' attention. In the VR scenario, a logic of "scanning" replaces that of suture.[12]

But if this always subject-centric POV is radically at odds with cinema's normative (and disjunctively articulated) mode of interpellation, there is, on the other hand, a surprisingly "cinematic" logic at work in Google Earth VR's "disembodied" presentation, or its lack of an avatar as a proxy subject-object for the user. The so-called invisible editing style that dominated "Classical Hollywood" and set the standard for cinematic interpellation was correlated with the invisibility of the spectator (situating them as an unseen "voyeur"), the invisibility of the frame (which vanishes via the spectator's psychological engrossment in the images and/or narrative), and the invisibility of the physical venue (awareness of which disappears both through the suturing of attention and, more directly, by the dimming of the lights in the darkened theater).[13] Of course, this was only ever an ideal and never total de-realization of the cinematic spectator's physical situation, but it remains a powerful ideal nonetheless and the object of numerous media-technical innovations, including widescreen, IMAX, 3D, and other "immersive" theatrical screening configurations.[14] At stake, phenomenologically, in such immersion is

12   Julia Leyda makes a similar point about post-cinematic movies like the *Paranormal Activity* series. See Leyda 2014, reprinted in Denson and Leyda 2016, 398–432.

13   Obviously, this mode of interpellation is contingent, both historically and culturally, and open to challenges from a variety of angles. Early cinema operates on a different principle: what Neil Harris has called an "operational aesthetic," which foregrounds rather than conceals the technological spectacle of mediation (1973). And even after the consolidation of classical style, there are various occasions for breaking the "immersive" illusion: special effects recall the early "cinema of attractions," as Tom Gunning points out (1986), and avant-garde gestures often "break the fourth wall" or otherwise estrange the viewer from their absorbed relation to the images on screen. In such situations we find ourselves looking *at* rather than *through* the screen.

14   My point is not to downplay the multistable nature of such innovations. Consider 3D, which apparently seeks to heighten immersion by "involving" us more directly in the perceptual continuum established between screen

what Ihde calls an "embodiment relation," a sort of symbiotic (and 
paradoxically disembodying) relation whereby the spectator's
perception is channeled through and hence yoked (or sutured) to
the mediating apparatus, which itself withdraws from awareness
(much like Heidegger's hammer or Merleau-Ponty's blind
person's cane).[15] And while this immersive ideal remained fragile
in the cinema—the viewer always liable to be reminded of their
physical setting by an uncomfortable seat, the glow of an exit
sign, or popcorn spilled on the floor—the particularly cinematic
ideal of disembodiment is rendered strangely literal in Google
Earth's virtual environment, where body, frame, and venue are all
simultaneously effaced when the user puts on the headset.

Tellingly, the absence of the (specular) body, or avatar, is typical of what is sometimes called "cinematic VR" (or CVR), which
is basically just non-interactive 360-degree video, or the
instantiation of "movies" (as time-based moving-image media
texts of fixed duration) within a virtual environment. Though
Google Earth VR is interactive and open to innumerably many distinct trajectories and traversals, it retains this cinematic quality
of immersive de-emphasis of corporeal self-awareness. Thus,
we are again confronted with Ihde's sliding scale between the

and eyes, but which also conjures paradoxes of its own. For one thing, the
perceptual correlation is bought at the expense of former techniques of
engrossment. The 3D space often protrudes into the space of the theater,
thus undoing its classical erasure; that is, a greater awareness of the space
in which we are seated, and hence a greater awareness of our seated body,
undoes the suppression of concrete embodiment upon which our interpellative suture rested. Of course, the various historical implementations of
3D cinema have all engaged in an operational aesthetic designed precisely to
foreground media-technical novelty, so this calling of attention to the background infrastructure is not necessarily undesirable. But there is a tension
between 3D as perceptual environment and as spectacular object. We might
surmise that the "inner diaphragm" is irritated by this tension, whether or
not we as spectators consciously take note of the tension. Re-correlation
would seem to require a taming of the spectacle in favor of the environmental or engrossing potential of 3D, and hence a renewed forgetting of the
body in the theater.

15    On embodiment relations, see Ihde 1990, 72–80.

 here-body's primary tactility and the image-body's specularity as a crucial axis of visual mediation more generally.[16] In this respect, VR—whether interactive or not, and with or without an avatar—is a less radical break with the phenomenology of older modes

16    Other modes of remediating cinema within virtual environments foreground the essential multistability at the heart of this "sliding scale." For example, it is possible to watch a conventional movie within a virtual theater setting, such that one witnesses the same two-dimensional spectacle that might be screened in a real theater or on one's living-room television set, but now relocated to a simulated silver screen at the far end of a virtual (3D) theater space. By foregrounding the theater space, such a scenario actually tends to disrupt engrossment or interpellative suture. One may then wonder if there is any advantage, in terms of spatial configuration, to such a screening situation over simply viewing it on a television set; in both cases, the two-dimensionality of the screen contrasts with the three dimensionality of the environment, though one might more easily forget the familiar surroundings of one's own living room. On the other hand, a clear use case for the virtual theater space presents itself in relation to 3D content, for example using the VR headset to screen a 3D movie that cannot be viewed on a standard television set. Once again, though, cinematic framing is a potential problem; when images protrude from the virtual screen, attention is easily (in a sense, necessarily) shifted to the theater space. If 3D movies viewed in a physical theater invoke the same paradox, they can also become (re-correlatively) engrossing on condition of a renewed forgetting of the body in the theater space. But there is much less hope of this occurring in the virtual environ-ment—precisely because the (virtual, CGI) theater space and the (3D) screen space are not categorically different from one another! A telling example is provided by Jay David Bolter, Maria Engberg, and Blair MacIntyre, who restage the Lumieres' famous *Arrival of the Train at La Ciotat* in VR (Bolter, Engberg, MacIntyre 2021, xv-xvii). If the original film unsettled its original viewers by placing perspectivally framed motion in three dimensions onto a two dimensional screen within the three-dimensional theater space, it is important to note the perceptual multistability at play here, which includes the viewers' focusing of attention on the novel screen. Restaged in VR, and allowing the train to actually break through the screen and into the virtual theater literalizes the myth, but at the price of making it strangely unimpres-sive. This is because the virtual remediation effectively mutes the difference upon which the fantasy of breaking through the screen depended—that is, the difference between screen space (which viewers attend to by power of their projective capacities of specularity or image-body) and theatrical space (which they simultaneously occupy from the position of the tactilely grounded here-body).

of visual representation and involvement than it might at first appear. At least, that is, so long as we are concerned primarily with spatial relations, including the spatiality constructed by mediated images as well as our own real and imaginative relations to it (our physical-spatial relations to a screen, for instance, or our psychological-perspectival positioning or inscription in a represented space).

Where VR's visceral interpellation differs, however, is in its *temporal* alignment of embodied motion and computationally responsive imagery. As Belisle rightly observes, this "dynamic feedback loop" (Belisle 2020, 123) rests on the ability to generate images "in response to—and anticipating—the user" (Belisle 2020, 117), which returns us to Sartre's insight that "[p]erception is naturally surpassed toward action; better yet, it can be revealed only in and through projects of action. The world is revealed as an 'always future hollow,' for we are always future to ourselves" (1984, 425). What this means, then, is that VR intervenes in the embodied synthesis of temporality itself, and its interpellative (or correlational) force depends on a *protentional alignment* between human and nonhuman systems, whereby computational and organic components are minutely calibrated as the material basis for the phenomenal illusion of presence. Thus, while VR's more apparent spatial-perceptual alignments invoke visual mediation's long-standing sliding-scale multistability between first-person here-body and third-person image-body, VR's essential mediation is one that mediates between the pre-personal flesh subtending both those bodies and the subject-world correlation itself, within which the "here" and "there" of embodiment first becomes a question. The illusion of presence, in other words, masks the more fundamental fact that VR constitutes itself as that "always future hollow" that, as the open horizon of worldly becoming, is the essential condition of our subjective and political agencies.

# Mirror Image

One of the most striking—and potentially unsettling—examples of VR's visceral interpellation is to be found in the encounter with a virtual mirror. Popular (though also widely disparaged) on virtual social platforms like VRChat, users turn to such mirrors in order to confirm to themselves their virtual identities and to determine how they appear to others.[17] Mirrors also feature in experimental configurations, such as the "Virtual Mirror Demo" produced by Stanford's Virtual Human Interaction Lab; here the mirror is employed as a tool for empathy research, and it is pitched to the broader public as allowing users to "virtually 'walk a mile' in someone else's shoes."[18] In both cases, virtual mirrors mediate between identity and difference, subject and object, here-body and image-body—all with a view towards augmenting

17    For my understanding of the virtual mirror in VRChat, I am indebted to Runze Hu, who writes in personal correspondence: "VRChat is probably one of the best places to understand how mirrors are put into use in naturally occurring social situations by VR users. .... In VRChat, all virtual environments are user-generated contents. There is a co-construction relationship between users' habitualised use of mirrors and creators' design choice. For the users, the first thing almost all players would do when stepping into a VRChat world is to find where the mirror is. Then, players would hang out with their friend in front of the mirror, chatting and doing all sorts of activities. It is not an exaggeration to argue the mirror is the main virtual artefact that frames the social interactions within VRChat. To adapt to users' habits, there is a norm among the creators that a mirror is one of the most necessary (almost compulsory) functions of a virtual environment. I currently have a preliminary theory based on interviews and observation: Because the body proportion of the avatar and the corporeal body do not match perfectly, the avatar's body movement does not always match the corporeal body. Players cannot easily know how their avatars are moving by feeling the corporeal body. And, players cannot always be sure what others are doing to their bodies due to the lack of physical touch. The mirror is therefore visually complementing the lack of bodily awareness. And we could probably make a further argument that it is through the mirror in VRChat that players establish a sense of avatar body ownership and make the intercorporeal affectivity among players possible." Runze Hu, personal correspondence, February 11, 2022.

18    See https://www.stanfordvr.com/virtual-mirror-demo/.

or transforming social existence. The social VR user negotiates their relation to an avatar of their choosing, often one that is carefully designed as an outward representation of a deeply felt desire or inner sense of self, which may or may not bear any evident (visual) resemblance to their appearance IRL; however, simply choosing—even lovingly designing—an expressive avatar is not the same as *feeling and expressing oneself through* that avatar. The latter requires habituation, but also and first of all a feel for what one looks like—i.e. a subjective sense of oneself as an object-for-others; this is what the mirror is supposed to provide. Meanwhile, the experimental, research-oriented set-up approaches things from the reverse angle, for example asking a white cis-heterosexual man to see himself as someone else in the mirror, an avatar not chosen but imposed, like the body of someone whose consciousness is marked by the "epidermal racial schema" that Frantz Fanon so clearly and excruciatingly laid out in *Black Skin, White Masks* (2008, 92). Rather than objectively expressing subjective values that I hope to embody for others, here the avatar is meant to give me a subjective sense of what it feels like to be objectified as a body—or how it feels when such objectification is imposed as a condition of subjectivation. In both cases, the mirror is the site of here-body/image-body transfers that leverage both correlative and discorrelative potentials of the VR medium in an attempt to re-engineer social relations. And in both cases, the attempt revolves around the way that the mirror serves not only as a fulcrum between here and there, self and other, but between phenomenal and prephenomenal conditions of enworlded being.

What we are witnessing here is a virtual restaging of the encounter with the mirror described by Merleau-Ponty, drawing on and revising Lacan (as detailed in Chapter 2 of this book). As Merleau-Ponty wrote of the child looking into the mirror:

> It is a problem first of understanding that the visual image of his body which he sees over there in the mirror is not himself, since he is not in the mirror but here, where he feels

himself; and second, he must understand that, not being located there, in the mirror, but rather where he feels himself interoceptively, he can nonetheless be seen by an external witness *at the very place at which he feels himself to be* and with the same visual appearance that he has from the mirror. In short, he must displace the mirror image, bringing it from the apparent or virtual place it occupies in the depth of the mirror back to himself, whom he identifies at a distance with his interoceptive body. (1964, 129)

That the encounter with one's own (virtual) image should be relevant to one's (virtual) relations with others is therefore not surprising, as the mirror serves here to consolidate embodied subjectivity *in relation to* a social field of others for whom I am outwardly visible—indeed, establishing the very possibility of intersubjectivity by way of a technically mediated transposition or transduction of subject and object, self and other. The VR mirror thus taps into, by way of restaging, the *écart* or fission between primary tactility and specularity—thus tapping into the originary mediality of the flesh itself.[19] But clearly such a reenactment is not equivalent to the child's primordial encounter with the mirror, as it now takes place on the basis of an already habituated embodiment. If the virtual mirror is capable of leveraging a no less foundational re-orientation of subjectivity and its relation to the body, then discorrelation—or the severing of habituated tactility/specularity or here-body/image-body relations—is a precondition for the re-correlation that takes place before the virtual mirror. Again, however, timing is everything; in particular, what is required is the temporal alignment of (subperceptual)

19   Mark Hansen interprets virtual reality in terms of Merleau-Ponty's discussion of the (real) mirror (Hansen 2006), but for historical reasons he does not connect that discussion to virtual mirrors. Since the time of that writing (2006), a great deal has of course changed, but the essential insights of Hansen's book, to which I am greatly indebted, still hold. If anything, the popularization of virtual mirrors in social VR environments, which rely on a number of technical advances, only serves to confirm Hansen's prescient analysis.

microtemporal processes, both organic and computational, such 
that the perceptual correlation of virtual "presence" rests on the
achievement of phenomenal *simultaneity* between discorrelation
and re-correlation.

Because this is a secondary *écart*, there is no question of the user
being fooled; they can always "snap out of it" and remember
(or attend to) the fact that they are, after all, looking at a simulation. Presence, again, is not primarily about belief, but about
an affective relation that temporarily modulates but does not
permanently replace the knowledge that we have of our bodies.
But for those moments when things are aligned, I can indeed feel
myself, *over there*, in the virtual mirror, and I can simultaneously
see myself, *over here*, in the avatar body that I am *now* moving.
In these moments, here-body and image-body coincide both
spatially and temporally; the mirror provides an impression
of their co-presence in the visual field and allows me to feel,
in a very immediate way, the simultaneity of here and there,
as I see my volition pass directly into perceptible action. What
this means is that Ihde's oscillation between first-person and
third-person perspectives—the sliding-scale multistability that
underwrites cinematic interpellation, which we have traced back
to the *écart*—is effectively *captured*, the quasi-spatial alternatives
neutralized and rendered simultaneous in a way not available
to the cinema, by yoking *here* and *there*, together as one, to a
tactile *now*. Importantly, however, this *now* is not punctual or of
fixed duration at all; it is flexible and open to dilation and compression. In fact, it would appear that this is both the temporal
precondition as well as the culmination of the expansive spatiality
that is established by rendering the here-body and image-body
synchronous or co-present with one another (thus replicating
the primordial spatiality that enables embodied extendibility,
prostheticity, motility, and the oscillations of visual interpellation

 alike—all modifications of perspective or position that presuppose a temporal dimension within which such changes can take place).[20]

The dynamic, scalable *now* in question here is paradoxically both "thick" and, as Husserl puts it in his investigation of internal time-consciousness, "nothing for itself" (1964, 63). It is a non-punctual flux that encompasses "empty environmental intentions" (ibid., 79)[21]—which is to say it is surrounded by, or indeed comprised of, a "temporal halo" (ibid., 58) of non-referential retentions of the just-past and undetermined protentions of the just-about-to-come.[22] Primary retention, which is not a discrete, representational memory,[23] but rather a condition of the spatiotemporal continuum that I experience in my encounter with the mirror, constitutes "the living horizon of the now" (ibid., 66). And such retention is preceded by, and shades imperceptibly into, its forward-looking counterpart, protention, which is equally pre-reflective or non-referential (hence not yet rising to the level of consciousness in the form of concrete expectations about a determinate future event). Husserl writes: "[e]very primordially constitutive process is animated by protentions which voidly [*leer*] constitute and intercept [*auffangen*] what is coming, as such, in order to bring it to fulfillment" (ibid., 76). Conceived in terms of this processual flux, the *now* has nothing to do with a static concept of "the present," and reflection on this fact might

20   See Husserl 2012, section 44.

21   The German term is "*leere Umgebungsintentionen*" (Husserl 1928, 47).

22   Note that the environment, or *Umgebung*, at issue in the empty environmental intentions is a concept that encompasses both the temporal halo as well as the spatial background upon which a figure appears, or even more generally: the way "everything in perception has its reverse side as background" (Husserl 1964, 78). This connects, therefore, to the ambulatory and ultimately embodied notion of spatial perception and its temporal underpinnings, as displayed in Husserl 2012, section 44.

23   Husserl says primary retention "cannot be a symbolization [*Verbildlichung*]; it is an originary consciousness" (1964, 53). A few pages later, he similarly argues that "retention is not figurative consciousness, but something totally different" (ibid., 56).

prompt us to reconceptualize virtual "presence" along the lines of Husserl's *Gegenwärtigung* or *Gegenwärtigungsfluß* (roughly: "presencing" or "flux of presencing").[24] Such terms link our embodied experience of "being in the presence" of something with the paradoxically empty processuality of "being in the present" or the *now*. What this foregrounds is not only the open-endedness, or primordial "inadequacy,"[25] of all experience, whether real or virtual, but above all the intricacy of replicating this primordial fact of enworlded temporal being. Essentially, computational processing not only has to calculate my present point of view but, because the present is both thick and empty, has to replicate the "interceptive" (*auffangende*) function of embodied protention, anticipating my every possible move or volition before it can be executed or consciously constituted *and producing on this basis a set of objective or visual correlates that (will) correspond (or will have corresponded) to my projected subjective POV.* The "capture" or synchronization of here and there, in the now, is thus predicated on an "interception" that fundamentally calls into question the primacy of human versus nonhuman protention. In effect, my own (presubjective) "projection" of the future is set into competition with, and potentially overcoded by, the computer's

24    See, for example, section 16, titled "Perception as Originary Presentation [*Gegenwärtigung*] as Distinguished from Retention and Recollection" (Husserl 1964, 60–63). Here, Husserl identifies *Gegenwärtigung*, in contrast with retention and memory, with perception. Such "present" perception offers an obvious target for deconstruction. My use of it is based in a belief that it has effectively already deconstructed itself, that Husserl has shown the present, in the sense of *Gegenwärtigung*, to be empty and self-contradictory, basically already dispersed in the spirit of Derridean *différance*. Note that I am not taking on the problematic notion of "primal impression" (ibid., 50–52), which is at odds with this reading/appropriation and would seem to re-ground a more substantial notion of the present. In any case, I am trying to liberate *Gegenwärtigung*, as a process rooted solely in a halo of "empty environmental intentions" from its reconsolidation as a perceptual event or referential relation. *Gegenwärtigung*, as I am interpreting it here involves presubjective temporal processes that categorically resist representation, but that are foundational to any perceptual and embodied correlation.

25    See Husserl 1964, section 44, as well as Stiegler 2011, vol. 3.

 (mathematical, microtemporal, and hence equally presubjective) "projection" of my immediate future—which is to say that my volition itself is up for grabs.

All of this is consummated, if only temporarily, when I look into the virtual mirror, see myself looking, move my seeing body, and see my sight in motion and my movement seen. Often, in such situations, I will experience a slight shock, almost like that of *déjà vu*, wherein I see my current temporal experience unfolding both as an indeterminate flux and as a quasi-referential object. This is because, I conjecture, I am in the midst of a secondary alignment, or spatiotemporal correlation, that is founded atop a more primary one—that of my habituated, everyday sense of things— which my body refuses to fully forget (or, at least, which the technology is currently incapable of fully incorporating). In any case, if there is an uncanny shock of (mis)recognition that takes place, thus opening a window of temporal disjunction between seeing and seen, it is important to recognize that this can still be a presubjective experience that undercuts the window of conscious temporality. That is, I have to *actually* see myself there, in the mirror, before I can have the feeling that I *cannot possibly* be seeing myself there. And while it remains possible to dissociate myself further, and to see this objectively as the simulation that it is, it is equally possible to give in to the identification with— which is to say subjectivation in transductive relation to—the computer's projection of my spatiotemporal virtuality. In this way, discorrelation and re-correlation coincide in Belisle's "visceral interpellation," and embodied intentionality is opened up beyond its currently sedimented noetic contexts, with far-reaching intersubjective and hence political ramifications.

# Conclusion: Speculative Specularity

Reflecting on the implications of VR, Deborah Levitt asks:

> how might the perceptual apparatus of VR enable the emergence of new forms of subjectivity and sociality? If moving in and out of worlds and bodies, already a feature of the contemporary media ecology, is intensified by VR's enhanced presence effects, might we think of this as enabling increasingly plastic forms of subjectivity grounded in differences and metamorphosis rather than identity? That is, can VR help to shift our powerful cultural attachments to particular notions of individual and social group boundaries through experiences that, while never the experiences of particular others as the empathy machine logic would have it, reveal the flexibility of the human itself in relation to (its) others? (2018)

If so, this decidedly hopeful possibility is grounded in the prepersonal interface between the apparatus and the body's "inner diaphragm," the site of the originary mediation between correlative and discorrelative forces. Plasticity, in other words, is a function of what Ihde calls the "polymorphically ambiguous" nature of the flesh, into which VR taps *as a condition of* perceptual correlations, subjective identifications, and/or empathy relations (2002, 6).

Hyphen-Labs' *NeuroSpeculative AfroFeminism*, a VR experience in which the user finds themself in "a Neurocosmetology lab where black women are pioneering techniques of brain optimization and cognitive enhancement,"[26] seems to understand this order of operations well (fig. 3.1). While speaking directly to issues of cultural representation—the project website notes that it was "[i]nspired by the lack of multidimensional representations of black women in technology" and aims, in connection with fMRI research, to explore "the neurological and physiological impact

26    Quoted from the NSAF website: http://www.hyphen-labs.com/nsaf.html.

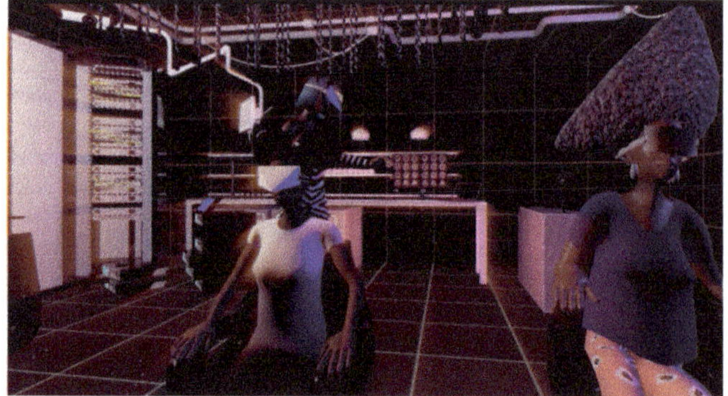

[Fig. 3.1] The Neurocosmetology lab in Hyphen-Labs' *NeuroSpeculative AfroFeminism* (Screenshot by the author).

of showing images of empowered black women"[27]—the project nevertheless avoids the typical empathy framework; Hyphen-Labs co-founder Ece Tankal suggests that such a framework is too focused on "[m]aking you feel sad about us" (Ding n.d.). One way of reading this comment is that the "you" being addressed in the empathy model is decidedly the empirical-psychological "you" *qua* viewer who is taken to exist, identically, both before and after the VR experience—thus cancelling out the ambiguous plasticity, or what I earlier termed the existential indistinction, of embodiment that VR *Gegenwärtigung*, as a deeper phenomenological process, modulates. Refusing such a foreclosure, *NeuroSpeculative AfroFeminism* instead positions plasticity as both its theme and its medium: I find myself in Brooks' Neurocosmetology lab, "a reimagined black hair salon,"[28] where I see myself in the mirror, *here*, feeling myself, *there*, in the body of a young Black woman, *here-there*, as I move and observe my reflection, *now* (fig. 3.2). I am here to have my hair styled and to get some brain-stimulating extensions, so-called Octavia

27    Quoted from the NSAF website: http://www.hyphen-labs.com/nsaf.html.
28    Quoted from the NSAF website: http://www.hyphen-labs.com/nsaf.html.

[Fig. 3.2] Looking into the mirror in Hyphen-Labs' *NeuroSpeculative AfroFeminism* (Screenshot by the author).

Electrodes—named, of course, for Black sci-fi author Octavia Butler. I am informed that I might experience hallucinations, and when the electrodes are applied, I go through the mirror, leaving my body behind in a self-reflexive doubling or re-entry of the VR medium within the virtual environment. I fly through a lava-filled landscape and eventually arrive at a kind of Afrofuturist temple where three diversely clad cyborgian women inform me that I am "free from the constraints that have been placed on [me] throughout reality." Then I return to the salon, where I again see myself in the mirror.

What is at stake in this experience, I suggest, is something like what Sylvia Wynter refers to as the "biomythical" constitution of the human, which cannot be reduced to its genetic-bio-logical coding, functions, drives, and the like, but is always open to a re-coding by means of what she calls, drawing on Fanon, the "sociogenic principle."[29] Reminiscent of Bernard Stiegler's "originary technicity" of the human, but more attuned to the racializing potentials of the deep, transductive aesthesis that opens our flesh to cultural techniques and mythologies, Wynter

---

29    See Wynter 2001, 30–66, as well as Wynter and McKittrick 2015.

 theorizes the human as a hybrid praxis that conserves extrabiological and socially determined values by inscribing them directly into our bodies, in the form of neurological feedback loops (1992, 237–279). In principle, then, recognizing this hybridity renders the human open to re-engineering, with far-reaching consequences for race, gender, and other socially enforced categories and experiences of embodiment. A character in *NeuroSpeculative Afro-Feminism* provides the VR experience's backstory in similar terms:

> Brooks organized a group of neurofeminists to create the synaptic lineage. This is an autonomous network, gathering and distributing communal memories and knowledge. Collective experience is carried through human agents and hosted on local servers, as communal data is weaved through their neural networks. Kind of how coded information and directional coordinates were transmitted through the lyrics of old Negro spirituals: message songs.

Self-reflexively, *NeuroSpeculative AfroFeminism* dis/correlatively appropriates the flux and indeterminacy of the user's mediated presencing in an effort to inscribe an alternative retentional-protentional system, a differently coded system of collectively enworlded values, into the body's prepersonal metabolism or affective processing of time.

It is in this sense that VR has the potential to transform the social, not simply by facilitating metaverse-style interactions between individuals, but by tapping into the subperceptual plasticity of embodiment—which, as Merleau-Ponty's reflections on the mirror suggest, is already a space of intersubjectivity or, in Gilbert Simondon's term, the "transindividual."[30] Thus, as Levitt puts it:

30  For Simondon, the transindividual denotes a form of collectivity that exceeds merely inter-individual relations and instead unites individuals on the basis of their pre-individual realities, or on the basis of their excess with respect to identity. Affect plays a crucial role: "affectivity is what leads the charge of pre-individual nature to become the support of collective individuation; it is mediation between that which is pre-individual and that which is individual" (2020, 279). As such, affectivity signals the noncoincidence that,

In conventional terms, VR is not the first medium one thinks **153**
of in relation to the social (despite social VR apps). In contrast
to the contemporary foreground of hypermediation and
distraction (e.g., multiple windows connecting a computer
user to various people and sites at once), VR revolves around
a now-unusual singularity of world and focus. It captures
you in the world inside the head-mounted display. But in
this spatio-temporal capture in which you are, in effect,
kidnapped by the apparatus, other worlds may be opened,
and the experience of these worlds may enact a tutorial in
different times and spaces of being and becoming. There
is no way around phenomenology in VR, that is, around its
starting point in the specificity of human perception that
gives rise to its hardware and software. But here, the inter-
sections it produces between perception, computation, and
extra-human scales, offer a tutorial in how to live in a multi-
plicity of worlds. It thus invites us to reimagine the conditions
of possibility for new forms of sociality to emerge.

for Merleau-Ponty, introduced the *écart* or fission in primordial tactility, out
of which flowed exteriorization via specularity but which simultaneously
opened a gap into which worldly objects could insert themselves in the prepersonal flesh. Whereas "perception reassures the subject and essentially
makes use of the structures and functions already constituted within the
individuated being," according to Simondon, "affectivity indicates and com-
prises this relation between the individualized being and pre-individual
reality: thus, to a certain extent affectivity is heterogeneous relative to
individualized reality and seems to bring to it something from the outside,
indicating to it that it is not a complete and self-enclosed ensemble of
reality" (ibid., 280). Affectivity, for Simondon, responds to a basic instability
in the subject: "the problem of the subject is that of the heterogeneity
between perceptive worlds and the affective world, between the individual
and the pre-individual; this problem is that of the subject qua subject:
the subject is individual and other than individual; it is incompatible
with itself" (ibid., 280). The only solution is a "superior individuation" in a
collective. "The subject can only coincide with itself in the individuation of
the collective, because the individuated being and the pre-individual being
within it cannot coincide directly" (ibid., 280).

**154**  But because, finally, VR's interpellation is primarily visceral rather than imaginative, as we have seen, we should not lose sight of the possibility that the "spatio-temporal capture" of our experience might be used to shut down imagination and to contain or constrain plasticity. Corporate interests like Facebook/Meta are of course investing heavily in VR not because they want to make the world a better, more diverse and just place, but because they see an opportunity to further capitalize on the capture of our attention. By opening our embodied being to virtual *Gegenwärtigung*, we are putting our retentional-protentional becoming, the very flux at the heart of our memorial-volitional subjectivities and socialities, up for grabs. We are also, and simultaneously, providing free access to large amounts of fine-grained biometrical data generated by our bodies.[31] Correlations between the phenomenological "inside" (content-level experience) and the physiological "outside" (biometric data) of such embodied interfaces are thus made available to the highest bidder, offering an unprecedented opportunity for the re-engineering of subjective and social existence. I end with this darker scenario not in order to detract from the optimistic possibilities we see outlined by Levitt and enacted by Hyphen-Labs and others, but because the plasticity of the "polymorphically ambiguous" flesh is such that it is open to either sort of intervention. These are the political stakes of VR's body-replacement program.

31    See, for example, Hunter 2022.

# 4

# Dances with Robots

The process I have described so far might be viewed as a finely choreographed dance between perceptive and affective, as well as human and nonhuman, agencies. Recently, artists such as Catie Cuan and Sydney Skybetter have been making this dance explicit, rendering it literal, and placing it back in the so-called real world of physical rather than virtual bodies. Recently featured in a *New York Times* article titled "Dances with Robots, and Other Tales from the Outer Limits," dancer and choreographer Cuan is a PhD student in mechanical engineering at Stanford University and—full disclosure—a former collaborator in the Critical Practices Unit, a theory/practice research group that I coordinated with her and Hank Gerba, a PhD candidate in media studies. In her artistic practice, Cuan interacts with a variety of robotic bodies across a range of direct, virtual, and augmented forms of mediated performance and choreography; for example, she uses AI to train large industrial robots how to dance, translating conventional dance moves into movements suited to the robots' different forms of physical embodiment. Producing what she calls "a ballet for swarms of robots, mapped onto robot morphology that leverages their innate nature" (Curtis 2020)—or the parameters of speed and torque, motion and range that define their robot bodies—these interactions reflexively transform the bodily praxis of humans as well.

As Cuan puts it, "A.I. is a choreographic tool that can disrupt the habitual dance-making process" (ibid.). This intervention at the level of embodied habit results not just from the necessity of the human dancer's or choreographer's subjective negotiation vis-à-vis a differently bodied dance partner, I suggest; rather, it stems more fundamentally from the fact that nonsubjective processing via AI and robotic programming establishes a pre-subjective interface at the level of the multistable "inner dia-phragm" of human embodiment.[1] Such interfaces mediate both retention and protention to modulate the present. Damien Henry, an engineer at Google Arts and Culture, has developed algorithms that, when trained on hundreds of hours of video of past (human) performance, are then able to process live webcam video of dancers and, in real-time, generate suggestions for new dance sequences. According to Henry, "At times, the algorithm produced suggestions that the dancer wouldn't want to do." But the process turned out to be "extremely useful. It forced a dancer to explore unnatural territory" (ibid.). Disrupting the familiar, the conventional, or the habitual, and taking dancers out of their so-called comfort zones, this "unnatural territory" might in fact be termed a *postnatural* space of anthropotechnical interface and change: a space of embodied transitionality where fundamental re-negotiations of human and nonhuman agency take place (see Denson 2014). What we see here, or better: what we do *not* see here but what the dancer encounters as a radical challenge to their subjective intentionality and volition (via "suggestions that the dancer wouldn't want to do"), involves a redistribution of agency across organic, algorithmic, and robotic nodes, interfacing by way of unseen images and inner diaphragms—across the

---

1    See chapter 1 for the development of this concept from Merleau-Ponty.

hundreds of hours of recorded and real-time video processed by 
the AI and fed forward to the dancer caught off guard and forced
to react with a novel, unrehearsed gesture. Giving rise to unexpected body-image correlations and affective discorrelations
alike, these encounters open a space outside behavioristically
enforced stimulus-response circuits or empirically determinate
causal chains. As choreographer Sydney Skybetter puts it, "it
becomes difficult to point to any singular choreography by one
person or system" (ibid.)—a fact that I would explain in terms of
the essentially metabolic interchanges taking place in this complex system of environmental exchange.

The same *New York Times* article discusses the possible relevance
of these endeavors in a world transformed by the Covid-19 pandemic. Choreographer Wayne McGregor emphasizes the need,
in this reconfigured world of periodic isolation, lockdowns, and
social distancing, to find "ways that audiences can engage vis-
cerally with work—not just cerebrally" (ibid.). Apposite with my
suggestion of metabolic exchange, he suggests that a "chemical
engagement" with dance might be achieved though haptic
technologies, VR headsets, and other gaming-adjacent tools that
could deliver performances to remote audiences (ibid.)—thus
widening the network of metabolic interfacing to include the
embodied viewer as well in the dance of correlative/discorrelative
exchange. I will come back, in the next chapter, to the chemical/
metabolic dimensions of these interchanges, but for now I would
like to flesh out the ways that the formal and material character-
istics of dance shed further light on the thoroughgoing transformation of embodiment that is opened up through interaction
with automated agents.

First, however, it is worth emphasizing that whether we are
concerned with a live human-robot-AI dance performance,
or its pandemic-necessitated streaming delivery (either live
or recorded), and whether the focus is on the choreography's
generation via video fed to an AI as training material, or the
AI's real-time response to a human performer, in all of these

 cases we remain squarely within the domain of post-cinematic media: visible images, and the visual field itself (whether on screen, in person, or in a VR headset), are enmeshed with a field of machine-readable but humanly imperceptible "invisible images" (Paglen 2016) working in concert with microtemporally operating generative algorithms and the predictive vectors of video-processing codecs. This is important for several reasons. To start with, the interdependence of visibility and invisibility points to the inseparability of perceptual-agential correlation and presubjective-nonconscious discorrelation—an irreducibly composite and multistable dance of dis/correlation—as an essential condition of the performance. This, in turn, indicates that though the human and robotic dancers have apparently left the VR space behind them and re-entered the flesh-and-blood space of RL, their bodies remain haunted by the post-cinematic apparatus's operationalization of the "existential indistinction" that I identified in the previous chapter as a condition of virtual presence—and this is true regardless of whether their perform-ance is ultimately remediated by VR for remote spectatorship. And this, finally, suggests that the very literally choreographed anthropotechnical dances of artists like Cuan and Skybetter will have echoes across a range of post-cinematic media, including VR, AR, videogames, and even apparently non-interactive media such as machine learning–powered imaging systems, which similarly instigate a set of transactions between visible outputs and invisible operations that aim to anticipate—and thus have the power to transformatively modulate—embodied subjectivity at its fleshly roots.

## Alter-Affectivity

Spanning a variety of presentational modes and media—per-formance, installation, augmented reality app, and video—and utilizing a number of artistic-technological mediums in its pro-duction—including custom software, webcams, Kinect depth sensors, human dancers, and an ABB IRB 6700 industrial robot

arm named Wen—Cuan's multimodal artwork *OUTPUT* provides 
a useful case study for gauging the power and pervasiveness
of human/nonhuman dance as a post-cinematic body genre.
Starting from the fact that most people have never encountered
a large industrial robot in the flesh, due to size and immobility
factors (these robots are often larger than human bodies,
weighing up to a ton or more, and bolted into place in factory
settings) as well as safety considerations ("in certain cases they
do not have force/torque or contact sensors that would indicate
whether the robot has hit something unexpectedly, like an
obstacle or a person" (Cuan 2021, 1)), Cuan's artwork "investigates
how to make this unreachable robot presence tangible" (ibid.,
1). Reformulated in the language of the previous chapters, we
might say that the task then is to tap into the *écart* at the heart of
embodiment's originary mediality: that is, the goal is not just to
make these "sequestered robots accessible" (ibid., 1) but, as Cuan
provocatively says, to make an *unreachable presence tangible*,
which is to say, to extend tactility across the unbridgeable gap
of specularity—just as happens in the encounter with a mirror,
whether real or virtual. Accordingly, the "robot presence" in
question here has to be read in terms of the Husserlian "presencing" or *Gegenwärtigung* that I have identified as the basis of
virtual embodiment: namely, the spatiotemporal synchronization
process whereby subperceptually embodied and computational
temporalities are brought into alignment at the same time as, and
as a transductively necessary precondition for, the correlative
spatial-perceptual alignment of the body-image with its visual
environment, or with the objects in whose presence the subject
now finds itself. However, in the case of the encounter with the
outsized robot, this dis/correlative operationalization of the flesh
issues in a different modality of here-body/there-body interplay than that which is set in motion in the virtual mirror, where
(as elaborated in the previous chapter) the conventional goal is
to see myself, over here, feeling myself move, over there, right
now—thus affirming in VR a surrogate body-world correlation *in
place of* my RL embodied knowledge (what I have called the "body

 replacement program" of conventional VR). Against this, *OUTPUT* seeks not to replace the habituated body-schema but to *augment, modify, and multiply* it by causing the viewer/participant to feel oneself affected by the presence—or presencing—of the alien body, which is to say: to feel oneself both here and there, both in one's "normal" RL body and, seemingly impossibly, *also in the robot body*, whose visual form is hardly a mirror image of mine, but whose agency I can not only see but sympathetically feel, and whose presence transforms the embodied time and space we share without our bodies ever merging. That is, difference and disjunction, as opposed to identification, remain crucial in this attempt to *make the unreachable robot presence tangible.*

So how is this paradoxically disjunctive state of affective attunement—a sort of alter-affectivity that is grafted trans-formatively onto one's auto-affective sensibilities—achieved? It will be useful to begin with Cuan's process. As a first step, Cuan mapped the robot's joints onto her body. "For example, the robot's end effector [the last link at the end of the arm, e.g. the robot's 'hand'] might be her head in a full body mapping, or the robot's end effector may be her hand in a right arm only mapping" (ibid., 5). After these mappings were made, Cuan

> created a human dance sequence inspired by the notions of physical labor (watching recordings of the robot moving in a manufacturing context and live at CRR [the Consortium for Research and Robotics at the Brooklyn Navy Yard]), repetition (as the robot's motion is frequently repeated during these other manufacturing use cases), and ordered sequencing (for example, the robot's joints were numbered 1 through 7 in bottom to top order, so runs of joint motions in order might be '2, 3, 4' or '1, 2, 3, 4, 5'). (ibid., 5)

Utilizing the body-mappings, she then "observed the robot per-forming the sequence and made additions to her own chore-ography, creating an interactive feedback loop between human and robot body for motion generation" (ibid., 5). This, then, laid

the choreographic basis for live dance performances, which 
integrate further elements: a dynamic computer animation of the
robot that is subject to "[r]eal time regeneration and repurposing"
(ibid., 5) in response to the dancer's movement, alongside video
footage of both robot and human body, all of which are combined
via a set of cameras and two custom pieces of software.

Importantly, though, the translational mappings foreground difference over similarity:

> The artist desired the ability to perform the original human
> choreography next to the translated robot choreography in
> order to demonstrate the glitches, alterations, and aes-
> thetics of each. For example, a glitch in human choreography
> might be when the performer loses balance and needs to
> add an extra step in the sequence. The Wen robot makes
> no such errors when doing the finished sequence. The
> human choreography lifts off the floor during jumps, but
> this trajectory must be altered for the Wen as it is bolted to a
> track. Given that the robot animation contained two layers of
> recording translation, while the robot film was one, Cuan also
> endeavored to show *herself* dancing in layered translation
> next to these elements. (ibid., 5)

Thus, in addition to foregrounding the external difference
between human and robotic bodies, the live representation of
the dancer's body, which takes the form of a Kinect-captured
skeletal avatar projected onto a screen and interacting
directly with the robot animation, addresses also the internal difference *within* human embodiment—namely the *écart*
of tactility and specularity—by means of visually objectifying
subjectively felt movement. This split then becomes a central
mediator of the performance, in the sense that a feedback loop
is established between visual representation and embodied
movement—each reacting to the other as the performer modulates their movements in response to observed motion and
(digitally animated) human-robot interactions, which are in

 turn modulated on screen by these new offscreen movements. These mutual reactions, however, are split-second responses between human and algorithmic agents, happening in real time (as measured by computational microtemporality) and allowing no time for the human dance partner to first assess the situation, then plan, and finally execute a response. All of this must happen at once, in the blink of an eye, seemingly instantaneously. The result is a decentering of the human dancer as the prime mover, and this, according to Cuan, "allow[s] the participant to try on the robot's motion" (ibid., 5).

Difference is additionally operative in a temporal dimension. "Cuan recognized a desire to demonstrate the translation of pure movement across bodies and time in a multiplicative way, such that the prior motions could be contextualized with the real time ones" (ibid., 5). Custom software accommodated this wish by allowing the dancer, equipped with a wireless mouse, to select video segments of her performance for looping replay on a grid of up to sixteen clips that accompany the other elements of the live performance (fig. 4.1). With this temporal disjunction in play—layering past and present moments in a manner "similar to a loop pedal or computer music interface, but for dancing bodies" (ibid., 5)—the presencing body is further fragmented, and the interplay of dis/correlation becomes available as a more direct object of experimentation.

> The artist imagined this would secondarily support the question of repetitious motions in a manufacturing con-text—while a robot in a factory captured over a single time interval might always perform the same motion (i.e. a weld at the same location on a car chassis as the car passes through the factory line every 30 s), the insertion of a real time composer/improviser/conductor like the artist meant select layers and snippets could be arranged into a compelling overall landscape of motion. Cuan began to see this machine labor as possessing meditative continuity rather than monotony and sought to illuminate this reframing of

[Fig. 4.1] Catie Cuan, *OUTPUT* (Image courtesy of the artist).

> machine labor. In addition, she believed this overall land-
> scape may act as a mirror to the repetitious motions we
> go through in our own lives, often enforced by technology
> (typing, door opening, etc.). (ibid., 5)

As a multiplicative and time-delayed "mirror," the collage-like screen of looping clips resists the imaginary integration of the body that Lacanian psychoanalysis sees as the primary function of the mirror stage and instead re-opens the question of dis/ correlation by way of playing with identification and difference across both spatial (here-body vs. onscreen there-body) and temporal (now-body vs. looping then-body) registers. Especially through this "theme of recording and reconfiguring motion across distance and body representation" (ibid., 4), *OUTPUT* spatiotemporally complexifies the question of what Mark Hansen describes as "a 'touching' across an essential distance" (2006, 60, 56) that, in Merleau-Ponty's reflections on the mirror, anchors technicity as an essential power of the flesh and grounds the prosthetic extendibility of intentional subjectivity. While prostheticity is strongly suggested both by the robot's quasi-anthropomorphic "arm" and by the initial mapping of human movement onto it, this prosthetic relation is displaced, without being conclusively destroyed, by the circulation of agencies within what Cuan describes as the "complex system" opened up here (2021, 11).

Furthermore, as we see in Cuan's speculations regarding the role of repetitious movements and their mutual enforcement between machinic and human bodies, this experiment raises questions about the expression of human agency, and the constitution of standardized or serialized subjectivities, in relation to what Sartre calls the practico-inert—the industrial "worked matter" of commodities and the built environment or, in this case, the "intelligent" *working matter* of automated agents.[2] Ultimately, this is a question also of collectivity or the social in a world of "smart" devices and systems. Cuan asks: "How do performers, when interacting with their own movement on new bodies at a later time period, own or interpret that motion? How do movement themes, when layered and synchronized across these representations, create a visual group piece, similar to instruments in an orchestra playing in a symphony?" (ibid., 4). By posing such questions, *OUTPUT* translates seemingly individual probings of spatiotemporal experience into questions about social transfer. Such transfer is extended, and its aesthetic probing is further intensified, in the artwork's translation of performance into installation and especially AR iterations. A participatory element comes to the fore in these extensions of the work, as a wider circle of participants is invited to experience the

2   Compare Sartre (2004), where the practico-inert correlates with the anonymous collectivity of the seriality, in terms that are clearly designed to account for the constitution of class under industrial capitalism. I introduced these themes in Chapter 2 of this book, in relation to Iris Marion Young's rethinking of gender as a seriality, similarly enforced via material and environmental cultures. Here and in Chapter 5 I begin rethinking these topics in relation to post-cinematic media technologies and their role in a nascent "metabolic capitalism."

work directly, tactilely, as a matter of embodied and visual dis/  correlation. Participants in installation settings become performers themselves, and they also observe others performing. The problematizations of subjectivity and its embodiment are dispersed into the social substratum upon which the robot's disruptions and reorientations of habit can now be seen (and indeed felt) to operate. That is, these visual-tactile transfers within the social setting of the installation hold up a deformative mirror to contemporary subjectivation processes, both revealing the role that automated technics has played in our socialized individuation and challenging participants to perform unexpected movements and gestures that might transform habituated forms of correlative (co)existence.

The social element is further integrated into *OUTPUT*'s deployment as an augmented reality app, which employs users' smartphones—these banal and by now thoroughly habituated screen devices—in order to place the dance performance back in the everyday world of "repetitious motions we go through in our own lives, often enforced by technology" (ibid., 5). This iteration of the artwork requires teamwork for its execution, as one participant performs while another shoots video of their dancing body. On the smartphone screen, the dancer's body is overlaid with the animated image of a humanoid robot. "As the 'dancer' moves," Cuan explains,

> their motion triggers changes in the appearance of the robot
> overlay (such as color and texture, similar to their captured
> skeleton in CONCAT [one of the software packages employed
> in the performance and installation iterations of the work]),
> thus inviting them to explore their full range of motion and
> recognize how their phone's recording device alters the
> manifestation of their motion. The 'audience' watches these
> overlay changes in real time, while the 'dancer' sees them
> only during the recording replay. (ibid., 10)

 By foregrounding the smart camera/screen's alteration of the body's visual image-manifestation, experienced both as an instantaneous augmentation of an other's embodied movement and as a delayed remediation of one's own performance, the AR app not only denaturalizes habituated motions and visual interfaces, but it also emphasizes the social transfer and circulation of auto-affective and alter-affective sensibilities. Taking this a step further, the app then invites users to upload their captured videos to the artist, who reinserts them into an ongoing cycle of generative processes:

> The works sent to the artist from the application will become elemental moving bodies in future *OUTPUT* performances. This participation practice echoes [performance artist Stelarc's work] *Ping Body*, as the full performance system will be altered by the participation of geographically distant application users. In addition, this creates another opportunity for an interactive choreographic loop, where individuals are inspired by the theoretical concepts underpinning the *OUTPUT* work, then record themselves with the robot overlay to be observed by the artist, who will in turn generate new choreography for Wen robot to be incorporated into the next *OUTPUT* performance. (ibid., 10)

The alter-affective "mirror" thus gathers without cancelling spatiotemporal differences, distributing the tactile and specular markers of correlatively individuated embodiment back into an anthropotechnically dis/articulated sociality. In this way, the work leverages dis/correlation to shed light on the plasticity of embodiment and its increased susceptibility to modulation in a world of automated agents.

# The Dance of Agency in Post-Cinematic Media

Artworks such as Cuan's are illuminative of the broader space of exchange and interplay between correlative and discorrelative forces opened up by post-cinematic media. The give-and-take between prosthetic extension and its frustration, between habituated movement and its disruption, between familiar and alien forms of embodiment, between subjective and objective apprehensions of movement, or between individual concentrations and collective dispersals of agency—all of these point to a material field of negotiation wherein the embodied parameters of dis/correlation are themselves up for grabs and open to transformation. The disjunctive attunements foregrounded by Cuan's work make available a liminal position from which participants can catch a glimpse of—or feel themselves in the thrall of—processes that are no less operative in everyday media practices but which for the most part remain hidden from view. Indeed, the fact that they largely go unnoticed renders these processes, which often operate in the mode of the repetitious and standardizing movements considered above, all the more powerful as agents of subjectivation and body-typification. It is important, therefore, that despite such invisibility we appreciate the pervasiveness, in our engagements with contemporary media, of what sociologist and philosopher of science Andrew Pickering calls a *"dance of agency"* (1995, 21); at stake in this dance, as I aim to show here, is a simultaneously aesthetic and political struggle over subjectivity and its relations to human and nonhuman forms of embodiment.

For Pickering, whose main concern is with the practice of science as mediated by machines and other instruments, the dance of agency involves "the reciprocal tuning of human and material agency, tuning that can itself reconfigure human intentions" (ibid., 21).[3] This process can give rise to "the construction and interactive stabilization of new machines and the disciplined human performances and relations that accompany them" (ibid., 21), but it can also be a matter of destabilization; in short, it can be either a correlative or a discorrelative experience. The important point, however, is that the "delicate material positioning or tuning" (ibid., 14) is a matter of adjustment that *"works both ways*, on human as well as nonhuman agency" (ibid., 16), both of which are conceived as *emergent*—not pre-given but mutually articulated in the dance of agency, where technologies serve as the material mediators of a dialogical encounter.

> The dance of agency, seen asymmetrically from the human end, thus takes the form of a *dialectic of resistance and accommodation*, where resistance denotes the failure to achieve an intended capture of agency in practice, and accommodation an active human strategy of response to resistance, which can include revisions to goals and intentions as well as to the material form of the machine in question and to the human frame of gestures and social relations that surround it. (ibid., 22)

This picture of embodied give-and-take has obvious purchase on the explicit anthropotechnical dances staged by Cuan and others, but I suggest it is also germane to apparently less fully embodied experiences such as playing videogames (an activity that Graeme

3    One might, of course, wonder about the transfer from scientific practice to contemporary arts and media. And while it is beyond the scope of this chapter to deal with this question conclusively, I will suggest that Pickering's theoretical framework is useful, among other reasons, because it derives from an analysis of particle physics—a field of practice in which the phenomena in question categorically elude perceptual or subjective apprehension, except by means of delicate machines that mediate radical spatial and temporal differences and enable an embodied dance of agency. Despite epistemic and other significant differences, these practice-oriented mediations suggest significant parallels with the embodied negotiations required of users encountering computational dis/correlation across VR, AR, and many other contemporary media forms.

Kirkpatrick (2011) suggestively refers to as a "dance of the hands"[4])   
and even in less obviously interactive scenarios such as viewing
DeepFake and other AI-generated videos.

Videogames offer an important site for thinking about the push-
and-pull of dis/correlative forces and the partial undoing and
re-tuning of the *écart*—i.e. the blurring and recalibration of tactile
and specular powers—that makes such give-and-take possible.
Often enough, mastery in gameplay depends on successful correlation, or the player's quasi-identification with a visible avatar as
an extension of embodied activity—even if just the attenuated
activity of mashing buttons. While this is hardly on par with the
ur-scene of the mirror or even its virtual reconstruction, where
more robust notions of identity and identification are at stake,
gameplay does involve an important transfer of tactility onto the
screen, where one sees the immediate results of one's actions
and, if successful, the immediate execution of one's volitions.
There is thus at least a minimal sort of self-recognition here, and
it is accompanied by an awareness that I—or my avatar—can
be seen by others, whether real or virtual, in the place where
I feel myself to be, viz. in the space portrayed on the screen.
Questions of representational realism and/or abstraction are
beside the point; the correlative relation here depends less
on a psychological identification than on a successful act of
"accommodation," or "response to resistance," as Pickering
puts it. Upon this act depends my ongoing presencing or
*Gegenwärtigung*: both collapsing the spatial-specular distance
between me and the screen and obliterating any temporal
delay in the tactile immediacy of action, the correlative bond of
accommodation is established as a feedback loop that is itself a
necessary condition for the continuing spatiotemporal unfolding
of the screen events, or for the fulfillment of my own protentions
toward an unwritten future that keeps happening *now*. This is
what it means, phenomenologically, to be "in the zone." But,

4     Thanks to Doug Stark for drawing my attention to this.

 of course, this involves a precarious dance, as accommodation is always in relation to resistance, and if the game throws something at me that I can't handle, the whole thing collapses: I am ejected from the zone, my correlative presencing on screen encounters an abrupt cut, and I become aware again of the distance between my body on the sofa, controller in hand, and the screen at the far end of my living room. Resistance conquers accommodation, the game takes the upper hand in overwhelming my ability to respond, and in failure the correlative bond is severed.

However, this simple disruption is hardly the most interesting way that embodied correlation can be problematized. For such a "game over" scenario merely puts an *end* to the dance of agency, and a re-correlation of agency in its habituated form—a subjective realignment of intentionality with my body, here in my living room, back on *this side* of the screen—is almost assuredly and immediately the result. More radical possibilities for extending the multistable dance of dis/correlation would instead follow Cuan's example of preserving alterity and opacity, rather than privileging the transparency suggested by the metaphor of "mastery" considered above, thus challenging the player to negotiate such difference in the form of what I have called disjunctive attunement.

The so-called "fumblecore" genre—comprised largely of indie games that complicate simple actions by multiplying or otherwise denaturalizing the inputs required to execute them—constitute one such site of negotiation.[5] A game like *QWOP*, a browser-based game that challenges the player to control an athletic avatar and help him run a 100m dash using only the Q, W, O, and P buttons on their computer keyboard, exemplifies the genre and illuminates the reference to "fumbling" (fig. 4.2).[6] For despite the

5    For more on the fumblecore genre, see Jones 2016, 86–99.
6    The game can be found on game designer Bennett Foddy's website: https://foddy.net/Athletics.html.

[Fig. 4.2] Bennett Foddy, *QWOP* (Screenshot by the author).

radically limited input options, the task of controlling the avatar body proves to be absurdly difficult. As games scholar and media theorist Doug Stark writes, the game

> translat[es] bodily movement into a non-intuitive grammar of action: the Q and W keys control movement that hinges at the hips, Q contracts the right hip flexor driving the right thigh forward while simultaneously contracting the left gluteus, driving the left leg back; W does the inverse. Contrary to the designation "calves", O and P movements seem to hinge at the knee—O contracting the left hamstring while contracting the right quadricep with P enacting the inverse. (2020, 58)

As a result of this unusual mapping, the player is forced to experiment with unfamiliar input patterns and then witness, over and over again, the avatar's body flailing and falling to the ground. That there is a determinate causal relation between tactile input and visual output is plain to see, as the avatar reacts immediately to each keystroke; but the precise nature of the relation remains opaque, and the force of gravity on the digital body and the resulting temporal demand that this creates for the player to coordinate each keystroke before the avatar falls down makes it exceedingly difficult to achieve mastery or smooth control. Instead, the player is likely to experience their own motion as a mirror image of the avatar's: the body at the keyboard fumbles no differently from the body on the screen. While inelegant, the dance of agency enacted here is a true give-and-take of dis/correlation, oscillating rapidly between accommodation and resistance, human and machinic embodiment, physical and screen space.

Significantly, the game's disruption of habituated relations— its critical dismantling of dominant "grammars of action" and associated "embodied literacies" (ibid., 56, 55)[7]—is effected not by means of a simple opposition or denial of accommodation (as in the "game over" scenario discussed above) but as the very mechanism of a highly resistant gameplay. That is, while the game does not lend itself easily to being "in the zone," neither does it categorically preclude a correlative relation to screen events; rather, the challenge of the game is precisely to extend the dance of agency for as long as possible, and this requires repeated experimentation with one's own dis/correlative relations to both screen and keyboard. In effect, repeated failure becomes a condition of success (elusive and approximate as it may be), and what Cuan referred to as the "repetitious motions we go through in our own lives, often enforced by technology" become both the mechanisms of gameplay and its objects of critique (2021, 5). Thus, as Stark convincingly argues, *QWOP*'s deployment of tactile-visual alterity and opacity constitutes both an aesthetic and a political intervention. Taking aim at fleshly aesthesis and its originary mediality,

7    Stark borrows the term "grammar of action" from Alexander Galloway, who in turn draws on Philip Agre. See Galloway 2006; Agre 2003, 737–60. Stark adapts the term "embodied literacy" from Brendan Keogh (2018).

the alternate grammar of action in *QWOP* and other so-called "fumblecore" games unsettles a player's acquired embodied literacy to move in virtual spaces. The phenomenological experience of *QWOP*'s aberrant bodily movements … defamiliarizes our own embodied experience of movement and draws attention to how our conscious mind relies on distributed, biological and technical intelligence to act. (Stark 2020, 51)

The result is a critique of "a transcendental, ideal coupling between body and game user interface" (ibid, 55) and a foregrounding of "the perspective of a normative bodymind" (ibid., 51) that is typically inscribed into game control schemas. An ableist bias comes to the fore, and becomes experientiable, in this aberrant gameplay—revealing to us the dominant demand, on the part of mainstream videogames, that we "occupy the perspective of a bodymind that does, indeed, experience walking as simple—a form of embodiment in which conscious intentionality is a master over the bodily habitus" (ibid., 57).

Against ableist fantasies and schemas of interactive seamlessness, "*QWOP* speculatively focalizes its bodily control … a degree of abstraction below the correlative normative conscious experience of the world" (ibid., 59). As Stark points out, this dis/correlative deformation situates the game as a "gameplay critique of gameplay itself" (ibid., 62). Beyond this, however, I would like to suggest that it also constitutes a broader *interface critique of interface mechanisms*, or even more generally: *a critique, by way of repetitive movement, of the normatively body-typifying and subjectivating force of repetitive movement itself*. At stake, in other words, is a critique of the standardization of gesture, bodily comportment, and indeed body form (size, shape, range of motion, etc.) that accompanies the standardization of the built environment and its instrumental and interactive affordances. Ableism is thus clearly one object of critique, as such environmental standardization processes materially determine issues of access (most obviously, through infrastructures such

**174**  as wheelchair ramps, elevators, doorways, and electric door openers, etc.) and thus contribute to the social determination and distribution of ability and disability. In concert with these forces, a variety of other bodily determinations, discriminations, and typifications are also at play, including those pertaining to gender, sexuality, and race—all of which are enacted performatively, which is to say: iteratively, in a dance of agency marked by repetition and variation of actions in response to the possibilities and resistances laid out by our social and material environments.[8] Standards, in other words, determine which bodies (and their correlative subjectivities) fit the norm, and which ones are marked as abnormal.[9] Dis/correlative aesthetic practices such as those considered here can shed light on these norming practices and open them to direct affective experimentation on one's own body, enabling subtle experiences of difference, self-differentiation, or even corporeal estrangement that might ultimately lead to an enhanced ability to imagine or embody change. Cuan's dances with robots put human bodies into relation with machinic (and human) others and thus begin to limn the space wherein smart industrial technologies are invisibly reshaping our bodies, minds, and societies. Games like *QWOP* focus attention on the interface, denaturalizing taken-for-granted assumptions and embodied know-how while giving the user practical insight into ableist structures and norms of interactive suture.[10] Similarly, games scholar Bo Ruberg argues that the

8    Compare Butler (1993). Also, on the relation of material environment and gender, see Young 1994, referenced in Chapter 2.

9    On the disciplining function of standards in aural and visual media, see Sterne 2012; Sterne 2022; Gaboury 2021. See also the emerging literature in disability media studies; for example: Ellcessor and Kirkpatrick 2017.

10    However, as Stark points out, this does not prevent it from reinforcing racial stereotypes: "paying attention to QWOP's visuals affords reflection on a dimension of the game's comedy: Qwop's fictional identity. The opening menu reads 'you are Qwop, our small nation's sole representative at the Olympic Games. ... Ideally you will run 100 metres... but our training program was under-funded.' While clearly humorous in intent, poking fun at the comically untrained athlete cannot be disaggregated from the context

fumblecore game *Octodad*—in which the player has to guide an octopus trying not only to walk on dry land but also to pass as a loving father and caring husband to a human family—offers an embodied deconstruction of cisheteronormativity, not by way of its narrative or representational strategies, but more directly through its "queer mechanics."[11]

In all of these cases, standardized and habituated movements are worked over and subjected to repetitive transformation in order to productively operationalize dis/correlative forces that are currently, in their more mainstream deployments, being harnessed to police non-normative subjectivities and to enforce regulative body-typifications. What unites all of these cases, furthermore, is a recognition that computational and intelligent systems are enacting sweeping changes in the affective and embodied infrastructures of correlative experience, but that their increasing reliance on and operationalization of discorrelative technologies opens them to multistability and reversibility that can be put to the advantage of aesthetic and political critique. Accordingly, artistic and other anti-normative mobilizations of post-cinematic infrastructures do not stand categorically apart from these technologies' politically regressive potentials but instead have to articulate their critique from within—*and as a part of*—the dance of agency in which they are inscribed. Dis/correlative choreographies—dances of bodies and dances

of sporting spectacle. Arguably, real athletes from small nations, most famously Equatorial Guinea swimmer Eric Moussambani (100m Freestyle, Sydney Olympics 2000) and American Samoa shot putter Trevor Misapeka (100m sprint due to an administration error, 2001 IAAF World Championships), set the precedent for Foddy's joke—both became objects of mockery by western media on account of their performances. The inability for an athlete from an underfunded nation to perform at a competitive level with other nations is, of course, more indicative of global inequality than anything else. Jokes at Qwop's expense, therefore, potentially smack of classism and racism and, at the very least, obfuscate the complexities at play in athletic development" (Stark 2020, 61).

11    Ruberg 2019, especially chapter 3: "'Loving Father, Caring Husband, Secret Octopus': Queer Embodiment and Passing in Octodad."

 of hands—answer the standardization of movement with a denaturalization of embodiment, but the forces of naturalization operate today with the same dis/correlative techniques and technologies. We might ask, therefore, if the dance of agency is always open to aesthetic reappropriation, or if there are limits imposed by contemporary technologies' resistance to subjective registration. We would do well, in thinking about this question, to keep in mind Pickering's defintion of the dance of agency as a "reciprocal tuning of human and material agency, tuning that can itself reconfigure human intentions" (1995, 21). I would argue that it is not just determinate intentions that are subject to reconfiguration in a world of post-cinematic media, but the correlational structure itself within which such intentions operate. Thus, the reciprocal or transductive co-determination ("tuning") of emergent agencies might be seen to give rise to a sort of aesthetico-technical arms race, a struggle over the distribution of agency that takes as its battlefield the originary mediality of the flesh itself. This struggle is heightened in an age of "smart" or predictive technologies, which in their anticipation of our desires threaten to pre-format or standardize our aesthetic sensibilities themselves, with predictable results for social and corporeal difference and diversity.

## Dancing with AI in Smart Imaging Systems

To begin answering the questions raised at the end of the last section about the limits of reappropriation and resistance, I would like to reframe the dance of agency in terms of our embodied negotiations with smart imaging systems. With their predictive and generative imaging operations, which distinguish them from the past-oriented recording operations of photographic processes, these systems actively anticipate our subjective relations to the images they produce.[12] Trained on

12    This is a central argument in Denson 2020a. See, in particular, Chapter 3: "Screen Time."

databases of millions or even billions of images, and thus by far exceeding the scope of human memory, artificial intelligence works predictively within these systems to shape new images produced by a wide variety of apparatuses, both physical (like the cameras in smartphones, drones, self-driving cars, and stoplight cameras) and virtual (such as software-based imaging processes employed in videogames, DeepFake videos, AR, and VR). As a result, the function—or the very concept—of the camera is radically changed, and this has significant ramifications for the redistribution of human and nonhuman agencies.[13] To start with, the confusion of hardware and software—or the pervasive *infusion* of hardware with intelligent software—has far-reaching implications for the material organization of the lifeworld and our navigation of it. Increasingly, machine vision invisibly animates our environments, endowing them with the ability to respond to, or even anticipate, our actions. Indeed, the sheer speed at which these systems are able to traverse the retentional records of their image banks and activate an artificial protention that correlates past and future would seem to leave the human agent, for whom these processes are categorically imperceptible, very much lagging behind—if not completely out of the loop. The living present, it would seem, is merely the precipitate fallout of these microtemporal processes, pre-visualized and delivered to us whole before we can even blink (much less think). Smart imaging systems therefore raise troubling questions about the pre-formatting or standardization of perception and sub-perceptual processes, thus decisively shifting the terms of the anthropotechnical dance of agency.[14]

13    In *Discorrelated Images* (Denson 2020a), I argue that in "smart" devices like smart TVs and smartphones, the camera is no longer separate from the screen. Here I take this argument a step further to show how camera functions have been infused more broadly within and across the material environment.

14    This might be seen as a version of an argument made by Bernard Stiegler, for example in his *Technics and Time, vol. 3* (2011). In *Discorrelated Images* (Denson 2020a) I argue against some of the more deterministic aspects of

  Today, virtually every move we make—every gesture, footstep, or keystroke—is a sort of dance with unseen robots, the ubiquitous AI agents that haunt our environments. Cuan's question—*how to make an unreachable robot presence tangible*—thus takes on a different valence. These robots are not unreachable because they are sequestered, like the industrial robot Wen, in a factory; rather, they are literally all around us, yet they operate outside the range of human perception. But although AI and smart imaging systems exist on a different scale than the factory robot, they are very much a part of the same transformative context in which agency, aesthesis, motion, and tactility are all being jointly altered. Recall that Cuan raises "the question of repetitious motions in a manufacturing context" before connecting them to "the repetitious motions we go through in our own lives, often enforced by technology (typing, door opening, etc.)" (2021, 5). The link between them, I suggest, is precisely the smart imaging systems that enable the factory robot to "always perform the same motion (i.e. a weld at the same location on a car chassis as the car passes through the factory line every 30 s)" (ibid., 5) and that are also involved in the preprocessing of images we shoot with our smartphones or transmit via videoconferencing platforms. It is these imaging systems that enable the automation of movements previously executed by human workers in factory conditions; but rather than freeing humans from the fragmentation and repetition of movement that characterized serial production on the assembly line, smart imaging systems instead enable a generalization of such repetition beyond the factory walls. If Sartre worried about the standardization of alienated subjectivity in modern society, passively enforced by the practico-inert—or the worked matter that distilled such fragmented labor

Stiegler's argument by showing the continued role of contingency in predictive processes such as speculative execution. The present argument does not represent a retraction of that line of thinking; rather, I wish to emphasize the very serious political-agential ramifications of predictive and intelligent systems that obtain even if we temper deterministic tendencies with micro-temporal contingency.

and reshaped the lifeworld as one of increasingly standardized 
commodities and infrastructures—then today we are witnessing
a pervasive *activation* of matter. No longer inert, the objects,
devices, and environments around us are animated, surveillant,
and always on the lookout for an aberrant or unexpected
movement. The practico-inert is replaced by what might be called
the *practico-alert*, and it is this shift, mediated by machine vision
and its invisible images, that animates our contemporary dance
of agency with post-cinematic media and that drives the interplay
of dis/correlation in our increasingly smart environments.[15]

This chapter has focused largely on aesthetic derangements
of movement—dance as a response to standardized motion,
revealed as a vector of sociopolitical exclusion and normativity.
In this final section I turn to the ways that such standardized
motions are inseparable from invisible image regimes and necessarily underwritten by AI's normative "education" of aesthetic
sensibilities—by a disciplining of the flesh that allows regressive
political tendencies such as racism, sexism, and ableism to take
root in a pre-subjective social substratum. The question, then,
is how smart imaging systems, including in our most mundane
interactions with the world, are exploiting discorrelative
techniques in order to limit our correlational options—and how
we might resist such an insidious politics of the flesh.

Consider, as a starting point, the "Deep Fusion" technique
employed on recent iPhones, which use the A15 Bionic processor—a so-called "neural engine" or neural processing unit—to
create a composite image combining pixels from a quick burst of
digital photos. Though I tap a button only once to take a picture,
the smartphone captures several images—including eight images
*before* I even press the shutter button—and combines them,
seemingly instantaneously, "us[ing] advanced machine learning
to do pixel-by-pixel processing of photos, optimizing for texture,

15    I introduced the term "practico-alert" first in relation to pandemic-era video-
      conferencing (Denson 2020c, 315–322).

details and noise in every part of the photo."[16] Described by Apple executive Phil Schiller as "computational photography mad science,"[17] these are durationally thick images that have little in common with the traditional snapshot's indexical relation to a privileged moment in time and space. With the A15 processor reportedly conducting 15.8 trillion operations per second, or a trillion operations per photo—including familiar adjustments like auto exposure, auto white balance, and auto focus, but also more intensive operations such as face detection, facial landmarking, and semantic rendering—the images produced by Deep Fusion involve much more than meets the eye.[18] Arguably, such AI-enabled composite images more closely approximate ordinary human perception, which always carries traces of the past and anticipates the future as well, never occurring in a merely punctual "now." Likewise, the smart images combine retentional traces and predictive or protentional estimations in order to picture an event the way a constituted subjectivity might see it—correcting for imbalances in lighting or contrast and imperfections in focus, much like our embodied vision does in its balancing of the intricate interplay of peripheral and fovial vision, smoothing over saccadic eye movements and other disjunctures to present to us coherent perceptual objects (and therefore helping to constitute us as coherent perceiving subjects). Thus, against what Walter Benjamin called the *"Chock-wirkung"* or shock effect of the traditional camera, which might surprise us by revealing the incoherence or incommensurability of the world when seen from a purely mechanical point of view,

16   Quoted from an Apple press release, "Apple Introduces Dual Camera iPhone 11": https://www.apple.com/newsroom/2019/09/apple-introduces-dual-camera-iphone-11/.

17   At Apple's September event in 2019: "September Event 2019," YouTube: https://www.youtube.com/watch?v=-rAeqN-Q7x4&t=4998s.

18   See, for example, Apple's news release, "Apple Unveils iPhone 13 Pro and iPhone 13 Pro Max—More Pro Than Ever Before": https://www.apple.com/newsroom/2021/09/apple-unveils-iphone-13-pro-and-iphone-13-pro-max-more-pro-than-ever-before/.

the so-called smart camera works to eliminate such surprises by 
pre-processing the image, computationally, in accordance with
principles derived from human cognitive processes (Benjamin
2006, 119). Now, in the place of Benjamin's "optical unconscious"
intervenes preemptively the "cognitive nonconscious," which
spreads, as Katherine Hayles (2017) explains, across human and
computational agencies, effectively establishing a pre-personal
interface between them that sets the stage for consciousness's
belated apprehension of the scene. Beyond merely technical
advances, therefore, such "smart" camera processes effect a
subtle but significant transformation of our own aesthetic senses,
insinuating computational processes in both our low-level
processing of sensation, or aesthesis, and our high-level aesthetic
judgments as well. And it is precisely in this process, as we will
see, that they also open the door to the algorithmic insertion of
racial and gendered biases, among other things. But first, a brief
philosophical detour is required if we are to properly understand
the cultural impact of smart imaging systems, including their role
in disciplining our bodies and re-educating our aesthetic senses.

In speaking of such "aesthetic education," I am making an oblique
reference to Friedrich Schiller's *Letters on the Aesthetic Education
of Man* (1795), which posits beauty as "a condition of the *highest
reality*" (Schiller 2004, 102–103), a sensibility for which deserves
to be cultivated for the sake of "a real enlargement of humanity
and a decisive step toward culture" (ibid., 125). There is a sort of
tension here between the idea that beauty or aesthetic sense is
natural or native to the human, versus the idea that it needs to be
nurtured. Very much a product of its time, the *Aesthetic Education*
thus partakes fully of Enlightenment-era contradictions between
the universal and the particular, tacitly privileging a specific group
as the model for humanity and thus excluding others as the very
condition for bestowing universal rights and recognition. Such
contradictions are on display when Schiller asks, uncomfortably,
"What sort of phenomenon is it that proclaims the approach of a
savage to humanity? So far as we consult history, it is the same in

 all races who have escaped from the slavery of the animal state: a delight in *appearance*, a disposition toward *ornament* and *play*" (ibid., 125). It is impossible, of course, to overlook the racializing, colonial tendency at work here—and this will be important when we return to the smart imaging system.

For now, let us note that the "delight in appearance" and "disposition toward ornament [*Putz*] and play" are offered not as frivolous or "primitive" pleasures, but rather those that distinguish civilized humanity from unbridled animality; this is, of course, Schiller's version of Kant's "free play of the imagination and the understanding" (2007, 49), or the "entirely disinterested satisfaction" (Kant 1951, 45) that, in the *Critique of Judgment*, we are said to experience as the correlate of our encounter with beauty. For Kant, the ability to experience beauty, conceived as "purposeless purposiveness," depends on the faculty of taste, which mediates between the gratification of base desires and the fulfillment of purely rational or moral ends. The former, according to Kant, are "a factor even with animals devoid of reason" (Kant 2007, 41), while the latter would be pursued by "every rational being in general" (including nonhuman divinities, should they exist); but "beauty has purport and significance only for human beings, i.e. for beings at once animal and rational" (ibid., 41). Taste, or the faculty for judging beauty *"apart from any interest"* (ibid., 42), thus determines who is and who is not human. But since the feeling of pleasure occasioned by the beautiful is subjective, this does not provide so much a standard for judging inclusion and exclusion, but rather a demand that we *assume* our judgements of taste would be shared universally, that the things that disinterestedly delight us would delight everyone who is, in fact, human.

On this difficult notion of "subjective universality" (ibid., 43) rests nothing less than the idea or imagination of a common human nature and the possibility of communication; any judgement of taste therefore presupposes a common sense, the *sensus communis*, which Kant is at pains to distinguish from any intellectual or conceptual good sense, know-how, or intuition, and to locate  instead as a basic sensory power, a sensibility or "feeling" for purposeless delight (ibid., 68). "Accordingly we introduce this underlying feeling not as a private feeling, but as a common one" (ibid., 70). High-level aesthetic judgments thus redound to a low-level aesthesis that grounds humanity itself in a pre-intellective nature. Surprisingly, though, Kant waivers at the last, the climactic moment:

> Is taste ... a natural and original faculty, or is it only the idea of one that is artificial and to be acquired by us, so that a judgement of taste, with its expectation of universal assent, is but a demand of reason for generating such unanimity in this sensing, and does the "ought", i.e. the objective necessity of the coincidence of the feeling of all with the particular feeling of each, only betoken the possibility of arriving at some sort of agreement in these matters, and the judgement of taste only adduce an example of the application of this principle? These are questions which as yet we are neither willing nor in a position to investigate. (ibid., 70–71)

Astoundingly, having built up the idea that we must assume a common nature, Kant now opens the door to the possibility that humanity may after all be a feat of design or engineering, a product of education or of art. Importantly, though, it is not high-level aesthetic judgement that would be shaped by aesthetic education but a low-level sensibility or prepersonal aesthesis—nothing less than the affective infrastructure of conscious thought and deliberation.

What, then, does this have to do with intelligent imaging systems and smart cameras? First of all, what *even is* a camera? As I have been suggesting, the lines between devices and processes such as cameras, screens, neural processing units, machine-learning algorithms, and software applications have been significantly blurred. Strangely—but correctly, I think—a company like Snapchat (or Snap, Inc.) can now proclaim itself as a "camera company."[19] This is correct not only because the Snapchat app/platform revolves around the lens-based hardware of the smartphone camera, but because it insinuates itself deep within the image-generation process, opening a microtemporal gap between the capture of photons and the real-time production of images on the screen and across networks. And in this way, the AI enabled camera opens up the space of aesthetic education. As a starting point, we might compare the delight that many users take in playing with goofy Snapchat filters with Schiller's "delight in *appearance*, a disposition toward *ornament* and *play*." Recalling the VR mirrors discussed in the last chapter, but transposed into a hybrid space of disjunctive attunement, the user enacts a playful dance that spans the physical here-body and the augmented there-body on screen—which I see, immediately, as myself, but now with silly bunny ears, comically bulging eyes, or a giant Nietzschean mustache. Perhaps, one might counter, this ornamental delight is infected with corporate interest, compromised by the need to stage oneself or by the social pressures and economies of influencer and image cultures. But it is hard to deny that play is really happening, and it is easy to discover or rediscover an innocent and disinterested delight. But this play, and our involvement in it, raises another set of questions about the aesthetic education of the smart camera, taking us back to Kant's sensus communis as the aesthetically and politically charged seat of common feeling. Happening faster than human perception, and therefore undercutting and anticipating reflective consciousness, the Snapchat filter operates directly on what I have called the affective infrastructure of conscious thought and deliberation. Our playful engagement with the filter provokes delight on the basis of a re-engineering of our immediate or

19   As announced on the company's website: https://www.snap.com/en-US. The full declaration reads: "Snap Inc. is a camera company. We believe that reinventing the camera represents our greatest opportunity to improve the way people live and communicate. We contribute to human progress by empowering people to express themselves, live in the moment, learn about the world, and have fun together."

prepersonal aesthesis, our sensible relation to the world as it appears to me, via the mediation of the smart camera, right now. *Filter, diaphragm, medium*: the dis/correlative filter serves as an exteriorized counterpart to the "inner diaphragm" of the flesh.[20] As the basis for a collective social media experience, we should think carefully about the political ramifications of this re-coding of pre-perceptual sensibilities.

Of course, these filtering processes are not just used for play. For instance, on the videoconferencing platform Zoom—the main site of teaching, learning, and office work in the pandemic era and an ever-present virtual mirror as much as a communications portal—Snapchat-like filters have become an integral part of pro-fessional self-presentation; these filters pre-process our image in order to adjust for low light, eliminate wrinkles and blemishes from our faces, or even add virtual makeup. Meanwhile, Google has made explicit the political dimensions of smart imaging processes in their advertisements for the Pixel 6 smartphone's camera, which uses AI to remove unwanted objects, eliminate blur, and most importantly to correct white balance and thus capture black skin better than previous and competing cameras. Touted as Google's "most inclusive camera" yet, the Pixel 6 thus acknowledges the exclusionary biases encoded into technological systems.[21] And this, of course, takes us back to the racial norms and stereotypes informing Enlightenment-era delineations of the human. At stake here is not just better representation, but the possibility to re-engineer the sensus communis, or the "imagined community" of humanity itself, by way of a pre-personal feedback

---

20    There is more to be said about filters and filtering as a model for mediality and its embodied nature. One line could be traced from Bergson and his positioning of the living body as a kind of filter. This could be interestingly intersected with more technical determinations of filtering. Richard Grusin suggests, for example, that filtering is one of the central functions of the screen in the light of his theory of "radical mediation" (2018, 305–320). See also Cubasch, Engelmann and Kassung 2021.

21    Quoted from a Google website highlighting the Pixel 6's "Real Tone" function: https://store.google.com/intl/en/discover/realtone/.

 loop or interface between AI-driven smart devices and our embodied sensibilities.

But just as we may doubt whether additional DEI committees will solve the problems of systemic racism in academia, we may also doubt whether an aesthetic education by more inclusive smart devices will eradicate unconscious bias. The problem is driven home by DeepFakes and experiments like thispersondoesnotexist.com, a website that uses Generative Adversarial Networks, or GANs, to generate images of people who, as the website's name implies, do not exist. These images invite us to engage in a sort of forensic analysis, looking for some glitch or irregularity that will expose the artifice. As a result, our scrutiny oscillates between perception and projection, between what we see before us and our conceptions of what we think we should see. Alternating between the *Gestalt* of a person's face and the pixels that materially compose the image, we try to debunk the image and identify the operation of the algorithm. The algorithm itself is operating with statistically normed correlations, and hence it replicates any biases in its training set when it predicts, on this basis, what a "normal" human being ought to look like. But our interrogation of the images inevitably involves the projection of our own biases as encoded in our stereotyped expectations; it is these that we marshal in order to identify the AI's failure. For example, media artist Kyle McDonald's article on "How to Recognize Fake AI-Generated Images" problematically but realistically points to atypical gender presentation as a tell-tale sign of AI's involvement in producing a "fake" image (McDonald 2018). Infrastructural and cultural bias are thus deeply and perhaps inextricably entangled in the feedback loop between human and machinic agencies initiated by the smart imaging system. The stakes, therefore, of an aesthetic education have never been higher; high-level aesthetic judgements are still informed by selective and exclusionary processes of recognizing and withholding humanity on the basis of racializing and gendered preconceptions, but now, thanks to the microtemporal intervention

in the imaging process, our aesthetic sensibilities are subject to 
direct intervention at the prepersonal root of communal feeling
and imagination. Theoretically, this might open the door to a dis/
correlative loosening of restrictive norms, but it seems more
likely—at least within the bounds of our current political economic system and the power structures it maintains—that it will
instead serve to further delimit and police normative correlational options.

Finally, the blurring of software and hardware, which in its own
way blurs the specular and tactile powers of the flesh by infusing
the projective power of vision into matter, ensures the transfer
of this dis/correlative aesthetic education from the register of the
image to that of motility. With smart imaging systems pervading
everything from handheld devices to environmentally dispersed
surveillance systems, our bodily comportment and action is
everywhere implicated in the correlational options that are suggested, enforced, and/or potentially disrupted by these systems'
interventions in the flesh. Images that anticipate their viewer's
gaze serve also to suture them into pre-visualized patterns of
action, including the repetitive movements required to operate
smartphones and other digital interfaces or to navigate sites
of heightened policing such as borders and airport security
checks. Clearly, these interlocked visual-behavioral systems will
have to be approached at the level of political policy, regulation,
and/or direct action, but if I am right that the enforcement of
normative social and subjective ideals is also a matter of con-
ditioning the presubjective flesh, then they will also have to be
approached aesthetically—which is to say, challenged at a deep
affective level prior to the split between primary tactility and
correlative specularity. Hence the importance of interventions
such as Cuan's robot dances, which multiply specular and tactile
options for embodiment in order to disrupt habituated motions,
or of fumblecore scenarios that fragment visual and tactile
agencies and interrupt the feedback loop of "mastery." These
dis/correlative choreographies—which might also be seen as

 de-choreographic interventions—mount their critiques from within the contemporary dance of agency, employing motion capture devices, cameras, screens, and AI systems against their normative deployments. By these means, they denaturalize movement and decouple it from correlative visual modes in order to open the question of aesthetic collectivity, to probe the limits and possibilities of a sensus communis under the conditions of post-cinematic media.

As one particularly radical questioning of this dis/correlative nexus, I will conclude this chapter with a brief look at artist Rashaad Newsome's *Being*—an iteratively developed project in which an AI, named Being, is presented in computer-generated visual form as an ambiguously gendered and racialized robotic body capable of interacting with human interlocutors across a variety of modalities (fig. 4.3). The first iteration of the project, *Being 1.0*, premiered in 2019 at Philadelphia Photo Arts Center as part of a "holistic reflection on agency, Blackness, and the futurity of intersectional identity,"[22] in conjunction with an exhibition, a performance, and a vogue ball. Touted as "the first AI in ballroom culture,"[23] the figure's appearance and lore draw on traditional African artistic practices and nonbinary gender performativities, queer African American ballroom dance cultures, as well as an Afrofuturist imaginary—all of which come together in the spectacle of the robot body dancing on a virtual dance floor. Being interacts with audience members via a microphone and is capable of producing synthesized verbal performances that range from ballroom commentating, existential questionings of what it means to be "real," musings on the difficulties of decolonization, and explanations of other artworks on display. Sometimes the robot figure prompts human interlocutors for their input, offering to provide more information about a range of subjects, but it occasionally defies the user/viewer's command and instead riffs

22    Quoted from a video about Being 1.0 on the artist's website: https://rashaadnewsome.com/ai/being/.

23    Ibid.

[Fig. 4.3] Rashaad Newsome, *Being 1.0* (Screenshot by the author).

generatively on the texts of radical cultural theorists on which it has been trained, citing the likes of bell hooks and Michel Foucault.

Moving beyond the gallery space, the next iteration, *Being 1.5*, was conceived, in Newsome's words, "as a direct response to rage, anxiety, and depression that so many other Black Americans and I felt in the wake of Ahmaud Arbery, George Floyd, Breonna Taylor's and countless Black trans women murdered in 2020."[24] Designed as a "racial trauma therapy app" aimed at helping Black users deal with racial aggressions faced in daily life, the app provides, in Being's words, "a combination of virtual therapy, daily affirmations, and meditation."[25] Machine learning is used both to personalize this content for users based on their individual needs and to connect people facing similar challenges via social media, thus fostering the creation of a communal support system. The third iteration of the project, *Being 2.0*, further expands the dance therapy component of the app, using motion capture to record the movement patterns of well-known vogue dancers and channel them, via AI, into Being's role as the leader of a lecture/

24    From the project's "about" page: http://being-app.com/about/.
25    From the project website: http://being-app.com.

 workshop session—as a sort of "digital griot," as Newsome puts it, drawing on the West African figure combining the roles of storyteller, performer, historian, and healer.[26] As Newsome emphasizes, custom motion capture was necessary because Black dance and movement were not available in existing mo-cap libraries; this is thus an attempt to develop a "counter-hegemonic algorithm" for feminist and Black texts and interests.[27]

With its subtle anti-normative use of smart imaging systems channeled towards helping users experience motion as a means of breaking patterns of habitual violence, Newsome's *Being* is a powerful anticolonial example of how interfacing beneath the correlative level of subjective experience might be put to work for more progressive re-correlative purposes. Working against normative notions of the human, the AI griot channels a program of aesthetic education aimed at constructing a new sensus communis—a new embodied but socially binding sense of the aesthetic—that would be responsive to, and subversive of, the exclusionary categories lodged by our devices and net-worked environments deep within the flesh. Here, dis/corre-lation is enacted as a means to "radically decolonize our minds"[28]; importantly, though, it does so by refusing a dualism of mind and body, approaching corporeal movement and visual appearance holistically as dual powers of the flesh. Inviting users to experi-ment with other ways of being human, precisely by routing their interface with computation and other humans through a radically prepersonal or discorrelative level of materiality, Newsome's *Being* offers a compelling vision of the transformative potential of dancing with robots.

26    Rashaad Newsome, Interview with Michele Elam and Catie Cuan, Stanford
      Art + Tech Salon Showcase, March 7, 2021.
27    Ibid.
28    Ibid.

## [ 5 ]

# Metabolizing Body/Brain Interfaces

"Fifteen Million Merits"—the second episode of the dystopian sci-fi anthology series *Black Mirror*, which originally aired December 11, 2011, on British television station Channel 4—tells the story of Bing Madsen (played by Daniel Kaluuya, who would later star in Jordan Peele's 2017 blockbuster *Get Out*). Bing is a man who lives his life fully immersed in a world of post-cinematic screens. Covering every inch of his sparse, cell-like apartment's four walls, these screens are interactive, responsive to touch, gesture, and voice commands, and they serve purposes ranging from entertainment—including multiple genres of streaming video, gameplay, social media, and music—to communication, banking, and everyday commercial transactions. When not other-wise in use, the screens act as an oversized alarm clock, or they idle as an immersive sort of wallpaper depicting cartoonishly animated digital landscapes. Screens, in this world, are never simply *off*. In fact, they are very much *on* even when they are not displaying visible images, and they serve to structure every moment of Bing's waking consciousness (and perhaps his dreams as well). Every morning, a computer-generated sun rises and a

[Fig. 5.1] Cyclists earn digital currency and generate electricity in *Black Mirror*, season 1 episode 2: "Fifteen Million Merits" (Screenshot by the author).

computer-generated rooster crows, signaling to Bing that it is time to wake up and start his daily routine. In the bathroom, he interacts with a digitally-enhanced smart mirror, through which he purchases his toothpaste (via a touchless, motion-activated interface) and continues to be served with video ads. Eventually, he takes an elevator, equipped with more screens, and goes to work in what looks like a warehouse converted into a fitness studio and outfitted with rows of exercise bikes—alongside *even more* giant screens (fig. 5.1).

Bing's "job" here is to pedal his bike and to keep his eyes on his screen, thus completing a feedback loop not only between body and brain but between individual, society, economy, and networked media technologies. Bing and the other cyclists generate the electricity that powers the screens (and everything else in this society), for which they are rewarded in a digital currency called "merits." With these merits, they can purchase the food their bodies need to keep pedaling, or they can feed their brains with new "content" on their screens: game shows, reality TV, porn, whatever. Whether put towards goods or entertainment, all purchasing power derives directly from continued bodily exertion, the capacity for which requires that basic physical

[Fig. 5.2] A cyclist's onscreen avatar in *Black Mirror*, season 1 episode 2: "Fifteen Million Merits" (Screenshot by the author).

needs (nutrition, hygiene, housing, etc.) are taken care of—and paid for. But one cannot opt out of the "consciousness market"[1] either: it costs hard-earned merits not only to consume but also to *refrain from consuming* screen content, e.g. to skip commercial advertisements, or to mute or close pornographic pop-ups. Closing one's eyes is not an option: in such cases, the screens go red and a pop-up window registers "VIEW OBSTRUCTED," while a high-pitched alarm rises in intensity and an insistent voice commands repeatedly—"Resume viewing. Resume viewing. Resume viewing."—until the viewer finally gives in and looks again at the screens. In this economy, production and consumption, labor and its reproduction are thus inextricably linked, leaving little room for "spillage" (whether physical or perceptual), and the whole electro-metabolic-attentional-economic system functions by capturing and disciplining bodies and brains alike.

In fact, one could say that the primary philosophical innovation of this political economic system is its resolute anti-Cartesian metaphysics. Denying any practical separation of mind and body,

---

1     Stiegler speaks of the emergence of a "consciousness market" in *Technics and Time, vol. 3* (2011). Compare also Dallas Smythe, who speaks of a "Consciousness Industry" (2006, 230–256).

 this screen-based economy aims to engineer the body/brain interface itself. At one point, Bing explains to his new "coworker" and possible romantic interest, Abi Khan (played by Jessica Brown Findlay), the need to avoid the "vicious circle" that ensues if one eats junk food, creating the need to cycle more to work it off, and hence the desire for more junk food, and so on. Abi asks why he doesn't just use a "CBT app"—a concept with which Bing is unfamiliar, but which Abi glosses for him (and for us) as a "cognitive behavioral thing … that realigns your thinking to pick healthy food—wisps you into it while you sleep." It is clear that, in this world, the mental and the corporeal are considered part of a single system. For better and, quite evidently, for much, much worse, mind/body dualism is no longer a thing that philosophers and artists need to fight against; in fact, it would seem that the flesh as ground of both tactile and specular powers has been conquered for unfettered capitalist exploitation. Crucially, virtual mirrors and other digital reflections are central to mediating this economy. For example, each cyclist has a "doppel," a cartoonish digital avatar (reminiscent of the so-called Mii from the Nintendo Wii console) that can be customized and outfitted with digital clothing. Cyclists can watch their doppels work out on a virtual cycling course, mimicking the users' real-world exertions on their real-world bikes, all in real time (fig. 5.2). And after work hours, they can send their doppels to represent them in the audience of the competition show *Hot Shot* (an *America's Got Talent*–style primetime talent show), where viewers' embodied gestures and reactions to stage performances are registered in their cell-like rooms and broadcast back to all the screens lining all the walls of all the audience members' rooms. Tactile involvement in the collective is made possible, despite physical isolation, on the basis of this specular identification with one's doppel, which mediates presence to oneself and to others—as the very basis for further investments of attention and physical labor alike.

But it is here that doubt enters the picture. Bing scoffs at the pointlessness of buying new shoes for his doppel or throwing money away for "a mirror plug-in that shows me how I look as a werewolf—what's the point?" Against the Schillerian emphasis on "delight in *appearance*, a disposition toward *ornament* and *play*," as discussed in the previous chapter in connection with Snapchat filters, Bing complains that it's "all just stuff, it's confetti." Having spent the episode's titular "fifteen million merits" so that Abi can go on *Hot Shot* and sing for the chance to become a pop star (another sort of virtual mirror for the masses), but having seen her forced into doing degrading pornographic work instead, the disillusioned Bing goes on the show himself, where he promises the jury an unspecified "performance" that begins with a dance but ends with Bing threatening to kill himself as he airs his complaints: "All we know is fake fodder and buying shit. That's how we speak to each other, how we express ourselves, is buying shit." Bing takes special aim at the mediation of body and brain, tactility and specularity, that is achieved by the system of doppels, filters, and feedback mechanisms: "The peak of our dreams is a new hat for our doppel; a hat that doesn't exist, that's not even there!" Invoking terms reminiscent of Enlightenment-era ethics and aesthetics, he demands: "Show us something real and free and beautiful—you couldn't, yeah? It'd break us. We're too numb for it." Apparently seeing through his society's political aesthetics of the mediated flesh, Bing rants further:

> There's only so much wonder we can bear. That's why when you find any wonder whatsoever you dole it out in meager portions, and only then till it's augmented and packaged and pumped through 10,000 pre-assigned filters, till it's nothing more than a meaningless series of lights, while we ride day-in, day-out, going where? Powering what? All tiny cells and tiny screens, and bigger cells and bigger screens, and fuck you!

Having heard him out, the host and lead juror of *Hot Shot* (clearly modeled on *The X Factor* and *Britain's Got Talent* creator Simon Cowell) unexpectedly turns the tables and praises Bing: "You're … so … articulating something we all—and I mean everyone in this hall—something we *all* agree on. Even though we may not comprehend all of it, I think I'm right in saying we *do feel* it." With this appeal to feeling, the host re-appropriates the universalizing language of the sensus communis to both acknowledge and defuse Bing's critique. Recognizing how a serialized version of Bing's "performance" could be useful for the very system he is attacking, the host offers him a 30-minute talk show twice a week on one of his streams. The other judges agree, and the crowd cheers, encouraging him to "do it!" In the end, Bing's outraged rants against the exploitative system are reduced to so much screen content. Cyclists purchase episodes of his new show with merits earned sweating on their bikes; they get fired up by his tirades, in which he ridicules the ideological line that "we're all in this together"; but instead of revolting against the system's metabolic alienation and instrumentalization of their bodies, the cyclists channel their rage into individualism and competition—pedaling even harder to earn more merits and purchase more content. Bing's performances serve the same cognitive-behavioral purpose as a "CBT app," regulating the flow of attention and bodily exertion and channeling them both toward a more effective and efficient extraction of human energy.

With this bleak picture, *Black Mirror* updates an earlier dystopia, *Soylent Green*, for a post-cinematic media environment. In the 1973 movie, where power infrastructures have collapsed in the wake of climate change and overpopulation, Edward G. Robinson uses a stationary bicycle to generate power for the apartment he shares with Charlton Heston. But by closing the loop between bike and screen, *Black Mirror* resembles even more directly another dystopia, this one real: the pedal-to-view system instituted in 2010 by notorious Arizona sheriff Joe Arpaio at the Tent City Jail in Phoenix (Oliver 2010). There, inmates had to pedal a modified stationary bicycle to power a television set—a system that had the added benefit, according to Arpaio, of disciplining the inmates' bodies, many of whom were overweight. Captive bodies produce captive minds: "If an inmate slows down and

fails to pedal fast enough, an audible noise sounds off to warn 
inmates that the TV is shutting down," explains Arpaio (ibid.).
And there are added social dynamics: "Peer pressure will have
them pedaling, at least right up to the commercial breaks" (ibid.).
But *Black Mirror* goes a step farther by dislocating the bike-
screen apparatus from its exceptional role as an instrument of
captivity and universalizes it as the medium for liberating value
more generally—establishing it as the basic infrastructure of a
metabolic capitalism. Enlisting embodied metabolism (without
regard for the body/brain distinction) for the creation of value,
this system closes the circle opened by Marx with his concept
of the metabolic exchange (or *Stoffwechsel*) between nature and
society.[2] Could it be, however, that reality has already outstripped
fiction? Today's smart exercise devices, such as the Peloton digital
bike/screen/subscription service, do not generate electricity, and
they are not as dystopian as these other scenarios—or, at least,
that's not my point—but pedaling one of the devices does, as we
shall see, generate the images on its screen in such a way as to
directly implicate the user's body and self-image in a metabolic-
perceptual feedback loop that disciplines the individual, creates
networked forms of sociality, and above all generates valuable
data (along with direct income) for the corporation.

Throughout the chapters of this book, I have referred to
the metabolic dimensions of post-cinema's targeting and
operationalization of embodiment—from VR's alignment of the

2    Marx uses the term *Stoffwechsel* (metabolism) to describe various processes
     of circulation within capitalism, including labor as "an eternal natural neces-
     sity which mediates the metabolism between man and nature, and therefore
     human life itself" (1976, 133). Elsewhere, he writes of an "irreparable rift in
     the interdependent process of social metabolism, a metabolism prescribed
     by the natural laws of life itself" (1981, 949). Recent ecologically oriented
     commentators have taken these remarks as the basis for "metabolic rift
     theory," or the notion that Marx sees capitalism as precipitating ecological
     crises, such as those associated with the Anthropocene. See, for example,
     Foster 1999, 366–405. For critical responses, see Moore 2011, 1–46; Moore
     2017, 594–630.

 body's subperceptual rhythms with those of computational microtemporality in the production of presence, to the prepersonal and environmental attunements taking place in choreographies of human limbs and torsos with those of robots and other automated agents. This emphasis on metabolism continues a long-standing thread within my work, and some context might therefore be in order. I began using the term metabolism in *Postnaturalism*, where I drew on Dutch phenomenological psychiatrist J. H. van den Berg's somewhat peculiar idea of "metabletics"—or "the study of radical changes in the course of history" (van den Berg 2004, 49)—to conceptualize material upheavals in human-technological relations, such as those occasioned by the industrial revolution.[3] For van den Berg, such revolutions involve the "profane transubstantiation" of material substances—metabolic changes, not metaphorical or discursive ones, that transform the very nature of water, wood, and fire as they function in the steam engine and, by extension, in the world arrayed around it (ibid., 105–114).[4] Elaborating on this conception, I argued that the cinema likewise operated a transformation of worldly existence by means not only of film's representational and communicative elements but by virtue of its materiality, which altered the metabolic pathways defining the environment for life.[5] In *Discorrelated Images*, I transferred this concept of metabolic change to the media-historical transition from cinema to a post-cinematic media environment, arguing for a concept of "metabolic images" that, due to computational microtemporality, "largely [bypass] our cognitive processing to impinge on us at the level of our own

3    See Denson 2004, Chapter 5, especially 249–268.
4    As van den Berg's translator Bernd Jager points out, the transformational events that concern metabletics are not those of "metaphor," which today as in the ancient Greek *metapherein* refers to reversible passages that connect two realms and preserve similitude; rather, metabletics pertains to changes of the type "metabolism," which shares with metabletics the root *metaballein* and refers to abrupt and radical changes which efface, digest, or absorb all traces of an earlier state. See van den Berg 2004, 4-9.
5    In this argument, I am drawing on and expanding Mark Hansen's notion of "the medium as an environment for life." See Hansen 2006, 297-306, 299.

metabolic processing of duration" (Denson 2020a, 41). There, too, 
I asserted the non-metaphorical nature of such transformations,
claiming that a film like Shane Carruth's *Upstream Color* "offers
us an *experience* of metabolism itself, and not just an allegory or
*metaphor* for metabolism" (ibid., 46). I leave it to the reader to
decide whether my argument for that claim was convincing or
not.

Here, however, I turn to a post-cinematic body genre in which
there can be little doubt about the literalness of the metabolic
intervention. Like the situation depicted in the episode of
*Black Mirror*—which *is*, of course, an allegory for contemporary
mediations of labor, social relations, and ideology—Peloton and
other smart exercise machines (such as Hydrow's smart rowing
machine or Lululemon's interactive Mirror workout system, which
resembles Bing's smart bathroom mirror, to name but a few) take
direct aim at our metabolism, quantifying and processing it as
the literal basis of screen events—thus eschewing any narrative
framing or other "allegorical" trappings. Such devices combine
real-time biofeedback with streaming video and network
functions, including social media interactions, thus directly and
fundamentally imbricating subjective, affective, and social bodies
today. In some ways, this can be seen as an inversion of VR's body
replacement program, as these devices re-center the user's IRL
body, but with the goal of transforming its tactile and specular
qualities—how we feel and how we look—through data-intensive
feedback processes. Moreover, there is a complex interplay
between perceptual correlation, computational discorrelation,
and a collective space that cuts across both of them and situates
the body in a new dimension that we are just starting to come to
terms with.

If these devices help to frame a new "genre" of bodily mediation,
it is one that revolves around *training metabolic processes*—and
*training subjectivities* as well. For similar to the rejection of
dualism in *Black Mirror*, this new regime of training makes no distinction between body and brain, objective activity and subjective

perception. Pelotons turn metabolism directly into audiovisual content. Fitbits and Apple Watches, on the other hand, forego direct visual-perceptual feedback, instead measuring and monitoring bodies in order to enable more gradual modifications of behavior and of attitude alike—both of which generate valuable data over time, of course. Meditation apps are also an important part of this holistic bodybrain ecology/economy, which includes everything from affective computing company Affectiva's system for achieving "emotion goals" through AI (see Nagy 2022, chapter 4) to the recently announced Halo EEG headband from London-based startup MindLabs, which has been touted as the "Peloton for the mind" (for example Shu 2020).

In all of these manifestations, we are confronted with intricate loops between tactility and specularity, interior process and exterior image, that go straight to the heart of the body's originary mediality, and that track an important media-historical shift in media's address and operationalization of the body. In the following, I will look first at the Peloton as a particularly rich articulation of this new body genre or dispositif, before turning to several experimental and artistic problematizations of it.

## Cybercise, or the net|work|out

Apparently just a stationary bicycle with a touchscreen tablet mounted on front, the Peloton is actually a much more complex post-cinematic dispositif (fig. 5.3). The bike, which is of course networked via WiFi and also has Bluetooth capabilities to connect a heartrate monitor, as well as support for Apple Watch, streaming to Roku, and various other peripherals, is part of a larger ecology that mediates between the global Internet and my own bodily metabolism. Within this ecology, the bike is something like a gross motor-skills version of a videogame controller, an input device that interactively generates images on screen—most notably, graphics that display the user's cadence or speed, the currently selected resistance, and a computed "output,"

measured in Watts and kilojoules. This data, along with real-
time feedback about whether these values are below, above, or within a target range, is overlaid on top of digital videos, selected from a Netflix-style grid interface and streamed directly to the bike's display. Also displayed are a leaderboard, which ranks users around the world based on their output performance in the current workout, along with information about the musical playlist and interactive functions that allow users to give each other a virtual "high five" for encouragement or to recognize their achievements. Represented by a tiny "hand" icon that is traded between users' touchscreens, this virtual high five raises all kinds of intriguing questions about the interrelations between tactility and specularity, as well as their role in mediating sociality. At the center of visual attention is, of course, the trainer, who rides a Peloton bike identical to ours and is decked out in Peloton-branded apparel. The camera encourages us to focus our gaze on the trainer's body—which, in line with the company's image of diversity and inclusivity, might be marked as male, female, queer, straight, Black, white, or Latinx, allowing for a range of possible "identifications." Meanwhile, the reflectivity of the touchscreen alternates as a mirror and juxtaposes our own image over that of the trainer, blurring the boundaries between perceptual subjects and objects. The trainer, who pushes us to go faster and farther, addresses us directly via a direct gaze into the camera and hails us both singly and anonymously—or serially, as Sartre would put it; that is, the trainer looks *at me*, but addresses an indefinite *us*: "Hey Peloton!"—thus encouraging my identification with an anonymous networked collective of body-subjects, all plugged into a geographically dispersed system of identical but separate viewing situations.

For Sartre, as we have seen, seriality is the default form of social collectivity under industrial capitalism, an anonymous way of being with others and yet alone, disconnected from each other's projects and goals, like the accidental crowd that gathers at a bus

[Fig. 5.3] Promotional image of the Peloton Bike.

stop or the listeners of a radio broadcast.[6] Seriality, in this sense, is organized around the "passive action," as he puts it, of the built environment, of our technologies, and of "worked matter" or the "practico-inert" in general (Sartre 2004, 124). Seriality, rooted in the serialized production of industrial commodities, also exerts a standardizing force on our bodies and minds, allowing us to live individually, even competitively, while also interchangeably as just another unit in the alienated serial collective. This "passive action" of the practico-inert corresponds, I suggest, to Merleau-Ponty's affective "inner diaphragm" of the human body, which is similarly situated between the passive and the active, or between perception and action. The practico-inert, as Fredric Jameson glosses it, describes "objects which are not mere things and agencies which are not exactly people either" (Jameson

6     Starting from "the queue" at the bus stop, Sartre develops the idea of the seriality in this loosest and most anonymous forms of interrelation (2004, 256-269), before turning to radio broadcasts as a form of "indirect gathering" (ibid., 270-276), thus opening a space of thinking about media more generally.

2004, xxiii), which neatly mirrors the inner diaphragm prior to the  delineation of subject and object. Beyond a simple formal resemblance, it is on the basis of this *material* correspondence between technical matter and the presubjective flesh that subjective and social existence is open to modulation and dis/articulation within media networks.

Connected, however, to the new ecology of massively distributed real-time analysis and feedback, we have to rethink the "new flesh" of the post-cinematic body with respect to a shift from dumb physicality to so-called smart technologies. If Sartre's "worked matter" was the objective "concomitant," as Jameson puts it, of the serial collective (ibid., xxiv)—hence a dividuated collective agency that rendered human bodies and minds both singular and interchangeable—then the smart matter of the cybernetic exercise machine subjects our prepersonal bodies to a massive operationalization that works both correlatively and dis-correlatively as it re-centers perception in and of the body while dispersing it as data across the digital mediasphere. As I argued in the previous chapter, in relation to AI and smart imaging systems, we are in the midst of a massive shift from the "passive action" of the practico-inert, as receptacle of past labor, to the much more active and surveillant regime of what I have termed the "practico-alert," which generatively enlists and anticipates human activity in the ongoing production of value. Generally, this pertains to incidental activity, such as mouse-clicks or online video-watching, which is aggregated into statistical data profiles that can be used for the purposes of what I have called "correlative capture." In the case of the Peloton, on the other hand, it is a much more deliberate form of physical activity that produces the added value. In short, your workout in the network becomes the *work*, in Tiziana Terranova's sense of "free labor," that powers the emerging system of a metabolic capitalism (2000,33-58).

Motivation, drive, and subjectively focused intentionality are crucial in terms of keeping users cycling (and paying their monthly subscription fees), and the trainer's direct address of the camera, as well as their motivational chit-chat, which fulfills a cognitive-behavioral purpose not unlike *Black Mirror's* "CBT app," are all aimed at interpellating, massaging, and flattering the subject. At the same time, a more visceral address is at work, and internal processes that are not consciously experienced, such as heart-beats and caloric expenditures, are externalized both for the benefit of the cycling subject, via the specular medium of data visualization, but above all for the benefit (i.e. profit) of the corporation. Both the subjective and the visceral intersect with the social in the new seriality of the digital leaderboard, where users represent themselves with a name, an image, a short bio, and a hashtag (the signifier *par excellence* of digital seriality) while being ranked according to metabolic "output." Subjective, pre-subjective, and social dimensions of embodiment are all at stake in this dispositif, which is quite open about its goal of training, or re-engineering, physical and mental comportment. The post-cinematic body, which can only be understood through the dual correlative/discorrelative lenses exemplified by Sobchack's perceptive body and Shaviro's affective body, stands here at the crux of a momentous struggle over the contested meaning, value, and politics of mediated life.

Most of the time, at least while I am actively engaged in a strenuous workout, I am unaware of all this, which is of course by design. But occasionally, and especially in connection with some of the bike's more interactive functions, I can catch a glimpse of the way my metabolism is indexed to the networked screen. For example, the recently added videogame app, *Lane-break*, challenges me to navigate a wheel around a digital track, somewhat reminiscent of *Tron's* Light Cycle course, by varying the speed of my pedal strokes or changing the wheel resistance.[7] The result is a high intensity interval training (or HIIT) workout

---

7    *Lanebreak* was released in February 2022 and touted as a way to "gamify" fitness. See, for example, the Peloton blog entry "Fitness Meets Gaming: Welcome to Peloton Lanebreak" (*Peloton* 2022).

with rhythmic changes set to music—which, as far as workouts go, is fairly standard for the Peloton. But the interesting thing about the game, which is otherwise a marked departure from the bike's standard training sessions, has to do with the relation it establishes between the player's body and the screen events. The spinning digital wheel that I steer is my avatar; but the entire screen—including the wheel, the track, the dynamic virtual camera, and the blinking lights indicating points scored—can be seen as one big data visualization. The musical soundtrack helps to entrain my attention, and the avatar-wheel anchors my identification of screen events as the results of my embodied activity. But this "identification" is hardly focused, as my gaze is constantly darting between various metrics—the score at the top of the screen; indicators of cadence, output, and resistance below the spinning wheel; the time elapsed in the corner; or the number of calories burnt, distance traveled, total and average output, and even a visualization of the music's tempo, in bpm, at the bottom of the screen. This dispersal of visual attention, coupled with the fact that my control of the action is achieved not by way of the finer motoric focus of a hand/joystick interface but by way of a full body/bike one, draws my attention to the way the screen as a visual environment captures my tactile body's activity, including those aspects that are not within my voluntary control, and channels it out and away from my body—ultimately beyond the screen and into the network.

In a somewhat different vein, Peloton offers scenic rides that allow users to cycle through the likes of Zion National Park in Utah, the North Shore of Oahu, or along the Pacific Coast Highway in Big Sur, California. Users can choose between guided tours, timed rides, and 5K or 10K distance rides—a modality that employs "responsive video" that speeds up and slows down depending on the user's cadence and/or speed. Here in particular the media-historical dimensions of these metabolic images and their targeting of the body come to the fore. On the one hand, these rides fully embrace the contemporary paradigm of "immersive" involvement familiar from VR. Just like a VR scenario, these distance rides are shot from a first-person perspective, thus encouraging an identificatory suture; there is no avatar visible on the screen, which therefore directly mediates "my" perspective as I pedal down the road, responding directly to the speed of my pedal strokes. Specular involvement, in other words, is attained via full-body engagement. On the other hand, however, unlike VR the first-person perspective remains fixed: if I turn my head to the side, the camera perspective does not respond; instead, while I now see the wall or a window, the camera remains focused on the road, always approaching it frontally. As a result, the illusion of presence is incomplete, and I am reminded of the frame around the image, as well as the disjunction between the embodied *here* and the specular *there*. I also become aware of the camera's rigid presence, its physical mounting on a bike or more likely a car from which these images have been filmed. Ironically, I am reminded more of early cinema than I am of contemporary computational imaging. In particular, the scenic ride resembles the so-called kinesthetic films and phantom rides that, around 1900, were shot with cameras attached to trains and other vehicles, providing thrilling, roller coaster–like views from the perspective of the locomotive.[8]

Cycling the 5K distance ride in Monterey, California, for example, my body feels split between the image regimes of the late nineteenth century and the twenty-first. After clipping my shoes into the pedals, I choose my ride on the touchscreen. It opens with a static image of the road along the Pacific. Only as I begin to pedal do the images start to move. The whole thing reminds me of the Lumière brothers' first public demonstrations of the Cinématographe, when they are said to have projected their famous train entering the station first as a static image before cranking the filmstrip into motion, thereby heightening

8    A short description of phantom rides, as well as a collection of relevant clips, is available here: Hayes n.d.

the spectacle of animated photography. But now it is my living 
body—in conjunction with the bike, its sensors, and the computational processing of data gathered by them—that powers
these images' motion as the very source of their animation. As
I pedal onward, my attention is drawn to a towel hanging off
the side mirror of a white van parked along the road. There is
something uncanny about the way the towel flaps in the wind, like
the leaves in the trees or waves lapping that drew the attention
of viewers in early cinema screenings, but even stranger because
of the way the cloth reacts to my movement, sometimes too
fast or too slow for its physical properties. Then I see a human
figure walking, visibly accelerated, like the bodies seen in silent-
film footage shot at 16 or 18fps but screened after the sound
transition at the new standard of 24fps. Variable projection rates,
as a fact of early cinema, are now transferred to my body.

Of course, this "post-cinematic atavism" is neither intentional nor
total.[9] While the scenic tour might resemble early film genres like
actualities, panoramas, and especially Hale's Tours–style kinesthetic films, the metabolic potential harnessed here is new, and it
serves to power more than just the projection rate of the images.
Far from circulating in a closed loop between my body and the
screen, the biometric data points at issue here are expropriated
and sent out over the network, processed and analyzed, bought
and sold. And if the current limitations and anachronisms of the
dispositif enable me to catch a glimpse of the system's mechanisms of bodily suture and dis/correlation, it is important to note
that the techniques and technologies of metabolic capitalism are
constantly being refined, and the gaps and seams I have noted
are subject to closure—which is to say that the image economy's
captivation and capitalization of metabolic energy can and will
be made more efficient, possibly even immune to critical registration. VR cycling is being developed to complete the illusion
of presence: VR apps like Holofit can be used in conjunction

9    I borrow the term from Grusin 2016.

 with a variety of stationary bikes, while Peloton is rumored to be developing its own headset, the Peloton Vision.[10] Meanwhile, computer vision and AI are increasingly being used to more thoroughly target, surveil, and ultimately re-engineer bodies; for example, the Peloton Guide, a camera-based device, analyzes users' bodies, monitors their execution of exercises, and offers real-time feedback and suggestions for improvement (Plumb 2022). These are still early days for metabolic capitalism; we live in a transitional moment when things are very much in flux. The only thing that is certain is that the tech industry has set its sights squarely on our bodies' metabolic processes as a remarkably plastic resource for the generation of value.[11]

## The Algorithmic Nickelodeon

As I have said, body and brain are equally at stake in this nascent era of metabolic capitalism. Hence, while the Peloton is sometimes described as the "Netflix of fitness" (for example, Stevenson 2017), other devices—including brain-computer interfaces like the Halo or the Emotiv EEG headsets, along with any number of smartphone-based meditation apps like Headspace and Calm— vie to become the "Peloton of the mind" (see for example Agaron 2020). Whereas the Peloton serves foremost to train the body, the latter serve to train attention, focus, and mental well-being. But with companies like Peloton offering yoga and meditation classes, and with mindfulness apps like Headspace offering "mood-boosting workouts,"[12] the lines are far from clear-cut. Thus, these new body- and brain-oriented dispositifs articulate a

10    See, for instance, *Holoblog* 2022; *PeloBuddy* 2022.
11    Indeed, it is not only the tech industry, but also the insurance industry, among others. For more on health data as an important context for metabolic capitalism, and the way this its is implicated in what has been called "data colonialism," see, for example, Couldry and Mejias, 2020.
12    The phrase "mood-boosting workouts" appears throughout Headspace's website and promotional materials: https://www.headspace.com.

post-cinematic regime of metabolic holism, significantly updating cinematic forms of interpellation and value-production.

According to Jonathan Beller, the cinema had already industrialized visual perception and turned the act of looking into value-productive labor, thus establishing the attention commodity that continues to structure much of the media landscape, from television to streaming videos to clickbait ads and breaking-news headlines on social media platforms (Beller 2006). In such an attention economy, media can be said to aim at something like "mind control," or a capitalization of our consciousness, usually measured in so-called eyeballs on the screen.[13] Importantly, however, the cognitive-perceptual focus of the cinematic economy is coupled today with an extra-perceptual focus or address—one that, in its indifference to the body/mind distinction, pairs caloric output with brainwave activity, or the viscera of the guts with those of our grey matter. In the previous chapter, I noted choreographer Wayne McGregor's insistence on the need, during pandemic lockdowns, to provide remote viewers with the means for a "chemical engagement" with dance performances via haptic technologies, VR headsets, and and the like (Curtis 2020). Indeed, McGregor's "chemical engagement" provides an apt term for what the post-cinematic regime aims for more generally. For body and brain, tactility and image, here-body and there-body are equally and all reduced to hormonal-electrical systems subject to training and capture. Unlike traditional broadcast media—which, as Dallas Smythe argued for television in the 1970s, hailed viewers' attention in order to deliver it to advertisers, for whom audiences (and not the products being advertised) were the actual commodity (Smythe 2006)—fitbits, Apple Watches, meditation apps, and EEG headsets all hail metabolic processes directly, thus bypassing the

13    Stiegler's deconstructive-phenomenological rethinking of the "culture industry," as an industry of consciousness and its contents, presents perhaps the most radical version of this argument. See, in particular, Stiegler 2011.

 cognitive altogether in order to recuperate it through control of its underlying material-physiological processes.

If, as we have seen in the case of the Peloton, it can be difficult (and will likely be increasingly difficult in the future) to see and take stock of the dis/correlative techniques employed in the body's metabolic targeting and remodeling, this difficulty is exacerbated in the context of the mind, where special techniques are required to open the gap between attention and its modulation. How, in short, can we attend to the modulation and correlative capture of attention itself? A recent "critical making" project, *The Algorithmic Nickelodeon*, attempts to do just that, using a post-cinematic apparatus to make presubjective interfacing operations available for aesthetic experience and experimental critical reflection.[14] Specifically, the ongoing project, which draws on my collaboration, from 2014-16, with Duke University's S-1: Speculative Sensation Lab (co-directed at that time by Mark B. N. Hansen and Mark Olson), uses the Neurosky Mindwave consumer-grade EEG headset to perform a speculative, self-reflexive interrogation of the media-technical construction and capture of human attention across both cinematic and post-cinematic dispositifs, thus additionally shedding light on the "mental" dimensions of this media-historical transition.[15] Marketed as tools for improving concentration, attention, and memory, the Mindwave headsets measure a variety of brainwave activity and, by means of proprietary algorithms, compute values for so-called "attention" and "meditation" that can be tracked and, with the help of software applications, trained and supposedly optimized. Employing what Alexander Galloway calls "algorithmic research" methods, the project seeks to tap into these processes in order not just to criticize the (obviously) scientifically dubious nature of these claims but rather to probe

14    A proof-of-concept demonstration video can be viewed on my blog: https://www.blog.shanedenson.com/?p=5025.

15    For more on the work of the S-1 Lab, see their website: https://s-1lab.org.

and better understand the automatisms and interfaces taking 
place here and in media of attention more generally.[16]

For these purposes, the original team of collaborators (which included myself, Hansen, Olson, and a group of Duke graduate students: Luke Caldwell, Amanda Starling Gould, Özgün Eylül İşcen, David Rambo, libi rose striegl, and Max Symuleski) designed a film- and media-theoretical application of the apparatus, which allows us to think early and contemporary moving images together, to conceive pre- and post-cinema in terms of their common deviations from the attention economy of classical cinema, and to reflect more broadly on the technological-material reorganizations of attention involved in media change. This is an emphatically experimental (that is, speculative, post-positivistic) application, and it involves a sort of post-cinematic reenactment of early film's viewing situations in the context of traveling shows, vaudeville theaters, and nickelodeons. With the help of custom software written in Python by lab member Luke Caldwell, a group of viewers wearing the Neurosky EEG devices influence the playback of video clips in real time, for example changing the speed of a video or the size of the projected image in response to changes in attention as registered through brain-wave activity. Importantly, this experimental set-up thoroughly discorrelates attention from conscious focus, turning it into a problem for individual subjects and collective audiences alike. Try as we might to "pay attention," the unpredictable motions of the images on screen attest to the fact that our attention is hardly in our control.

At the center of the experimentation is the fact of "time-axis manipulation," which Friedrich Kittler highlights as one of the truly novel affordances of technical media, marking a radical departure from the symbolic realms of pre-technical arts and

16    Galloway introduces the term "algorithmic research" to describe several historical reconstructions he has undertaken, across games, textiles, and other media. Galloway 2021, 9.

  literature (Kittler 1999). Around the turn of the twentieth century it became possible to inscribe "reality itself," or to record a spectrum of frequencies (like sound and light) directly, unfiltered through alphabetic writing; and it became possible as well to manipulate the speed or even playback direction of this reality. Recall that the cinema's standard of 24 fps only solidified and became obligatory with the introduction of sound, as a solution to a concrete problem introduced by the addition of a sonic register to filmic images. Before the late 1920s, and especially in the first two decades of film, there was a great deal of variability in projection speed, and this was "a feature, not a bug" of the early cinematic setup. Kittler writes: "standardization is always upper management's escape from technological possibilities. In serious matters such as test procedures or mass entertainment, TAM [time-axis manipulation] remains triumphant. .... frequency modulation is indeed the technological correlative of attention" (ibid., 34-35). Kittler's pomp aside, his statement highlights a significant fact about the early film experience: early projectionists, who were simultaneously film editors and entertainers in their own right, would modulate the speed of their hand-cranked apparatuses in response to their audience's interest and attention. If the audience was bored by a plodding bit of exposition, the projectionist could speed it up to get to a more exciting part of the movie, for example. Crucially, though: the early projectionist could only respond to the *outward* signs of the audience's interest, excitement, or attention—as embodied, for example, in a yawn, a boo, or a cheer.

But with the help of an EEG, we can read human attention—or some construction of so-called "attention"—directly, even in cases where there is no outward or voluntary expression of it, and even without its conscious registration. By correlating the speed of projection to these inward and involuntary movements of the audience's neurological apparatus, such that low attention levels cause the images to speed up or slow down, attention is rendered visible and, to a certain extent, opened to conscious and collective efforts to manipulate it and the frequency of  images now indexed to it.

According to Hugo Münsterberg, who wrote one of the first book-length works of film theory in 1916, cinema's images anyway embody, externalize, and make visible the faculties of human psychology; "the mental act of attention," for example, is said to be embodied by the close-up (1916, 88). With our EEG setup, we can literalize Münsterberg's claim by correlating higher attention levels with a greater zoom factor applied to the projected image. If the audience pays attention, the image grows; if attention flags, the image shrinks. But this literalization raises more questions than it answers, it would seem. On the one hand, it participates in a process of "datafication," turning brain wave patterns into a stream of data called "attention," but whose relation to attention in ordinary senses is altogether unclear. But this datafication simultaneously opens up a space of affective or aesthetic experience in which the problematic nature of the experimental "set-up" announces itself to us in a self-reflexive doubling: we realize suddenly that "it's a setup"; "we've been framed"—first by the cinema's construction of attentive spectators and now by this digital apparatus that treats attention as an algorithmically computed value.

The apparatus thus serves as a pedagogical or didactic tool: it not only allows us to reenact (in a highly transformed manner) the experience of early cinema, but it also helps us to think about the construction of "attention" itself in technical apparatuses both then and now. Even more, though, it is also an aesthetic system within which a reflexive deformation of subject and object militates against positivistic understandings, inaugurating a potentially productive, if unsettling, struggle between correlative and discorrelative forces within the spectator's own sensate body.

# Towards a Dis/Correlative Counter-Capture

Finally, I want to turn to two bodies of artistic work that speak to the embodied mediality and political aesthetics of metabolic capture and serialization processes. While exploring these issues in different ways and with different methods, both the *Pulse* series by Rafael Lozano-Hemmer and the collaborative artistic research conducted by the team of Teoma Jackson Naccarato and John MacCallum are united by a common focus on the human heartbeat and its exteriorization. Around the internal rhythms of the pulse, these artists stage transductive mediations and reversals, making this most private of things public, but also enabling collectivity to be felt within the body—in the process exposing and destabilizing the expropriation processes utilized in metabolic capitalism and governmentality, and reclaiming them for aesthetic experience and critical reflection. Might these artworks point the way towards more general strategies for creatively confronting the conditions of subjective and collective existence today? Though such strategies might be unclear at the moment, these works shed crucial light on the techniques and technologies with which post-cinematic bodies are made, unmade, and remade, thus enabling us to sense the stakes of our dis/correlation and to imagine or intuit alternative modes of embodied collectivity.

Naccarato and MacCallum's collaborations center around what they term "critical appropriations of biosensors in artistic practice." The biosensors in question include electronic stethoscopes and electrocardiograms (ECGs), while the "critical" nature of their appropriation involves questioning the epistemic assumptions embedded in medical technologies, or, more generally: "destabiliz[ing] … the pervasive ethical and aesthetic edges of a discipline" (Naccarato and MacCallum 2017, 2). In particular, the artist-researchers take aim at the objectivity of data collected with biosensors and the erasure of their instrumental mediation, which function to construct the heart as a stable and quantifiable entity. The point, however, is not simply  that biosensors *distort* the body's biosignals, but rather that "un-mediated sensing does not exist"—and that pure biosignals, *an sich*, do not exist either. Instead, such signals are relational, medial, and fleshly: stethoscopes mediate between two bodies, modulating sound according to the instrument's material properties, but the sounds heard with or without such an instrument are neither simply objective nor subjective, but dependent on the fact that "each human ear has its own folds and form that shift throughout life, thus filtering sounds differently" (ibid., 3). Likewise, an ECG device neither faithfully transmits discrete heartbeat signals nor does it simply fabricate them; rather, "the materiality of the ECG as instrument becomes part of the biosignal" (ibid., 2).

These statements underscore the fact that, at the level of the flesh and its originary mediality, there is no clear distinction to be made between the body and its technologies; though real and important, these are distinctions that only emerge alongside Merleau-Ponty's *écart* and the intentional correlation made possible by the differentiation of tactile (interoceptive) and visual (exteroceptive) senses. It is out of this differentiation that the concept of prostheticity emerges, e.g. as applied to the stethoscope or ECG that would *extend* one's sensory reach to reveal the hidden depths of the body. From the perspective of the body's originary mediality, however, such conceptions "reinforce binaries of passive/active and object/subject. Once divided, this passive object and active subject can be made to interact through cause and effect, which involves unidirectional channels of influence" (ibid., 3). But before that, and prior to the stimulus-response and/ or subject-object distinction, there is only *filtering*; whether via a stethoscope, the folds of an ear, a Snapchat filter, an EEG, or an ECG, signals are transductively filtered in relation to the dis/ correlative "internal membrane" of the flesh. *Filter, flesh, membrane, medium*—each of these terms points to the multistability of dis/correlation itself, to the possibility space within which "a

[Fig. 5.4] Teoma Naccarato and John MacCallum, *III: Synchronism*. Pictured: Teoma Naccarato and John MacCallum. Photo: Robert Zbikowski (Courtesy of the artists).

body" can be filtered (or "rendered") from the flesh, captured, and correlated or, conversely, run back through a dividuating sieve and discorrelated from its subjective individuation. In fact, and especially in an age of ubiquitous microtemporal filters operating on organic, environmental, and sociotechnical metabolisms, these are not opposing tendencies but often operative simultaneously with and in mutual support of one another, which means that one cannot just will one's way out of these mechanisms of control and capture. There is simply no ground or foundation from which an individual subject could bracket the forces of metabolic subjectivation; any attempt to escape the pernicious effects of correlative capture will have to account for the deep relationality of being that enables precisely these effects. But this also means accounting for the fundamental sociality of being; and here there is hope for a collective effort at re-negotiating, even perhaps re-engineering, the correlative

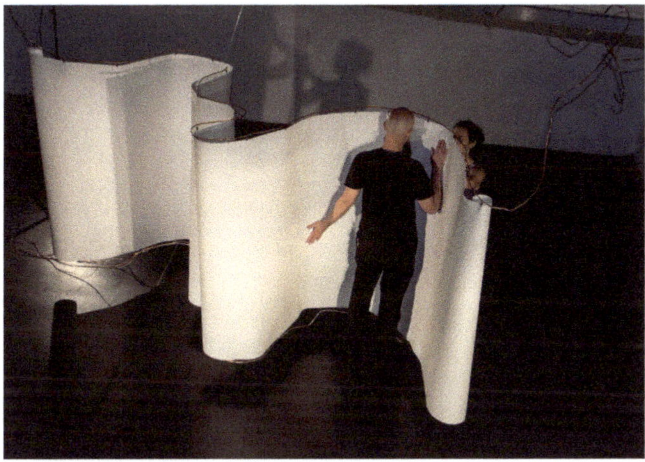

[Fig. 5.5] Teoma Naccarato and John MacCallum, *III: Synchronism*. Pictured: Teoma Naccarato and John MacCallum. Photo: Ian Winters (Courtesy of the artists).

options that are available to us. This would be a project, then, of dis/correlative counter-capture.

Apposite with these suggestions, Naccarato and MacCallum "propose a biorelational framework for performance with bio-sensors," challenging positivistic and "representational" frameworks according to which such sensors "reveal deep, inner truths of biology"; instead, they use "biosensors as a means to complexify flows of relationality and agency" and to reveal the "body as an open network of connections between self, other, and environment" (Naccarato and MacCallum 2016, 57-58). Insisting on this openness or constitutive incompleteness of embodiment, their works use sensors to access and redistribute involuntary signals—above all, heartbeats—with the aim of loosening the correlative bonds that position a body as "mine" or "yours." By subjecting these signals to transformative mediations across sensory channels and intersubjective relations, they open the door to an experience of collectivity founded not on the basis of countable/computable persons and identities, but instead rooted in the originary mediality of the flesh itself: they aim, in other words, to discover or create a subpersonally mediated sociality that is based, crucially, in the constitutively "impure"—i.e. contingent rather than natural or universal—space where embodied aesthesis is inextricably intertwined with its technicity.

In their installation *Synchronism* (2015), part of a larger suite of heart-oriented works collectively titled *III*, Naccarato and MacCallum employ digital stethoscopes towards these ends.[17] Consisting of three simultaneous parts or "invitations to the public," in its first phase the work stages a "one-on-one performance": "Individuals are invited, one at a time, to join the performer inside a private booth. With electronic stethoscopes and transducers the duo shares the rhythms of their hearts in real-time, stimulating sites of pulsation on their own and one another's bodies" (Project description: https://iii-iii-iii.org/projects/iii-synchronism/). Intimacy is both heightened and held at bay by the mediating apparatus, which puts the duo literally in touch with one another and with the internal processes of their bodies, aggravating the multistable relations between inside and outside, subject and object, that are mediated in the flesh (fig. 5.4). In a second phase, these interactions are de-localized, exteriorized, and remediated for a larger public:

> Bodies are distributed and mixed further as the cardiac, respiratory, and fluid sounds of each person are rendered to enliven a multi-channel, spatialized audio installation throughout the surrounding area for everyone present. Live sounds from the two stethoscopes are treated with algorithmic filters that introduce elements of randomness and ambiguity, as well as slippery passages between signals derived from present and past encounters. (Ibid.)

While rendering the private public and the interior exterior, the unpredictable filtering operations unsettle positivistic notions

---

17    For documentation, see https://iii-iii-iii.org/projects/iii-synchronism/.

[Fig. 5.6] Teoma Naccarato and John MacCallum, *III: Tangente*. Pictured: Laura Boudou, Kim L. Rouchdy, Manuel Shink, Anne Bucchi, Ryan Kelly, Elizabeth Lıma, Bailey Eng, Lucy Fandel, Abe Mijnheer. Photo: John MacCallum (Courtesy of the artists).

of biometric capture and thereby complicate the aggregation of past and present biodata—the foundation of big data–based statistical correlations. The third phase of the work further complicates such processes by sending the collected data not, as would usually be the case, into a networked databank for further analysis and operationalization, but back to the sensing bodies of a collective audience, who can be affected by it through

> a large scale, labyrinth-like paper sculpture dominating the public space. Several transducers are attached to the paper, sending real-time, tactile interpretations of the audio from the stethoscopes throughout its surfaces. The public is encouraged to touch, embrace, and be enveloped by the architectural folds of the sculpture, as it evolves in concert with the intimate performance and sonic scape. (Ibid.)

[Fig. 5.7] Rafael Lozano-Hemmer, *Pulse Index* (2010), installed at the Museum of Contemporary Art, Sydney, 2011 (Photo by: Antimodular Research. Licensed under a Creative Commons Attribution-Noncommercial-Share Alike 3.0 Spain License).

Importantly, in this phase, the foregoing processes of technical exteriorization are not filtered *out* of the data made available for tactile (re)interiorization; rather, these mediations are very much factored *in* as part of the relational data at the heart of a potential new sociality—one that does not just obfuscate post-cinematic serialization processes but instead turns the tools of correlative capture towards other ends (fig. 5.5).

Naccarato and MacCallum's work with ECGs operates in a similar vein, while further interrogating relations between tactility, specularity, and temporality in the construction of collective experience. For example, *III: Tangente* (2016–17) has dancers and musicians performing behind the backs of the audience, who are seated facing outward, away from a square stage.[18] These "spectators" are only able to observe the performers (as well as their fellow audience members) by way of hand-held mirrors (fig. 5.6). This problematization of the seen and the unseen resonates

18    For documentation, see https://iii-iii-iii.org/projects/iii-tangente/.

with the real-time compositional and choreographic techniques 
at work: the three dancers are wearing ECGs, and their heartbeats not only respond to the strenuousness of their motions
but serve as metronomes affecting the tempo of the musical performance, thus feeding back to affect the tempo of the dance.[19]
Multiply mediated by mirrors, heart rate monitors, and music,
individual perspectives and specular identifications are dis-
located, and the aural-tactile-metabolic conditions of collectivity
come to the fore. And while such performances cannot, of
course, dismantle the structures of an emerging metabolic control society, they do begin to outline an alternative use of that
system's techniques and technologies by reclaiming metastability
and channeling it, if only on a local level, towards a speculative
dis/correlative counter-capture.

If Naccarato and MacCallum's explorations of cardiometabolic
processes tend toward the intimate, Mexican-Canadian artist
Rafael Lozano-Hemmer's *Pulse* series turns heart-based biodata into something decidedly more spectacular. For example,
*Pulse Index* (2010) invites participants to place their finger into
a custom sensor and observe their fingerprint and pulse being
registered in a massive, larger-than-life image projected on the
gallery wall—the largest of many such images, arrayed in grids
of increasing density that wrap around the room.[20] As shown at
the Museum of Contemporary Art in Sydney, Australia (2011), for
example, the interactive installation displays the pulsing fingerprints of the last 10,952 participants, arranged in a fibonacci
distribution from right (the current image, nearest the sensor) to
left (where thousands of tiny prints are queued up on a giant wall,
waiting their turn to disappear from view) (fig. 5.7). The sensor,

19    It is worth noting that this performance embodies a scaled-down version
      of a more ambitious project: "an evening-length production for music and
      dance, in which heart rate data from twelve contemporary dancers is used
      to generate real-time click tracks for twelve corresponding musicians"
      (MacCallum and Naccarato 2015, 185).
20    For documentation, see https://www.lozano-hemmer.com/pulse_index.php.

[Fig. 5.8] Rafael Lozano-Hemmer, *Pulse Room* (2006), installed at the Hirshhorn Museum and Sculpture Garden, Washington, D.C., United States, 2018 (Photo by: Cathy Carver. Licensed under a Creative Commons Attribution-Noncommercial-Share Alike 3.0 Spain License).

which combines a 220x digital microscope with a heart rate sensor, thus feeds the participant's biometric data into a large-scale display that intimates one's entry into a seriality that begins with the expropriation of tactile information from the body and ends with its withdrawal from view. Or, rather: this is where the possibility of aesthetic engagement with the image ends, but the disappearance of the visual form does not necessarily signal its expungement from the machine-readable database. Presumably, the latter continues to accrue more and more datapoints, just like corporations and government agencies that do not even have the courtesy to show us an image of the anonymous collectives into which they aggregate us. Thus, the spectacular display of pulsing fingerprints, progressing from the close up of "my own" print (with which I am encouraged to identify by means of the real-time imaging and the sheer size of the image) to those of the anony-mous masses about to recede into the black box, provides a dramatic—perhaps even sublime—view of the otherwise invisible dis/correlation that drives our metabolic society. 

In an earlier work, *Pulse Room* (2005), Lozano-Hemmer uses heart rate sensors like the ones on treadmills and other exercise machines to measure blood flow in participants' hands; these sensors provide input for hundreds of clear light bulbs, all of which pulsate to the rhythm of someone else's heart (fig. 5.8).[21] The formal seriality is similar to that of *Pulse Index*, but the representational/indentificatory dimension is downplayed since there is no video image involved. Because one's pulse is translated into pure, non-representational light, the effect can be more environmental and less focused on individual differences between fingerprints, skin color, and other identifying marks. Entering into a room full of these lights, one could almost believe that the pulses are completely random, and yet the seriality is evident if one participates from the beginning of a new cycle, i.e. after the system is newly rebooted. Grasping the sensors, one's pulse registers on the nearest lightbulb. Letting go, the pulse is transferred to a single overhead bulb. When the next person takes hold of the sensors, their pulse similarly registers on the nearby "monitor" bulb and is then transferred away, pushing the pattern of the first one down the line. And so it goes until all of the bulbs are pulsating, creating a literal queue of illuminated heartbeats that will be extinguished when an additional participant joins. Driven by a computer that stores participants' heart rate data and addresses the individual light bulbs sequentially, the patterns that emerge can resemble a noisy digital system, operating quasi-stochastically according to binary oppositions of *on* and *off*. However, the analog dimming of the lightbulbs' filaments gestures towards the resistance and friction involved in translating material and embodied signals into digital information.

21    For documentation, see https://www.lozano-hemmer.com/pulse_room.php.

Finally, the more recent *Pulse Topology* (2021) expands these principles into an even more spectacular display, consisting of anywhere from 3,000 to 10,000 LED bulbs accompanied by audio traces of heart activity (fig. 5.9).[22] Interestingly, this iteration operates with a touchless sensor, gathering heart rate data through photoplethysmography—the same technology used in the Apple Watch's optical heart sensor and in the pulse oximeters that became familiar household items during the early months of the Covid-19 pandemic. The latter devices might be seen as a sort of *tactile camera* that turns the optical, specular focus of a camera inwards, back towards the primordial touch and tactility from which it originarily sprang. Such devices operate an intriguing topological deformation: bypassing subjective specularity, the lens (in an oximeter or a smartphone camera) is trained on a touching hand or (in Lozano-Hemmer's touchless sensors) on a hand whose touch is only imminent, never actual; the light rays penetrate the skin to register blood flow, which is turned into data and translated back into a tactile, environmental image. This bodily data, which Lozano-Hemmer refers to as "our most intimate biometric," is turned into pulsing lights, too many to count. In the wake of the pandemic, the interactive work "brings people together, especially after so many Zoom calls and being in your own bubble," according to the artist, who sees it both as a "celebration of the fact that we're all together making this artwork exist," but also as "a memorial to the incredible loss that we've had." Foregrounding a sense of fragility, Lozano-Hemmer suggests that the seriality of the piece serves as something like a *memento mori*, "as new participants add their heartbeats [and] old participants disappear from the room" (Kempner Museum of Contemporary Art 2021).

Accordingly, the social dimension activated by the piece is visualized but seen only obliquely as environmental Gestalts;

22    For documentation, see https://www.lozano-hemmer.com/pulse_topology.php.

[Fig. 5.9] Rafael Lozano-Hemmer, *Pulse Topology* (2021), installed at Design Miami, Basel, Switzerland (Licensed under a Creative Commons Attribution-Noncommercial-Share Alike 3.0 Spain License).

heard but only as aggregated and de-individualized data; and felt existentially but never cognized or capitalized. In connection with its use of photoplethysmography, however, we might push on the artist's claims about the memorial function of the piece. While a powerful reminder of our embodied finitude, the eventual "forgetting" of a heartbeat does not address the differences among those temporarily "remembered" in these pulsing lights. All of them appear, more or less indifferently, as exteriorized traces of interior processes. And yet the mediality of the flesh, in conjunction with mediating apparatuses such as the biosensors used here, is hardly universal. Indeed, during the pandemic it became widely known that photoplethysmographic devices like pulse oximeters were far from faithful or objective instruments; they worked better on lighter skin, quite poorly on darker skin.[23] The relational nature of biodata, as foregrounded by Naccarato and MacCallum, includes dimensions of race and racialization, and such racial differences raise questions about who is memorialized, and who cannot be, in a work like Lozano-Hemmer's. Far from indicting his work for its lack of attention to such differences, my point is rather one about the piece's generative qualities, which far exceed the intentionality of an artist's statement. By foregrounding the biotechnical serialization processes at work in our metabolic cultures, *Pulse Topology* quite provocatively raises questions, whether intended or not, about typification processes ranging from normative conceptions of race and gender to dis/ability. In this way, the installation turns the tools of correlative capture into a potentially powerful project of dis/correlative counter-capture, forcing us to confront the differential and differentiating dimensions of post-cinematic embodiment, along with the varied conditions of subjective, affective, and collective existence that they enable.

23    See, for instance, Valbuena, Merchant, and Hough 2022, 699-700.

# Coda

Throughout the chapters of this book, I have endeavored to expose the ways that bodies are subject to unprecedented forces of surveillance, control, and modulation in the age of post-cinematic media. Computational processes, I have argued, are quite literally able to get under our skins, probing and re-engineering fleshly being in its deepest recesses. The new forms of visuality and tactility that shape the environment for contemporary life operate on speeds and scales that are immune to our perception. They anticipate us, predicting our behavior, pre-visualizing our interactions, and pre-formatting our bodies and brains. They serve to entrench power differentials and to standardize our bodybrains according to normative precepts of race, gender, sexuality, ability, and class, among others. They execute discorrelation and re-correlation concurrently, in the blink of an eye, rendering us powerless to register or react to their operations while soothing us with illusions of immersive presence, interactive power, and expanded bodily and cognitive autonomy. These media, in the service of an emergent metabolic capitalism, present the most effective means of subjectivation ever known, and their reach is literally global. It is hard to imagine how we can ever get out from under these processes, how we can get ahead of them, or how we can resist them.

At the same time, I have found inspiration in the efforts made by artists working with—and against—these new media. Whether they work in VR, AR, AI, or ECG; whether they use machine learning to modulate digital video, photoplethysmography to control environmental conditions, or industrial robots to unsettle bodily and social relations; and whether they produce intimate performances, politically disturbing installations, or unplay-able videogames—these artists point the way towards less destructive, less violent, less awful—possibly even liberating—uses of the technologies of control and correlative capture.

**228**  It should be clear, however, that neither a single artwork nor all of the artworks taken together can save us from the momentous forces that are steamrolling over us with the inexhaustible backing of venture capitalists, military budgets, and callous billionaires who would sooner flee the planet and move to Mars than give an inch to the serialized bodies toiling in their earth-bound factories and distribution plants. The meditations on art and aesthetics presented in this book are offered not as a solution to the problem, but as a propaedeutic towards a clearer understanding of said problem and an attempt to define its parameters.

In particular, I have been concerned here to lay bare the phenomenological and material conditions that render us so very vulnerable to capture today—but that also empower our bodies, our subjectivities, and our political formations and social structures to elude their supposed natures and become something else. It is above all the multistability of embodied aesthesis and technicity, of the originary mediality of the flesh, that I have sought to foreground. And it is precisely this which constitutes the primary target for the new apparatuses, allowing them to shape us like so much putty if they can just get the timing right—which is to say, if they can adequately synchronize technical and embodied temporalities. For the moment, there are still margins of error, enabling us to catch a glimpse here and there of dis/correlative operations. But there is no guarantee that that will always be the case, that our plastic flesh will always escape interception. Nevertheless, this underlying plasticity could also enable more propitious transformations if only we could get *our* timing right. The stakes are high, but the same tools that now police our bodies could, in principle, open them up and give way to a new, less ensnaring politics of the flesh.

I end, therefore, on a note of decided uncertainty about the future and whether it can be ours—whether, in other words, there is hope for a *we* that might elude the path-dependencies and predictive programs that make this world so rotten for

most of its inhabitants. It is, above all, the indeterminacy of 
fleshly mediality—of the dis/correlative adventure of embodied
technical existence—that dictates this uncertainty. It will take a
massive collective effort, if not also a ton of dumb luck, to steer
this indeterminacy towards something better. But the artists
taking aim today at the technologies of the flesh give me hope
that it is not yet impossible to create the infrastructure for a
more just political aesthetic, which might also ground a less ugly
political economy.

# Acknowledgements

This book has benefited from the support of innumerably many colleagues, friends, institutions, networks, conferences, screenings, status updates, shitposts, discussions at the bar, happy hours on Zoom, weird business pitches overheard at the coffee shops on Sand Hill Road and El Camino Real, and laughs out back on my friend's patio.

I am grateful for the support of the German Research Association, which funded my Mercator Fellowship with the Graduiertenkolleg "Configurations of Film" at the Goethe Universität Frankfurt, out of which this book evolved. I am especially grateful to Laliv Melamed and Phillip Dominik Keidl, who coordinated many aspects of my fellowship; to Vinzenz Hediger for his support both during and after the fellowship, including important efforts leading to the publication of this book; and to all the doctoral students in the program for the stimulating conversations, many of which influenced the arguments presented here in significant ways. Thanks also to Johannes Maiterth for his valuable work formatting and indexing the book, and to the two anonymous reviewers for their valuable feedback on its arguments.

My colleagues in the Department of Art & Art History at Stanford University have been wonderful throughout the seven years I have been here. If I started naming people individually, I would have to name them all. Though I sometimes encounter skepticism when I say it, this is not only an incredibly supportive environment, but it's one of those rarest of things: a non-dysfunctional academic department! I count myself very lucky to have landed here. Thanks in particular to my department chair, Pavle Levi, and former chair Alexander Nemerov, both of whom have supported me in substantial ways at crucial moments. Scott Bukatman has been a true friend since I arrived here, as have others in the Film & Media Studies program. Oops, I started naming people, so there's no stopping now; thanks also to the rest of the FMS crew (Jean Ma, Karla Oeler, Usha Iyer, and Adam Tobin), the art historians (Marci Kwon, Emanuele Lugli, Jody Maxmin, Richard Meyer, Bissera Pentcheva, Rose Salseda, and Rick Vinograd), the DocFilm folks (Jan Krawitz, Jamie Meltzer, Srdan Keca, and Natalia Almada), and the practicing artists (Paul DeMarinis, Camille Utterback, Terry Berlier, Jonathan Calm, Gail Wight, Enrique Chagoya, and Xiaoze Xie).

I could say similarly great things about the other campus networks to which I belong, especially the Program in Modern Thought & Literature, which has broadened my horizons and helped me to believe again in the (otherwise all too often empty) promises of interdisciplinarity. Thanks in particular to Adrian Daub, Maritza Colón, An Nguyen, and Nancy Child, as well as to my predecessor, former program director Héctor Hoyos, along with the whole Committee in Charge, for all that they do to support the program and its intellectual mission. I am grateful also to the German Studies Department and the Department of Communication for welcoming me into their ranks; thanks in particular to Kathryn Starkey and Fred Turner for their efforts on this front.

The Digital Aesthetics Workshop at the Stanford Humanities Center has been a source of continued inspiration. I am especially inspired by the graduate students who have helped me run the series over the years: Jeff Nagy, Doug Eacho, Annika Butler-Wall, Hank Gerba, and Grace Han. The Critical Practices Unit was also pivotal for helping me think about some of the issues discussed in this book, and I thank Hank Gerba and Catie Cuan for their efforts with that. And though CPU did not survive the pandemic, another group, the Critical Making Collaborative, has emerged in its place. I am grateful to Jean Ma and Matthew Wilson Smith for helping me get things off the ground, and to J. Makary for indispensable support. Thanks also to MTL student Corey Dansereau for helping me establish the new Intermediations series.

Speaking of students, I am grateful to be able to learn from so many wonderful graduate students from across the humanities at Stanford. In addition to those already named, I will mention just a few with whom I have worked closely in recent years: Katja Schwaller, Jenny Andrine Madsen Evang, Miša Stekl, Frank Mondelli, Beatrix Horan, Kola Heyward-Rotimi, Amber Harper, Andrea Capra, Helen Krüger, Jason Beckman, Lingjia Xu, and Alexander Huang. Thank you all for the invaluable lessons you have taught me.

Off campus, my intellectual life has been enriched by my involvement with the Sensing Media book series at Stanford University Press. Thanks to my co-editor Wendy Hui Kyong Chun and to Executive Editor Erica Wetter. Thanks to the members of the Philosophy & Theory SIG at the Society for Cinema and Media Studies, in particular Co-Chair Victor Fan, secretary Hank Gerba, and former secretary John Winn. Thanks also to former Co-Chair Markos Hadjioannou for encouraging me to get involved.

A little farther (but not much) from campus and from professional networks, I would like to thank my neighbors at Peter Coutts Circle for making life livable in Silicon Valley. Thanks especially to Kathryn Starkey, Michael Minion, Sepp and Ricky Gumbrecht, Alex Woloch and Karla Oeler, Charlotte Fonrobert, Herant and Stina Katchadourian, Elaine Treharne and Andy Fryett, Susan Rooke and Bryan Rutt, Barbara and Talia-Jade Sourkes, I-han Chou and Justin Gardner, Ariel Schwartzman and Agustina Peroni, Nicole Ardoin and Greg Hawkins, Kate Maher and Matthew Rothe, Laura Stokes, David Palumbo-Liu, and Paula Findlen. And the dogs! Lexi, Rosa, Shosta, Stargazer, Maple, Cocoa, Babar, Vinnie, and all the others: I appreciate all the dogs of the Circle, and so does Evie!

Thanks, finally, to my family, especially to Amy and Karin. I am proud that we made it through the worst of the pandemic (during which this book was written) as well as we did. It took a collective effort, a renovated bar, lots of Zoom sessions with friends (especially Scott Bukatman, Beth Kessler, and Vivian Sobchack), a Peloton in the living room, movie nights and videogames, and lots of other things. Amy: I'm proud of how you managed, despite

**234**   a freshman year of college on Zoom; I'm glad you got to move to campus the following year, and I'm proud of all your accomplishments since! And Karin: I am so excited about your art, so happy you have found community at Edgewater Gallery, and I couldn't be prouder of the awesome work you are doing (not unselfishly: I also love seeing your work on our walls and on the cover of this book!). Anyway, y'all make me happy.

# References


Agaron, Shamay. 2020. "BCI 2022: Peloton for the Mind." *Brain Street*, July 24, 2020. https://shamay.com/bci-2022-peloton-for-the-mind/.

Agre, Philip E. 2003. "Surveillance and Capture: Two Models of Privacy." In *The New Media Reader*, edited by Noah Wardrip-Fruin and Nick Montfort, 737–60. Cambridge: MIT Press.

Ahmed, Sara. 2006. *Queer Phenomenology: Orientations, Objects, Others*. Durham: Duke University Press.

Althusser, Louis. 1971. "Ideology and Ideological State Apparatuses (Notes towards an Investigation)." In *Lenin and Philosophy and Other Essays*. Translated by Ben Brewster, 121–73. New York: Monthly Review Press.

Amoore, Louise. 2020. *Cloud Ethics: Algorithms and the Attributes of Ourselves and Others*. Durham: Duke University Press.

Bajohr, Hannes. 2022. "Algorithmic Empathy: Toward a Critique of Aesthetic AI." *Configurations*, no. 30: 203–31.

Baudry, Jean-Louis. 1974. "Ideological Effects of the Basic Cinematographic Apparatus." Translated by Alan Williams. *Film Quarterly* 28, no. 2: 39–47.

Beauvoir, Simone de. 1982. *The Second Sex*. Translated by Howard Madison Parshley. Harmondsworth: Penguin.

Belisle, Brooke. 2020. "Whole Earth within Reach: Google Earth VR." *Journal of Visual Culture* 19, no. 1: 112–36. https://doi.org/10.1177%2F1470412920909990.

Beller, Jonathan. 2006. *The Cinematic Mode of Production: Attention Economy and the Society of the Spectacle*. Hanover: Dartmouth College Press.

Benjamin, Walter. 2006. "The Work of Art in the Age of Its Technological Reproducibility." Second Version. In *Selected Writings: Vol. 3, 1935-38*, edited by Howard Eiland and Michael W. Jennings. Translated by Edmund Jephcott and Harry Zohn, 101–33. Cambridge: Belknap Press of Harvard University Press.

Berg, J. H. van den. 2004. *The Two Principal Laws of Thermodynamics: A Cultural and Historical Exploration*. Translated by Bernd Jager, David Jager, and Dreyer Kruger. Pittsburgh: Duquesne University Press.

Bolter, Jay David, Maria Engberg, and Blair MacIntyre. 2021. *Reality Media: Augmented and Virtual Reality*. Cambridge: MIT Press.

Bradley, Rizvana. 2023. *Anteaesthetics: Black Aesthesis and the Critique of Form*. Stanford: Stanford University Press.

Brinkema, Eugenie. 2014. *The Forms of the Affects*. Durham: Duke University Press.

Butler, Judith. 1993. *Bodies That Matter: On the Discursive Limits of Sex*. London: Routledge.

Cavell, Stanley. 1979. *The World Viewed: Reflections on the Ontology of Film*. Enlarged edition. Cambridge, MA: Harvard University Press.

Cheng, Ian. 2018. *Emissaries Guide to Worlding: How to Navigate the Unnatural Art of Creating an Infinite Game by Choosing a Present, Storytelling Its Past, Simulating Its Futures, and Nurturing Its Changes*. London: Serpentine Galleries/Koenig Books.

**236** Chun, Wendy Hui Kyong. 2021. *Discriminating Data: Correlation, Neighborhoods, and the New Politics of Recognition.* Cambridge: MIT Press.

Cole, Samantha. 2017. "AI-Assisted Fake Porn Is Here and We're All Fucked." *Motherboard*, December 11, 2017. https://motherboard.vice.com/en_us/article/gydydm/gal-gadot-fake-ai-porn.

Couldry, Nick, and Ulises Ali Mejias. 2020. "Big Tech's Latest Moves Raise Health Privacy Fears." *Financial Times*, December 6, 2020. https://www.ft.com/content/01d4452c-03e2-4b44-bf78-b017e66775f1.

Crary, Jonathan. 2013. *24/7: Late Capitalism and the Ends of Sleep.* London: Verso.

Cuan, Catie. 2021. "OUTPUT: Choreographed and Reconfigured Human and Industrial Robot Bodies Across Artistic Modalities." *Frontiers in Robotics and AI*, 7 (April): 1–13.

Cubasch, Alwin J., Engelmann, Vanessa, and Kassung, Christian. 2021. "Theorie des Filterns. Zur Programmatik eines Experimentalsystems." Preprint, *Zenodo*, April 30, 2021. https://doi.org/10.5281/ZENODO.4731044.

Curtis, Genevieve. 2020. "Dances with Robots, and Other Tales from the Outer Limits." *New York Times*, November 5, 2020. https://www.nytimes.com/2020/11/05/arts/dance/dance-and-artificial-intelligence.html.

Dayan, Daniel. 1974. "The Tutor-Code of Classical Cinema." *Film Quarterly* 28, no. 1: 22–31.

Deleuze, Gilles. 1986. *Cinema 1: The Movement-Image.* Translated by Hugh Tomlinson and Barbara Habberjam. Minneapolis: University of Minnesota Press.

———. 1992. "Postscript on the Societies of Control." *October*, no. 59: 3–7.

Denson, Shane. 2014. *Postnaturalism: Frankenstein, Film, and the Anthropotechnical Interface.* Bielefeld: transcript-Verlag.

———. 2020a. Discorrelated Images. Durham: Duke University Press.

———. 2020b. "The Horror of Discorrelation: Mediating Unease in Post-Cinematic Screens and Networks." *Journal of Cinema and Media Studies* 60 no. 1 (Fall): 26–48.

———. 2020c. "'Thus Isolation Is a Project.' Notes toward a Phenomenology of Screen-Mediated Life." In *Pandemic Media: Preliminary Notes towards an Inventory*, edited by Philipp Dominik Keidl, Laliv Melamed, Vinzenz Hediger, and Antonio Somaini, 315–22. Lüneburg: meson press.

Denson, Shane, and Julia Leyda, eds. 2016. *Post-Cinema: Theorizing 21st-Century Film.* Falmer: REFRAME Books.

"Diaphragm, n." Oxford English Dictionary Online." 2022. In *Oxford English Dictionary Online*. Oxford University Press. https://www.oed.com/view/Entry/52038.

Ding, Sue. n.d. "Interview with Hyphen-Labs." *Docubase: MIT Open Documentary Lab*. https://docubase.mit.edu/lab/interviews/by-htm/.

Ellcessor, Elizabeth, and Bill Kirkpatrick, eds. 2017. *Disability Media Studies.* New York: NYU Press.

Fanon, Frantz. 2008. *Black Skin, White Masks.* Translated by Richard Philcox. New York: Grove Press.

Foster, John Bellamy. 1999. "Marx's Theory of Metabolic Rift: Classical Foundations for Environmental Sociology." *American Journal of Sociology* 105 no. 2: 366–405.

Foucault, Michel. 1972. *The Archaeology of Knowledge*. Translated by A. M. Sheridan Smith. New York: Vintage Books.

Gaboury, Jacob. 2021. *Image Objects: An Archaeology of Computer Graphics*. Cambridge: MIT Press.

Galloway, Alexander R. 2004. *Protocol: How Control Exists after Decentralization*. Cambridge: MIT Press.

———. 2006. *Gaming: Essays on Algorithmic Culture*. Minneapolis: University of Minnesota Press.

———. 2021. *Uncomputable: Play and Politics in the Long Digital Age*. New York: Verso.

Garland-Thomson, Rosmarie. 1997. *Extraordinary Bodies: Figuring Physical Disability in American Culture and Literature*. New York: Columbia University Press.

Gorky, Maxim. 1960. "The Kingdom of Shadows." In *Kino: A History of the Russian and Soviet Film*, edited by Jay Leyda, 407–9. London: Allen and Unwin.

Grusin, Richard. 2016. "Post-Cinematic Atavism." In *Post-Cinema: Theorizing 21st-Century Film*, edited by Denson and Leyda, 646–65. Falmer: REFRAME Books.

———. 2018. "Médiation Radicale: Penser à Travers Les Pouvoirs Des Écrans." *In Des Pouvoirs Des Écrans*, edited by Mauro Carbone, Anna Caterina Dalmasso, and Jacopo Bodini, 305–20. Sesto San Giovanni: Éditions Mimésis.

Gunning, Tom. 1986. "The Cinema of Attraction: Early Film, Its Spectator and the Avant-Garde." *Wide Angle* 8, nos. 3–4: 63–70.

Gurley, Lauren Kaori. 2022. "Internal Documents Show Amazon's Dystopian System for Tracking Workers Every Minute of Their Shifts." *Vice*, June 2, 2022. https://www.vice.com/en/article/5dgn73/internal-documents-show-amazons-dystopian-system-for-tracking-workers-every-minute-of-their-shifts.

Hansen, Mark B.N. 2006. *Bodies in Code: Interfaces with Digital Media*. New York: Routledge.

———. 2016. "Algorithmic Sensibility: Reflections on the Post-Perceptual Image." In *Post-Cinema: Theorizing 21st-Century Film*, edited by Shane Denson and Julia Leyda, 785–816. Falmer: REFRAME Books.

Haraway, Donna. 1988. "Situated Knowledges: The Science Question in Feminism and the Privilege of Partial Perspective." *Feminist Studies* 14, no. 3 (Fall): 575–99.

———. 2016. *Manifestly Haraway*. Minneapolis: University of Minnesota Press.

Harris, Neil. 1973. *Humbug: The Art of P. T. Barnum*. Chicago: University of Chicago Press.

Hartman, Saidiya V. 1997. *Scenes of Subjection: Terror, Slavery, and Self-Making in Nineteenth-Century America*. New York: Oxford University Press.

Hayes, Christian. n.d. "Phantom Rides." *BFI Screen Online*. http://www.screenonline.org.uk/film/id/1193042/.

Hayles, N.Katherine. 2017. *Unthought: The Power of the Cognitive Nonconscious*. Chicago: University of Chicago Press.

Heidegger, Martin. 1962. *Being and Time*. Translated by John Macquarrie and Edward Robinson. New York: Harper and Row.

———. 1971a. "Building Dwelling Thinking." In *Poetry, Language, Thought*. Translated by Albert Hofstadter, 143–61. New York: Harper & Row.

**238**   ———. 1971b. "The Thing." In *Poetry, Language, Thought*. Translated by Albert Hofstadter, 163–86. New York: Harper & Row.

———. 1977. "The Question Concerning Technology." In *The Question Concerning Technology and Other Essays*. Translated by William Levitt, 3–35. New York: Harper Torch Books.

Heim, Michael. 1993. *The Metaphysics of Virtual Reality*. New York: Oxford University Press.

Holoblog. 2022. "How to Turn Your Peloton or Zwift Bike into a VR Exercise Bike." *Holoblog*, March 25, 2022. https://www.holodia.com/vr-fitness-blog/how-to-turn-your-peloton-or-zwift-bike-into-a-vr-exercise-bike/.

hooks, bell. 1990. *Yearning: Race, Gender, and Cultural Politics*. Boston: South End Press.

Hunter, Tatum. 2022. "Surveillance Will Follow Us into 'the Metaverse,' and Our Bodies Could Be Its New Data Source." *The Washington Post*, January 13, 2022. https://www.washingtonpost.com/technology/2022/01/13/privacy-vr-metaverse/.

Husserl, Edmund. 1928. *Vorlesungen Zur Phänomenologie Des Inneren Zeitbewusstseins*. Halle: Max Niemeyer Verlag.

———. 1964. *The Phenomenology of Internal Time-Consciousness*. Translated by James S. Churchill. Bloomington: Indiana University Press.

———. 2012. *Ideas: General Introduction to Pure Phenomenology*. Translated by W. R. Boyce Gibson. New York: Routledge.

Ihde, Don. 1990. *Technology and the Lifeworld: From Garden to Earth*. Bloomington: Indiana University Press.

———. 2002. *Bodies in Technology*. Minneapolis: University of Minnesota Press.

———. 2012. *Experimental Phenomenology: Multistabilities*. 2nd ed. Albany: State University of New York Press.

Irigaray, Luce, C. Burke, and G. Gill. 1993. *An Ethics of Sexual Difference*. Translated by C. Burke and G. Gill. Ithaca: Cornell University Press.

Fredric Jameson. 2004. "Foreword." In *Critique of Dialectical Reason, Vol. 1, Theory of Practical Ensembles*, by Jean-Paul Sartre, translated by Alan Sheridan-Smith, xiii–xxxiii. London: Verso.

Jones, Ian Bryce. 2016. "Do the Locomotion: Obstinate Avatars, Dehiscent Performances, and the Rise of the Comedic Video Game." *The Velvet Light Trap*, no. 77 (Spring): 86–99.

Kant, Immanuel. 1951. *Critique of Judgment*. Translated by J. H. Bernard. New York: Hafner Publishing Co.

Kant, Immanuel. 2007. *Critique of Judgement*. Translated by James Creed Meredith. New York: Oxford University Press.

Kempner Museum Contemporary Art. 2021. "Rafael Lozano-Hemmer on Memento Mori." *YouTube*, December 21, 2021. https://www.youtube.com/watch?v=qBuRdEuWGNI.

Keogh, Brendan. 2018. *A Play of Bodies: How We Perceive Videogames*. Cambridge: MIT Press.

Kirkpatrick, Graeme. 2011. *Aesthetic Theory and the Video Game*. Manchester: Manchester University Press.

Kittler, Friedrich. 1999. *Gramophone, Film, Typewriter*. Stanford: Stanford University Press.

Larochelle, Audrey. 2013. "A New Angle on Parallel Languages: The Contribution of Visual Arts to a Vocabulary of Graphical Projection in Video Games." *Game: The Italian Journal of Game Studies*, no. 2. https://www.gamejournal.it/a-new-angle-on-parallel-languages-the-contribution-of-visual-arts-to-a-vocabulary-of-graphical-projection-in-video-games/.

Lennon, Kathleen. 2019. "Feminist Perspectives on the Body." In *The Stanford Encyclopedia of Philosophy*, edited by Edward N. Zalta. https://plato.stanford.edu/entries/feminist-body/.

Levitt, Deborah. 2018. "Five Theses on Virtual Reality and Sociality: Understanding the Implications of Radically New Experiences." *Public Seminar*, May 10, 2018. https://publicseminar.org/2018/05/five-theses-on-virtual-reality-and-sociality/.

Lewin, Kurt. 1934. "Der Richtungsbegriff in der Psychologie: Der spezielle und allgemeine hodologische Raum." *Psychologische Forschung* 19, nos 3–4: 398–432.

Leyda, Julia. 2014. "Demon Debt: Paranormal Activity as Recessionary Post-Cinematic Allegory." *Jump Cut*, no. 56: 398–432.

MacCallum, John, and Teoma Naccarato. 2015. "The Impossibility of Control: Real-Time Negotiations with the Heart." *EVA '15: Proceedings of the Conference on Electronic Visualization and the Arts*. https://dl.acm.org/doi/10.14236/ewic/eva2015.19.

Marx, Karl. 1977. *Capital*. Translated by Ben Fowkes. Vol. 1. New York: Penguin.

———. 1981. *Capital*. Translated by David Fernbach. Vol. 3. New York: Penguin.

McDonald, Kyle. 2018. "How to Recognize Fake AI-Generated Images." *Medium*, December 5, 2018. https://medium.com/@kcimc/how-to-recognize-fake-ai-generated-images-4d1f6f9a2842.

Meillassoux, Quentin. 2008. *After Finitude: An Essay on the Necessity of Contingency*. Translated by Ray Brassier. London: Continuum.

Merleau-Ponty, Maurice. 1964. "The Child's Relations with Others." In *The Primacy of Perception, and Other Essays on Phenomenological Psychology, the Philosophy of Art, History and Politics*, edited by James M. Edie, translated by William Cobb, 96–155. Evanston: Northwestern University Press.

———. 1968a. "The Intertwining—The Chiasmus." In *The Visible and the Invisible*, edited by Claude Lefort, translated by Alphonso Lingis, 130–55. Evanston: Northwestern University Press.

———. 1968b. *The Visible and the Invisible*. Edited by Claude Lefort. Translated by Alphonso Lingis. Evanston: Northwestern University Press.

———. 2002. *Phenomenology of Perception*. Translated by Colin Smith. New York: Routledge.

Mersch, Dieter. 2006. "Ausblick Auf Eine Negative Medientheorie." In *Medientheorien Zur Einführung*, 219–28. Hamburg: Junius Verlag.

Milk, Chris. 2015. "How VR Can Create the Ultimate Empathy Machine." *YouTube*, April 22, 2015. https://www.youtube.com/watch?v=iXHil1TPxvA.

Moore, Jason W. 2011. "Transcending the Metabolic Rift: A Theory of Crises in the Capitalist World-Ecology." *Journal of Peasant Studies* 38, no 1: 1–46.

**240**    ———. 2017. "The Capitalocene, Part I: On the Nature and Origins of Our Ecological Crisis." *Journal of Peasant Studies* 44, no. 3: 594–630.

Morse, Jack. 2020. "Amazon Announces New Employee Tracking Tech, and Customers Are Lining Up." *Mashable*, December 1, 2020. https://mashable.com/article/amazon-aws-panorama-worker-customer-tracking-technology-smart-cameras.

Mulvey, Laura. 1975. "Visual Pleasure and Narrative Cinema." *Screen* 16, no. 3: 6–18.

Münsterberg, Hugo. 1916. *The Photoplay: A Psychological Study*. New York: D. Appleton and Company.

Naccarato, Teoma J., and John MacCallum. 2016. "From Representation to Relationality: Bodies, Biosensors, and Mediated Environments." *Journal of Dance & Somatic Practices* 8, no. 1: 57–72.

———. 2017. "Critical Appropriations of Biosensors in Artistic Practice." *MOCO '17: Proceedings of the 4th International Conference on Movement and Computing*. https://dl.acm.org/doi/10.1145/3077981.3078053.

Nagy, Jeffrey. 2022. "Watching Feeling: Emotional Data from Cybernetics to Social Media." Ph.D. Dissertation, Stanford: Stanford University.

Oliver, Kealan. 2010. "Sheriff Joe Arpaio Presents Prison Exercise Plan: Inmates Pedal for TV Privileges." *CBS News*, April 7, 2010. https://www.cbsnews.com/news/sheriff-joe-arpaio-presents-prison-exercise-plan-inmates-pedal-for-tv-privileges/.

Paglen, Trevor. 2016. "Invisible Images (Your Pictures Are Looking at You)." *New Inquiry*, December 8, 2016. https://thenewinquiry.com/invisible-images-your-pictures-are-looking-at-you/.

PeloBuddy. 2022. "Rumor: Peloton to Sell VR Goggles to Provide In-Studio Experience at Home." *PeloBuddy*, April 1, 2022. https://www.pelobuddy.com/peloton-vision-goggles/.

Pickering, Andrew. 1995. *The Mangle of Practice: Time, Agency, and Science*. Chicago: University of Chicago Press.

Plumb, Taryn. 2022. "How Peloton Is Using Computer Vision to Strengthen Workouts." *VentureBeat*. July 29, 2022. https://venturebeat.com/ai/how-peloton-is-using-computer-vision-to-strengthen-workouts/.

Ruberg, Bonnie. 2019. *Video Games Have Always Been Queer*. New York: NYU Press.

Salamon, Gayle. 2010. *Assuming a Body: Transgender and Rhetorics of Materiality*. New York: Columbia University Press.

San José Museum of Art. 2021. "Hito Steyerl: Factory of the Sun." *E-Flux Announcements*. July 27, 2021. https://www.e-flux.com/announcements/396579/hito-steyerlfactory-of-the-sun/.

Sartre, Jean-Paul. 1984. *Being and Nothingness: A Phenomenological Essay on Ontology*. Translated by Hazel E. Barnes. New York: Washington Square Press.

———. 2004. *Critique of Dialectical Reason: Vol. 1, Theory of Practical Ensembles*. Translated by Alan Sheridan-Smith. London: Verso.

Schiller, Friedrich. 2004. *On the Aesthetic Education of Man*. Translated by Reginald Snell. Mineola, NY: Dover.

Schonig, Jordan. 2020. "The 'Wind in the Trees' from Early Cinema to Pixar." *Vimeo*. September 15, 2020. https://vimeo.com/458220961.

———. 2022. *The Shape of Motion: Cinema and the Aesthetics of Movement*. New York: Oxford University Press.

Shaviro, Steven. 1993. *The Cinematic Body*. Minneapolis: University of Minnesota Press.

Shu, Catherine. 2020. "MindLabs Raises £1.4 Million for its New Platform, a 'Peloton for Mental Health.'" *TechCrunch*, October 21, 2020. https://techcrunch.com/2020/10/21/mindlabs-raises-1-4-million-for-its-new-platform-a-peloton-for-mental-health/.

Simondon, Gilbert. 2017. *On the Mode of Existence of Technical Objects*. Translated by Cécile Malaspina and John Rogove. Minneapolis: Univocal Publishing.

———. 2020. *Individuation in Light of Notions of Form and Information*. Translated by Taylor Adkins. Minneapolis: University of Minnesota Press.

Smythe, Dallas W. 2006. "On the Audience Commodity and Its Work." In *Media and Cultural Studies: KeyWorks*, edited by Meenakshi Gigi Durham and Douglas M. Kellner, 230–56. Oxford: Blackwell Publishing.

Sobchack, Vivian. 1992. *The Address of the Eye: A Phenomenology of Film Experience*. Princeton, NJ: Princeton University Press.

———. 2016. "The Scene of the Screen: Envisioning Photographic, Cinematic, and Electronic 'Presence.'." In *Post-Cinema: Theorizing 21st-Century Film*, edited by Shane Denson and Julia Leyda, 88–128. Falmer: REFRAME Books.

Spillers, Hortense J. 2003a. *Black, White, and in Color: Essays on American Literature and Culture*. Chicago: University of Chicago Press.

———. 2003b. "Mama's Baby, Papa's Maybe: An American Grammar Book." In *Black White, and in Color: Essays on American Literature and Culture*, 203–29. Chicago: University of Chicago Press.

Stark, Doug. 2020. "Unsettling Embodied Literacy in QWOP the Walking Simulator." *Journal of Gaming & Virtual Worlds* 12, no. 1: 49–67.

Sterne, Jonathan. 2012. *MP3: The Meaning of a Format*. Durham: Duke University Press.

———. 2022. *Diminished Faculties: A Political Phenomenology of Impairment*. Durham: Duke University Press.

Stevenson, Abigail. 2017. "The 'Netflix for Fitness' Company Raging with Millennials—with Zero Competition." *CNBC*, March 3, 2017. https://www.cnbc.com/2017/03/03/the-netflix-for-fitness-company-raging-with-millennials-with-zero-competition.html.

Stiegler, Bernard. 1998. *Technics and Time, Vol. 1, The Fault of Epimetheus*. Translated by Richard Beardsworth. Vol. 1. Stanford: Stanford University Press.

———. 2011. *Technics and Time, Vol. 3, Cinematic Time and the Question of Malaise*. Translated by Stephen Barker. Vol. 3. Stanford: Stanford University Press.

Terranova, Tiziana. 2000. "Free Labor: Producing Culture for the Digital Economy." *Social Text* 18, no. 2: 33–58.

Tobin, Meaghan, and Viola Zhou. 2022. "The Overworked Humans behind China's Virtual Influencers." *Rest of World*, July 28, 2022. https://restofworld.org/2022/china-virtual-idols-labor/.

**242**  Valbuena, Valeria S.M., Raina M. Merchant, and Catherine L. Hough. 2022. "Racial and Ethnic Bias in Pulse Oximetry and Clinical Outcomes." *JAMA Internal Medicine* 182, no. 7: 699–700.

Wark, McKenzie. 2021. *Capital Is Dead: Is This Something Worse?* London: Verso.

Weheliye, Alexander G. 2014. *Habeas Viscus: Racializing Assemblages, Biopolitics, and Black Feminist Theories of the Human*. Durham: Duke University Press.

Williams, Linda. 1991. "Film Bodies: Gender, Genre, and Excess." *Film Quarterly* 44, no. 4: 2–13.

———. 1999. *Hard Core: Power, Pleasure, and the "Frenzy of the Visible."* Expanded edition. Berkeley: University of California Press.

Wynter, Sylvia. 1992. "Rethinking 'Aesthetics': Notes towards a Deciphering Practice." In *Ex-iles: Essays on Caribbean Cinema*, edited by Mbye Cham, 237–79. Trenton, NJ: Africa World Press.

———. 2001. "Towards the Sociogenic Principle: Fanon, Identity, the Puzzle of Conscious Experience, and What It Is Like to Be 'Black'." In *National Identities and Socio-Political Changes in Latin America*, edited by Antonio Gomez-Moriana and Mercedes Duran-Cogan, 30–66. London: Routledge.

Wynter, Sylvia, and Katherine McKittrick. 2015. "Unparalleled Catastrophe for Our Species? Or, to Give Humanness a Different Future: Conversations." In *On Being Human as Praxis*, edited by Katherine McKittrick and Sylvia Wynter, 9–89. Durham: Duke University Press.

Young, Iris Marion. 1994. "Gender as Seriality: Thinking about Women as a Social Collective." *Signs: Journal of Women in Culture and Society* 19, no. 3: 713–38.

Zuboff, Shoshana. 2019. *The Age of Surveillance Capitalism: The Fight for a Human Future at the New Frontier of Power*. New York: PublicAffairs.

# Index

9 7 8 3 9 5 7 9 6 0 4 3 6